The Limerick

The Limerick
A History, 1820–1920

Bob Turvey

McFarland & Company, Inc., Publishers
Jefferson, North Carolina

LIBRARY OF CONGRESS CATALOGING-IN-PUBLICATION DATA

Names: Turvey, Bob, author.
Title: The limerick : a history, 1820-1920 / Bob Turvey.
Description: Jefferson, North Carolina : McFarland & Company, Inc., Publishers, 2024. | Includes bibliographical references and index.
Identifiers: LCCN 2024033205 | ISBN 9781476695594 (paperback : acid free paper) ∞
ISBN 9781476652801 (ebook)
Subjects: LCSH: Limericks—History and criticism.
Classification: LCC PN6149.L5 T87 2024 | DDC 809.1/75—dc23/eng/20240719
LC record available at https://lccn.loc.gov/2024033205

BRITISH LIBRARY CATALOGUING DATA ARE AVAILABLE

ISBN (print) 978-1-4766-9559-4
ISBN (ebook) 978-1-4766-5280-1

© 2024 Bob Turvey. All rights reserved

No part of this book may be reproduced or transmitted in any form or by any means, electronic or mechanical, including photocopying or recording, or by any information storage and retrieval system, without permission in writing from the publisher.

Front cover image: © ARTISTRY ACE/Shutterstock; limerick by the author

Printed in the United States of America

McFarland & Company, Inc., Publishers
  Box 611, Jefferson, North Carolina 28640
    www.mcfarlandpub.com

To my wife; who's long-suffering—though short.

(But I cannot suppress a mean thought.
As a Finn she can't see
What's attractive to me;
She likes limericks much less than she ought!)

Contents

Introductory Quotations	ix
Preface	1
Introduction	3
PART I—Suggested Sources of the Limerick Pre-1820	11
1. Not the Beginning!	13
2. Possible Limericks in English Prior to 1820	29
3. Possible Irish Origins Prior to 1820	38
PART II—Limericks from 1820 to 1920	53
4. The 1820s: At Last—Limericks!	55
5. The 1830s: Little Progress—On the Surface	62
6. The 1840s: Some Progress Comes to Light	65
7. The 1850s: The Calm before the Storm	73
8. The 1860s: The Limerick Explodes	82
9. The 1870s: The Limerick Develops	124
10. The 1880s: The Limerick Expands	151
11. The 1890s: Who Wrote What?	162
12. The 1900s: The Limerick Explodes—Again	175
13. The 1910s: The Limerick Does Its Bit	194
Appendix: Pre-1820 Verses in English Which Have Been Claimed to Be Limericks or Proto-Limericks	203
Chapter Notes	235
Bibliography	257
Index	261

Thanks

There was an old man who said, "WHAT!
I'm supposed to acknowledge a lot
Of folk who helped me,
With advice, given free,
And who shared some rare texts that they'd got?"

Mea Culpa

At long last this book's fully grown,
Based on wonderful things I've been shown,
By kind folk, far and near;
But I must make it clear—
All mistakes are entirely my own!

Introductory Quotations

The time has come for the Limerick to be studied analytically and historically. Canons are to be established, origins investigated, and the development of the species traced. Let us not neglect this, the latest expression of the soul of man.
—Christopher Morley, "The Limerick,"
The Haverfordian, January 1909.
More accessible in Christopher Morley,
Hostages to Fortune, 1925, page 10.

As to the first Limericks, and the origin of the name, there is positively no way to ascertain the facts.
—Carolyn Wells, *Book of American Limericks*,
G.P. Putnam's Sons, New York, 1925, Foreword, page iii.

The definitive work on the limerick will probably never be written.
—Anon, *The Limerick, A Facet of our Culture*,
privately printed, Mexico City, 1944, page 53.
(Actually A. Reynolds Morse, Cleveland, OH, 1948.)

If there's one thing about limericks you can't be, it's scholarly.
—John Armstrong, *There Was a Young Lady Called Alice, and Other Limericks*,
Dell Publishing, New York, 1963, page 11.

I shall waste no time discussing the origin of the limerick because nobody agrees on what it is. The Irish claim is strong. The English claim is strong, there is even a French claim—a sort of squatter's rights, based on hazy medieval tenure.
—Nefastus Dies, *Encounter* magazine,
January 1969, page 55.

Introductory Quotations

Once really immersed in the study of limericks, one finds that questions keep cropping up to which the answers are so generally taken for granted that few people even realise that they exist. Who invented the limerick—or did it simply evolve?
—Cyril Bibby, *The Art of the Limerick*, Research Publishing Company, London, 1978, page 9.

A really "authentic" history of the limerick does not, as far as I am aware, exist.
—Wim Tigges, "Explorations in the Field of Nonsense," Rodopi, Amsterdam, 1987, page 118, footnote 2.

Let each scholar put up in his cell
This motto to help him excel:
"The task you're pursuing
May not be worth doing,
But remember, it's worth doing well."
—A.N. Wilkins, *Mortal Taste*, Exposition Press, New York, 1965, page 39.

A little learning is a dangerous thing;
Drink deep, or taste not the Pierian spring.
—Alexander Pope, *An Essay on Criticism: Part II*, 1711.

Preface

The limerick verse form has been known and loved worldwide for over two hundred years. Fans have included presidents, prime ministers, kings, ambassadors, judges, Nobel laureates, bishops, geniuses, one certified lunatic and many millions of ordinary men, women and children.

Competitions requiring entrants to write a limerick date back over a century and are still popular today.

Books exist which contain thousands of limericks.

But:

- **Where did limericks come from?**
- **How did they develop?**
- **Why did they become popular?**
- **Why are they called limericks?**

When I first thought about these questions I was puzzled by the suggested answers. Some made no sense at all. Some flatly contradicted others. Often, little or no evidence was offered.

It became clear that I could live in ignorance of their history and development—or I could try to find what the answers were.

I therefore searched the great libraries of the world. I examined private book collections, newspaper collections, private correspondence and diaries. During this 30-year odyssey some fascinating people, stories, places, publications and limericks were found. And, I believe, an accurate picture emerged of how the limerick verse form developed historically.

This book paints that picture.

Introduction

I was perhaps ten when I came across my first limerick. A school friend told me a variant of the legendary "Young Man of Racine." This limerick is widely believed to have been written by the Hungarian polyglot genius and mathematician, John von Neumann. Modified for an English audience it went:

> A young man from near Aberdeen
> Once invented a wanking machine.
> On the ninety-ninth stroke
> The bloody thing broke,
> And whipped up his balls into cream.

Like most great limericks it was instantly memorable, so naturally the first thing I did when I got home was to recite it to my younger sister. Gratifyingly, she laughed. However, a little while later I heard her ask: "Dad, what's a wanking machine?"

My Early Exposure to Ideas about the History of the Limerick Verse Form

Over the years I learned many more limericks. I suppose I must have wondered in a vague way where they came from, who wrote them, and, of course, why they were called limericks. I didn't really pay much attention to the history of the verse form until I read a reprint of Langford Reed's 1924 *The Complete Limerick Book*, which I bought from the Hudson's Bay Company's department store when I lived in Montreal. This book contained Reed's attempt to trace the history of the limerick verse form. He seemed to appeal to odd sources in an attempt to show that the verse came from Ireland, via France. I remember thinking that his efforts didn't really sound convincing, or even logical, but I had no special knowledge to the contrary.

The next book to spur my interest in the history of the limerick was probably Gershon Legman's magisterial work, *The Limerick*. Due to censorship in the U.S. and UK it was first published privately in Paris in 1953. It initially existed simply as a collection of nearly 1,800 bawdy limericks, which Legman had collected from an impressive range of sources. When the book could be published freely after changes to censorship laws in the 1960s, Legman added an introductory text that was essentially an updated chapter he had written for his earlier work *The Horn Book*. The back cover of one edition described this as "a fascinating survey of the development of the limerick from the fourteenth century to modern times." Sixty-seven pages long, it bombastically rambled hither and thither in non-chronological order, willy-nilly throwing out "facts" and references, relevant or otherwise, to the matter being discussed. Legman's opinion seems to be that the limerick was essentially a dirty poem which had started life among the English drinking songs, especially those of the 1500s. The keen reader will notice that most—if not all—of the verses cited as evidence are not actually in limerick form, but Legman gets round this by calling this era the prehistory of the limerick. The chronology of Legman's argument is more than a little difficult to follow, as he leaps around between time periods. It's almost as if he tipped his research file cards on the floor and typed them up at random.

After reading Legman's introduction, I wonder if anyone could sit down and sketch out accurately just what Legman thinks is the chronology of the development of the limerick verse form, exactly where it originated, and why it became so popular. I know I would struggle. A gallant attempt was made in 1981 by George Belknap, who also suggested that Legman thought that limericks had reached their highest point of creativity in the seventeenth century and had been decaying ever since, a process continuing to the present day. However, as I said, the verses quoted by Legman don't even seem to be limericks, and as he only quotes a handful, how could he determine where the supposed high point was?

Early in his text Legman identifies several children's books published in the 1820s as containing the first real limericks, mentions that they inspired Edward Lear, then contradicts himself commenting that it was a reprint of Edward Lear's book of verse in 1863 [sic] in London which spurred a massive interest in the limerick verse form.

Interestingly, despite all his discourse that proto-limericks came from dirty English drinking songs many centuries ago, and that the original limericks were "an indecent verse form," Legman says that the Lear reprint was also responsible for the rise of the dirty limerick in the 1860s. He states that a 12-page document titled *A New Book of Nonsense* (London, 1868) was "the earliest collection of erotic limericks **known** to have existed." Astonishingly he states in the next line that "no sure trace of this brochure has survived except a bare reference to its title." In other words, he is claiming that this booklet is known to have contained erotic limericks—when no copy of it exists, no record of its contents exists, and no one alive has ever seen a copy!

You can see why at times I have wondered what to believe.

The year 1967 saw the publication of what is probably the most commercially successful historical limerick book ever published—that is, a book of limericks which also contains a history of the verse form. *The Lure of the Limerick* by William Baring-Gould ran into many editions. On the front of one such, a red ribbon proclaims it to be "The Bawdy World-wide Bestseller." On the back, following the price in several countries, is a definition of the contents so that bookshops and librarians can file it in the proper section—NONFICTION / HUMOR.

Limericks are true? What have I been missing all my life?

Actually, I'm sure the nonfiction designation refers to Part One of the book, where seven chapters trace what Mr. Baring-Gould thinks is the history of the limerick verse form. In a hundred-odd pages, in a more chronologically logical text than Legman's, the author runs through the main ideas suggested by earlier writers on the subject. Even so, it contains demonstrable mistakes of fact. The reader also gets the feeling that there is a lot more information which could and should have been included.

Dr. Cyril Bibby was one of the world's first sexologists and a man who led an interesting life, judging by his Wikipedia entry and his obituary in the *Times*. In 1978 he published *The Art of the Limerick*. Like others before him, Dr. Bibby described many aspects of the history and development of the limerick verse form. Unlike others before him, he was not content to just regurgitate these various ideas without examining them a little more closely. What he found disquieted him. Early in the book he writes: "It cannot be said that higher education has so far done much to promote scholarly study of the limerick. Indeed, to me as a scientist, accustomed to check and double-check assertions before presuming to put them to print, it came as rather a shock to find how frequently literary writers seem to quote and requote received statements without any properly rigorous investigation."

The good doctor then gives several examples of sloppy scholarship. Later he considers the origin of the word *limerick*, commenting: "Perhaps, faced now with two conflicting hypotheses, for neither of which there is any firm evidence, some scholar some day will really set to and solve the problem."

Bibby's book received an interesting review by Jeremy Treglown in *Books and Bookmen*, one part of which read:

He is concerned to offer a "serious study" of the limerick, expects "utterly honest criticism" and uses a great deal of space thundering at "so-called literary critics" and "pseudo-scholarly writers" who have failed, for example, to establish the etymology of the word *limerick* to his satisfaction. He hasn't got any further than these pathetic, craven freeloaders himself, it turns out—what he's waiting for is someone who will put in some proper research on this one.

In the meantime he hasn't much of value to say about the form, and his potentially interesting account of its history is submerged among examples of almost anything in the language that rhymes *aabba*.

Wow. Harsh. But a perceptive comment. Many writers do seem to collect "stuff" about limericks, and then arrange it in various categories in a show of "scholarship," without being able to critically examine whether or not it had a place in the history and development of the limerick verse form.

Some authors seem obsessed with one idea, which is promoted almost to the exclusion of all others. A good example can be found in Jean Harrowven's 1976 book *The Limerick Makers*. After dealing with a few proto-limericks in English, she makes an impassioned case for an Irish origin of the limerick. As I shall deal with this extensively, I will merely comment that the evidence presented is not examined critically, nor compared with any of the rival theories to see how it stacks up.

Why I Have Studied the History and Development of the Limerick

As the reader might imagine, I have always enjoyed reading, reciting and writing limericks. Many years ago I began to seriously wonder about their antecedents.

After reading so-called authoritative books and articles, I became completely puzzled as to what was true and what was false as regards the history and development of the limerick. Many suggestions offered in the literature were mutually incompatible. It was clear that some writers were blindly copying previous works, mistakes and all. Idle speculation was often presented as incontrovertible fact. Perhaps most astonishing of all were references which stated that a certain limerick could be found in a particular book, when merely opening the book proved categorically it was not present.

Somewhere along the line it became clear that I would remain in a state of puzzlement about the matter unless I set to and worked out for myself what the true history of the limerick verse form was. Almost without realizing it, that is what I have done. I certainly had no idea it would take so long.

My Approach

To date no one has collected every known fact, comment or opinion about the limerick, arranged this corpus into a chronological sequence and then examined critically what can be correct and what is implausible. In other words, no one has winnowed out the rubbish to expose the true story.

I therefore attempted to do just that: to try to collect everything known and said about limericks and see what the true story was. It is probably impossible to collect everything ever written about limericks, but I hoped I could find enough to allow me to understand the true story of the history and development of the limerick verse form.

When I started I had no preconceived idea as to what that story was; all that was clear was that limericks had either developed slowly from other verse forms, or they had been created fully formed somehow and somewhere. It was clear that at some point they became known as limericks and somehow they became popular. All I wanted to know was WHEN, WHERE, HOW and WHY.

I also wanted to look at the development of the verse form over the years, and to understand how it evolved into the complicated and wonderful object that we have today.

This took considerable time, as might be imagined. It was not enough, by the way, to merely read. Every so-called "fact" had to be checked. Every strongly expressed belief had to be proved or—what was often much harder—disproved. Eventually I believed that I had studied enough to actually have an accurate overview of the subject.

On the basis that others might be interested in my findings, I have created this book. It seemed to me that the only logical way to structure it was as chronologically as possible.

The scope of this book

After much deliberation I have limited the scope of the book to the first hundred years; a century has a nice round feel to it. Interesting things did happen in the subsequent years, but including them in this work would make it far too long.

I feel it is critical that any assertion I make can be traced back to the source I based it on. This is not possible with most earlier books. Accordingly I have appended extensive endnotes to most chapters.

Attributions

One of the great problems in limerick research is to find the author of any particular limerick. Rather than clutter up this book with the problems—and sometimes the excitement—involved in trying to run an author to earth, I have only attributed names to limericks where I have clear evidence. For limericks of unknown or uncertain parentage, rather than use *Anon* or *Unknown*, I have simply given no citation.

And the answers are?

I believe there were no real limericks before 1820. There were odd verses which came close to a limerick layout, but none of these, in my opinion, led to anything. That's an important point to make: if a limerick-like verse led to nothing, then it has played no real part in the history and development of the limerick verse form.

The first real limericks were contained in a group of illustrated children's books printed in the 1820s in London. Edward Lear was inspired by one of these books to write limericks in the 1830s for the small children of his artistic patron, the Earl of Derby. It was the publication of an expanded third edition of Lear's verses in 1861 which sparked a great interest in the verse form. The exact reason why this happened is debatable.

It is possible that the spread of the verse might owe a lot to the creation of what can be called personal limericks. These are verses in which the characteristics and foibles of a friend or acquaintance are included. They have the advantage of remaining in the friend's mind, although they are of little interest to others. With many such verses being created, it is possible that some really memorable gems were created, thereby allowing the limerick form to become much more widespread.

It can equally be argued that it was the creation of the dirty limerick—again, seemingly inspired by Lear's 1861 book—which caused the limerick to become popular.

Limericks were sung in convivial gatherings, originally in England. This, too, may be the reason for their popularity—especially if personal limericks were on the agenda for the crowd to enjoy.

After the 1860s there was no stopping the spread of the limerick. And unfortunately, there was no stopping the proliferation of silly ideas as to where they had come from and how they had acquired their name.

Three omissions

Three topics are not discussed in this book. First, I do not address the question of why limericks are called limericks. This is such a big subject that it would make this book twice as long. I have therefore written a separate work addressing this question.

I can answer it succinctly, though: limericks really do seem to have been sung to the beat of a now forgotten tune whose chorus was "Won't you come up to Limerick?" Boring as it may be, that is how they acquired their name. They were probably called limericks in the late 1860s, and probably in England.

The second omission is an in-depth description of personal limericks. I believe that one reason why limericks became popular and remain popular was the development of the personal limerick. This is where a listener's or reader's interest in the verse form is piqued when a verse is written specifically about them. I believe such people became kindly disposed to the old verse form and helped spread it. No one has ever suggested this idea before. To weave this idea into the current book would be to dilute the proposition; to add the text I have written on the matter would make this book too long.

Finally, I have not included an in-depth analysis of what a limerick actually is. Over the last 30 years I've had a great deal of fun attempting to categorize the old verse form, but again, to have included this text would have turned the current work into an encyclopedia.

PART I

Suggested Sources of the Limerick Pre-1820

Genuine limericks were published in several children's books in the 1820s, copies of which still exist. The purpose of this part of the book is to critically examine suggestions that limerick verses existed before these children's books were published. It is convenient to split this part into three chapters. These describe all sources that I know of which suggest there were limericks or limerick-like verses in existence prior to 1820.

Chapter 1 summarizes what might kindly be called "outlandish ideas."

Chapter 2 examines claims that the verses existed in English prior to 1820, and that these verses were either limericks or proto-limericks which developed into limericks.

Chapter 3 examines claims that verses in Irish Gaelic existed in limerick form prior to 1820, and that these verses gave rise to limericks in English.

Chapter 1

Not the Beginning!

A reader interested in when and where the first limericks were written can find a staggering array of suggestions. The following examples show that numerous corners of the world and several epochs of recorded history have been claimed. While most have probably been made tongue-in-cheek, some appear to be genuine suggestions. In any event, not one of the following is taken seriously by any limerick historian as indicating where and when limericks actually originated. I include them to show the range of what is on offer to the baffled reader.

Ancient Egypt

A 1975 American book suggested that archaeologists exploring King Tutankhamen's tomb had found on a mutilated wall the third and fourth lines of an ancient Egyptian limerick, which came out, through translation, as:

> She had for her clients
> Both pygmies and giants[1]

When a UK edition was published in 1978, a reviewer[2] for the *New Scientist* very properly pointed out that the author was that well-known maestro of English language wordplay and jokes, Willard Espy, and that it was most likely that he himself was the originator of the lines.

Although I am certain that no ancient Egyptian ever wrote a limerick, the singsong nature of their language was quite conducive to doing so. So much so, that Dr. Carol R. Fontaine, an assistant professor of the Old Testament at the Andover Newton Theological School in Massachusetts, created limericks in hieroglyphics for the express purpose of making it easier for her students to learn the symbols of this venerable script. She chose as her subject comments made by the powerful vizier Ptahhotep to Pharaoh Izezi about how he was getting too old for the job, and that perhaps the pharaoh might like to appoint a successor. Obviously a classical choice of subject matter, as can be seen in the 1981 article she published in *The Biblical Archaeologist*.[3]

There are, of course, some great limericks *about* Ancient Egypt:

> A Chinaman touring the Nile
> Said, "The Sphinx is no doubt all the style.
>   But yonder there be
>   Other ruins, I see,
> And I'll pyramid those for awhile."

In 1960 Bennett Cerf[4] attributed this limerick to one Frederick Van Horn. Other versions have two novelists touring the Nile, and a wise man exploring it. All, however, are agreed that they need to "peer-amid" the pyramids for a while.

Cerf is a quite unreliable source. The most likely author is Blanche Elizabeth Wade, over whose name the limerick stands in a 1901 reference.[5] This, incidentally, illustrates a perennial problem in limerick scholarship: proving who wrote what. We shall encounter more examples later.

Ancient India

Some brilliant American chemists have been very interested in limericks. One such was Gilbert Newton Lewis. Another was Henry Bohn Hass, who regaled friends and colleagues with many verses, including personal tributes and additional stanzas about the young lady called Wilde who kept herself quite undefiled. He also appears to have written the following classic:

> There was a young lady from Clyde
> Who ate some green apples and died.
>   The apples fermented
>   Within the lamented,
> Made cider inside her inside!

In between all this literary work he also invented the gas chromatograph, which is one of the bedrocks of modern chemical analysis.

For some unstated reason he thought that "the limerick is reliably reported to be found in Sanscrit in the Bhagavad Gita, the sacred writing of the Hindus which is at least 1700 years old and probably much older. Thus the claim that this form of verse originated in the English language is incorrect. It has, however, reached its greatest development in English speaking countries. Nobody knows how it came to be called Limerick."

This appears in a collection of his poems and limericks published privately in 1982.⁶ Not being too sure of the rhyme scheme of the Bhagavad Gita, I asked the then Boden Professor of Sanskrit at Oxford University if there were any limericks in it. (What is the point of having experts in arcane subjects unless you occasionally make use of them?) Professor Christopher Minkowski kindly replied to my enquiry and explained:

> If we go by formal metrical criteria, there are no limericks in the Bhagavad Gita. There are two predominating metrical forms in the BG, the so called shloka meter, which is made up of four lines of eight syllables each (most Sanskrit meters are syllabic), and the trishtubh, which is made up of four lines of eleven syllables each. So I don't know why Prof. Hass would have thought this, except that the pattern of light and heavy syllables in the trishtubh has a few overlaps with the pattern of the limerick: u _ u _ _ , u u _ u _ _ (where u is light and _ is heavy), but there is far from a perfect match. And [as] there is no end rhyme in Sanskrit, it being a language with inflectional endings, like Latin or Greek, there is no glory in it.

I think it's a pity that India is not the home of the limerick since some of the great limericks use Indian place names.

Persia

In 1912 a London magazine called *The New Age: A Weekly Review of Politics, Literature, and Art* contained a short contribution by P. Selver titled "Pastiche. Some aspects of the Limericks as a verse-form." This began with the observation:

> Now that the vogue of the limerick has become almost a matter of literary history some attempt should be made to discuss its significance more fully than has hitherto been done. The following brief indications may serve to draw attention to the large field for research that lies ready for treatment. It is to be hoped that before long some earnest critic will hasten to amplify and treat in greater detail a few of these scattered and imperfect notes.
>
> The literature of the subject is, of course, extremely scanty. A short account of the development of the limerick is given in Volume XII of Professor Heiligenberg's valuable "Englische Verslehre." But the happy flashes of the distinguished author's method are here almost entirely lacking. Most of his judgments are heavy and unconvincing, and he seems quite unaware of the leading part played by the limerick in the English poetical revival in the first decade of the twentieth century.
>
> As regards sources and origins, Professor Heiligenberg, usually so intrepid in this respect, will not commit himself far. He certainly hazards some conjectures about medieval Latin hymns and Leonine hexameters; but his pronouncements are so hedged in with reservations and restrictions that they cannot be regarded as the last word on the subject.⁷

Those who would like to study the eminent Professor Heiligenberg's pontifications for themselves are in for a long wait. The whole reference seems to be made up.

Selver's article then suggests that limericks came from Limerick, and would have been written in Erse. This idea, however, does not exclude other theories, and he says that by rewriting a typical limerick in a slightly different layout to the normal five lines—

> There was a young man of Kinsale
> With inordinate cravings for ale.
> It is dreadful to think that he so loved this drink
> As to swallow it out of a pail.

—this will immediately remind the reader of the layout and rhyme scheme of the *Rubáiyát of Omar Khayyam*. (Which indeed it does, but only of those verses in Edward Fitzgerald's "translations.") Some further speculations follow, of a doubtless erudite nature, and we are told that "the Oriental influences in the limerick are too marked to be entirely neglected."

A follow-up letter to the editor of the magazine says that several readers wrote to Selver, suggesting that he was right:

> A communication from Mr. Thomas Dodsley was particularly complimentary. It is noteworthy that my somewhat venturesome conjecture with regard to Oriental elements in the limerick are fully corroborated by Mr. Dodsley, who has a first-hand acquaintance with Persian poetry. In addition, he draws my attention to a few hitherto overlooked metrical peculiarities of the limerick, such as the occasional anacrusis in the second line, and the position of the cesura in the last line.[8]

The erstwhile author of the article is probably Paul Selver, who was a prolific writer and translator. In a 1926 book one of Selver's characters comments: "This rather reminded him of a mock essay on the origin and history of the limerick which Tancred had once written for *The Mistral*, and which, with its quotations from Persian and Gaelic bards, had been taken seriously by a number of respectable but obtuse readers."[9]

Again, the magazine referred to did not exist, so we may safely regard the whole affair as a spoof. Persian poetry did not give rise to limericks.

Which is perhaps another pity, since Omar Khayyam was the sort of chap who would have enjoyed a good limerick; for example, along the lines of:

> A remarkable race are the Persians,
> They have such peculiar diversions.
>   They screw the whole day
>   In the regular way,
> And save up the nights for perversions.

Chapter 1. Not the Beginning!

Well, as they say in Farsi: "The moving finger writes, and having writ, moves on." I've written all I know about the supposed Persian origins of the limerick, so I suggest we, too, move on.

The Glory That Was Greece

Aristophanes: Cloud cuckoo land

A book titled *Greek Social Life* was published in 1925. In one passage the author, F.A. Wright, a professor of classics, describes a typical evening's entertainment: drinking a good deal of weak wine, eating little, mainly talking, and a little singing. He further records:

> The invention of limericks also was a favorite diversion at ancient Athenian symposia, and Aristophanes at the end of *The Wasps* gives half a dozen specimens. Here is one of them:
>
>> An amateur, driving too fast,
>> From his car to the roadway was cast;
>> And a friend kindly said, as he bandaged his head—
>> "Mr. Cobbler, stick to your last."[10]

The Wasps was first seen on stage in 422 BC.

This verse was mentioned by H.I. Brock in his 1947 limerick book.[11] He went on to say that the Greeks didn't use rhyme, so consequently they didn't have limericks in the way we do. However, later books certainly gave the impression that Aristophanes wrote limericks. In 1963 Armstrong wrote that "the limerick existed, in one variant or another, as far back as [...] Aristophanes."[12]

William Baring-Gould commented on Wright's book in his hugely influential 1967 work, and his text reads as if the Greek original actually did contain limericks. If true, then these would arguably be the oldest limericks in the world. Baring-Gould also introduced a typo into the limerick, changing its meaning somewhat. The friend becomes less than sympathetic as "he banged" the driver's head. Presumably to knock some sense into it!

In 1978 Dr. Bibby quoted the limerick in its more kindly version, restoring "bandaged" for "banged." He then showed that the original verse was not in limerick form at all by the simple expedient of going back to the Greek. He found another translation which was much closer in form and layout:

> There was a man of Sybaris, do you know,
> Thrown from his carriage, and he cracked his skull,

> Quite badly too. Fact was, he could not drive.
> There was a friend of his stood by, and said,
> "Let each man exercise the art he knows."[13]

That last sentence, incidentally, should be pinned up on the wall of every author who ventures to write upon the noble subject of limericks.

Actually, many of the "classical poems" can be translated using the limerick format and rhyme scheme. Usually no claim is made by the author that the original was a limerick; merely that the limerick layout best conveys what one translator of *The Wasps* described as "the rambunctious energy and lyrical verve of its poetry."[14]

A good example is Gilbert Murray's 1909 translation of Aristophanes's *The Frogs* (first performed 405 BC), in which several of the verses are given in limerick form. As a contemporary review put it:

> Gilbert Murray's spirited verse translation of "The Frogs" of Aristophanes is a real pleasure. [...] He boldly adopts the Limerick meter, and we are led by facile, yet accomplished workmanship sometimes to doubt whether we are reading Gilbert or Gilbert Murray. We quote the opening of the chorus:
>
>> Frogs: O brood of the mere and the spring,
>> Gather together and sing
>> From the depths of your throat
>> By the side of the boat
>> Coax, as we move in a ring.[15]

Another good example of transliterating ancient verses into limerick form occurs at the end of the 1912 Selver article, although he of course *is* "claiming" that such verses are the predecessors of limericks. He writes:

> The Greek anthology contains many epigrams that might well be cast into limerick form. The *Epitaph on a Fowler*, by Mnasalcas, which in Garnett's translation reads thus:
>
>> Now may the swiftly-winging bird return,
>>   And sit in peace upon this pleasant plane;
>> Pimander now is ashes in his urn,
>>   Nor here will lift his limy rods again.
>
> may be freely rendered into a limerick, as follows:
>
>> A Greek, with the snares that he spread
>> Caught hundreds of birds, it is said.
>>   But what bird now cares
>>   For his lime and his snares?—
>> For wily Pimander is dead!

Perhaps that's taking transliteration one step too far. However, it's not a bad philosophical limerick, and there are a lot more philosophical limericks around than most people realize.

Stobæus

A seemingly authoritative letter in a 1933 magazine[16] suggested that Stobæus, a fifth-century AD writer, wrote a limerick in the third volume of his *Florilegium*. The Greek verse is given in "classical" limerick layout and the author comments that Porson, the legendary Greek scholar, had made marginal notes in his copy of Stobæus, writing "utter bosh" at the appropriate point. The letter writer suggested this was a prophetic nod toward Edward Lear's later work on limericks, such nonsense sometimes being called bosh.

A prose translation is given: "Eplithus carved the memorial that it might be an everlasting possession, but the citizens and all passers-by said, 'O all-abominable word [or thing].'"

Since the magazine in question was *Punch* and the letter writer signed himself "Marmaduke Monk-Howson, The Oaks, Bilgewater, nr. Bosham"—the average English reader would have recognized it for what it was: a spoof, although apparently it did cause one American academic to write a short note in *The Classical Journal*, which included the Greek limerick, and contained the legendary footnote: "The editions of Stobæus which are accessible to me here do not contain this quotation. Is this another example of *Punch*'s humor?"[17]

A fellow American put the matter to rest a few months later. W.A. Oldfather of the University of Illinois explained that the limerick was in all likelihood a spoof.[18] He further explained that the limerick was probably referring to a Jacob Epstein panel of the wood-sprite Rima, erected in Hyde Park, London, in 1925. This was received with less than rapturous praise from the public at the time. The two words—Epstein and Rima—were identified by Professor Oldfather in the original Greek limerick: Eplithus = Epstone = Epstein.

After that exposition the matter rarely troubled the reading public again, except once to summarize the whole affair, and to give a somewhat different translation: "Eplithos made the monument that it might be a possesion [sic] forever. But all the citizens and all the passers-by said 'O what an utterly horrible thing.'"[19]

Funnily enough, some erudite soul actually did write a limerick about the Epstein exhibit, although none of our classical authors seemed to know of it:

> There once was a sculptor of mark
> Who was chosen to brighten Hyde Park;
> Some thought his design
> Most uncommonly fine,
> But more liked it best in the dark.

And the origin of this gem? *Punch* magazine, June 3, 1925, page 595.

(For anyone wishing to see the offending panel, photographs exist in reference works[20] along with descriptions of the resulting imbroglio. The *Yorkshire Evening Post* gave as its considered opinion: "That isn't Rima. That's the soul of a ... poulterer's wife being conducted to hell by two frozen hen turkeys.")

Saint Thomas Aquinas

In days gone by the world and his dog spoke Latin, as exemplified by the expression *cave canem* found at Pompeii. Well, the educated world did, at least. One reason was because the church still ran in Latin. And one of the prayers in Latin has been suggested to be the oldest limerick in the world.

Some limerick students have become quite excited over the following verse, which is a prayer of thanksgiving used by priests after Mass. Widely attributed to St. Thomas Aquinas (1225–1274), it has the inadvertent form of a limerick:

> sit vitiorum meorum evacuatio
> concupiscentiae et libidinis exterminatio
> caritatis et patientiae
> humilitatis et obedientiae,
> omniumque virtutum augmentatio.

Some have struggled to translate the verse with their schoolboy Latin; however, parallel texts are widely available, so there is no real problem for the monoglots among us. A typical translation reads:

> Let it be for the elimination for my sins,
> For the expulsion of desire and lust,
> [And] for the increase of charity and patience,
> Humility and obedience
> As well as all the virtues.

The description of this Latin verse as "the first limerick" has been well-ventilated in both the popular press and the scholarly press. Let's look at a few references, in approximate chronological order.

The following, from an American review of Langford Reed's 1924 book on limericks, gives us two popular references for the price of one:

> "I have for my model," replied Angelicus, "none other than the great St. Thomas Aquinas."
> "Doctor Angelicus, I have always respected your veracity," remarked Primus Criticus, "but now—"
> The Doctor interrupted him by waving a copy of the *London Morning Post*

for December 30, 1924, in his face. "Here is my authority," said he. "It states that St. Thomas Aquinas himself was the perpetrator (shall we say unconsciously) of a pious limerick incorporated in the Roman Missal among the prayers to be said in the thanksgiving of the priest after his Mass. Word for word the verse falls into an almost perfect limerick form—"[21]

The verse appeared in the *Times* in 1935, where the Reverend Pizey described it as "a somewhat cumbersome Limerick."[22] This inspired a gentleman to write to an American magazine 11 years later. He described it as "A Saintly Limerick" and gave a translation in a limerick-like layout, which had neither the right number of feet in each line nor very good rhymes either.[23]

A 1946 issue of *John O'London's* popular weekly magazine contained the following remarks: "A CLERICAL friend has drawn my attention to what must surely be the most curious limerick in existence. It occurs in the Latin prayer written by St. Thomas Aquinas for thanksgiving after Mass. As it stands, of course, it is simple Latin prose; but I gather that all those who use the Breviary have noticed that in rhyme and rhythm it forms—a perfect limerick—in which form I print it here."[24]

The columnist concluded this description by asking if any reader knew of an older limerick.

The Listener magazine of 1951 contained a flurry of letters from correspondents all eager to tell what they thought was "the earliest limerick." Jack Werner[25] wrote in, suggesting Aquinas; he mentioned that the verse, which he quoted, would be appearing in his soon-to-be-published book. And it did indeed appear in *Small Latin and Less Greek*, his 1954 book.[26]

A 1953 article on the limerick in *The American Mercury* told readers that "the use of this metrical form has not always been profane and light-hearted. One of the most beautiful prayers of the thirteenth century, composed by St. Thomas Aquinas, and still used was as a thanksgiving after Mass, is in the meter of the Limerick."[27]

In 1963, one Hugh Ross Williamson of the Savage Club, London, wrote to *The Spectator* and enquired: "What is the date of the earliest limerick?"[28] He said he suspected St. Thomas Aquinas of introducing one deliberately as a mnemonic into one of his best known prayers, which he quoted, and ended by asking if anyone knew of an earlier example.

The verse appeared in *Notes & Queries* in 1968.[29] In this reference the author waxed lyrical about it and gave evidence that it was written in the twelfth century; Aquinas lived in the thirteenth.

Harrowven had it on page 13 of her 1976 book. A review of the 2004 reissue of Harrowven's book in the *TLS* commented on it, adding, "It is a curiosity of literary history (first recorded here, we dare say) that the earliest application of limerick meter should have occurred in a plea to resist all that the limerick became famous for."[30] Doubtless that statement will end up as an indubitable fact in some future book on the history of the limerick.[31]

Bibby printed the verse in his 1978 book on page 180.

In 1985 the subject was ventilated at some length in an American magazine for limerick aficionados.[32] In 2009 the magazine contained several translations of the verse into English, in limerick form. These came from the internet; most display only a vague relationship to the original text.[33]

A 2017 reference made a fair stab at rendering the verse into a limerick:

> May God's feast leave my vices depressed;
> May it quench the desires in my breast;
>   May my virtues gain clarity:
>   Humbleness, charity,
> Patience, and all of the rest.[34]

What Ronald Knox had to say about the matter

Unfortunately, none of the above authors, and the many others who in print and online have stated that Aquinas actually created a limerick, seem to know what Ronald Knox wrote about this verse in 1925 when reviewing Langford Reed's *The Complete Limerick Book*:

> The claims of antiquity made for [the limerick] are frequently fantastic. Thus you will hear it stated that it goes back to St. Thomas Aquinas. This legend is based on a passage in one of his prayers which does just convey the suggestion of a Limerick to a person unable to scan, or even to count. Here is an English Limerick made up on the exact model of the passage in question, scanning on the same principle syllable for syllable:
>
> > Once long ago there resided someone at Bibury
> > Who was much worried by someone's bringing a gross charge of bribery
> > Over some election festivities
> > Cause by his somewhat expensive proclivities,
> > The time he stood as a candidate for Highbury.
>
> If anybody likes to regard that as a limerick, let him.[35]

There's not much to say after that, is there?

Indeed, the only thing I can think of is to note that Knox uses the expression "you will hear it stated," which suggests that he might not have been the first to bring attention to Aquinas's so-called limerick. And indeed he wasn't—despite those who claim that he was. Spurred on by his remark, I ran to earth the following 1917 references: "And so it happens that we have Thomas Aquinas making and reciting very good limericks in his hours of recreation,"³⁶ and "It is a matter of historic tradition that St. Thomas Aquinas composed and recited very good 'limericks' in his hours of recreation and that they were highly appreciated by his brethren."³⁷

The origin of the claim

Further investigation suggests that the probable origin of the attribution is a short text in an April 1910 edition of a Catholic weekly review magazine published in London: "A clerical correspondent writes to point out that the following words from the Prayer after Communion by St. Thomas Aquinas, which is given in the Missal, when arranged as a verse fall into the familiar form of a Limerick."³⁸

At least one other magazine picked up this attribution and helped spread the word. In July 1910, a New York journal commented: "Scholars have often amused themselves by discovering unintended hexameters in sober prose authors, or in the English Bible; but it is left to the London *Tablet* to have discovered an actual limerick embodied in the Prayer after Communion by St. Thomas Aquinas, and given in the Missal. Put into lines it reads…"³⁹

The Council of Trent

This is not a local unitary authority that looks after an area of Nottinghamshire. Keen students of Catholic history will know that the Council referred to sat intermittently at Trento in Italy from 1545 to 1563, mainly in response to a growing popularity of Martin Luther's ideas. It considered such weighty matters as the condemnation of the Protestants, the banning of certain books, and a load of other doubtless important stuff.

Keen readers of the *Pastoral Music* magazine will probably have noticed the following article in a 1990 issue. After a few general remarks about how meetings of liturgical and musical people have a mainly serious side, the author comments that on occasion the delegates let their hair down and indulge in a little lighthearted behavior. Sometimes they produce jokes, drawings, photos and suchlike, which rarely get included in the official reports. He then comments:

> There is really nothing new about this; the same thing has been happening at serious church meetings for a long time, but only now are some of these artifacts coming to light. You might have seen the photos, for instance, of the vaguely suggestive mosaics depicting the participants of the Synod of Whitby (Yorkshire, 664). They were published in the volume *Erotic Celtic Mosaics* (London: Chad, Wilfrid & Associates, 1982). Or, for those who studied

decadent medieval Latin, there is the famous Latin limerick that shows the early impact of scientific method on popular consciousness. It first appeared, according to all reports, during Session 11 (1551) of the Council of Trent.

> Episcopus ven't in Majorcam
> Qui vidit feminam tarn pulchram
> Quam piscopus dixit....
> Well, you remember the rest.[40]

Further enquiries suggest that the whole article is a spoof. For instance, there is—alas—no book of erotic Celtic mosaics. The publisher's name seems a composite made up from the names of the chief protagonists at the Synod of Whitby. The name of the author of the article is a pen name of several worthy members of the National Association of Pastoral Musicians, whose contributions are otherwise anonymous.

I did write to the editor asking if the whole thing was a spoof, but in case it wasn't could he tell me the rest of the limerick? As expected, answer came there none.

China

A 2006 book designed to teach the elements of English grammar to reluctant and recalcitrant American children contains the comment that "maybe you have heard this already, but limericks were invented in twelfth-century China as a marching ditty for the army."[41]

If true, this would have occurred in the appropriately named Song Dynasty, a golden era when poetry, literature and culture flowered in a time of stability.

Armies do march to a variety of tunes. Many such tunes are accompanied by rude words. I rather like the idea of battalions marching along singing limericks in Chinese, but as far as I know no one has ever unearthed a priceless Ming limerick.

Holland

At a conference called Unity and Diversity in the Caribbean, held in Curaçao in 1983, the linguist Frank Martinus Arion of the University of the Netherlands Antilles presented a paper intriguingly titled "Creole Influences in European Limericks."

The abstract describing this paper starts by commenting that some odd rhymes such as *eeny meeny miny mo* have not really been understood. The Dutch-Antillean author (who had spent 26 years in Holland) then says:

Methodologically, the first strange thing to note is that up to now the similarity in the word material of these songs, though in different languages, has not been noticed. Another is that some of the Dutch ones clearly have the form of the so-called English limerick, a form that on second investigation was known and popular in Dutch literature long before the limerick became the quintessence of an Englishman's superior wit.

The nonsense theory does not seem to hold; above all, not in combination with the rather intricate limerick versification, and the Germanic trail also proves very awkward. Where, then, does the proud English wit (which was known in Holland long before it became English) really come from?[42]

Quite what this all means I'm not sure. Efforts to find the text of the presentation have been in vain. However, a chapter by Arion in a 1989 book is titled "Creole Nursery Rhymes in Dutch and the Origin of the Limerick."[43] This probably has a strong association with the presentation. Having looked at it I confess to being somewhat baffled, not least because it is in Dutch.

Arion's essay on children's verses originating from Dutch can be read in English in a 1998 work.[44]

Whether Dutch limericks had any part to play in the development of the English form I leave for others more learned than I to discover.

There are naturally limericks *about* the Netherlands:

> In Holland all clog dancers revel
> In jigs where they stamp like the devil.
>   But the land has been marred
>   By that stamping down hard;
> So it's flat and below the sea level.
> —Bob Turvey

In the country itself the verse form is alive and well and kept vocal, for example, by such eminently respectable public performers as Drs. Nagtegeijl and the Groninger Swaffel Choir, as can be seen online.[45]

France

The claim that France was the origin of limericks was not made by a man of French letters, but by a British belletrist. In his first book on limericks, Langford Reed says that Ireland was an early source for the singing of limericks, and that the first specimen ever composed was the old nursery rhyme "Hickory Dickory Dock." In the second edition of this book he writes: "Since the first edition of this book appeared, its compiler believes that he has been fortunate enough to elucidate a literary mystery that has puzzled the world for a good many years—that concerning the origin of the Limerick."

After describing some early English limericks, and the Church's involvement in limerick creation, he explores several venerable versions of "Hickory Dickory Dock," including a French version believed to be "hundreds of years old." Reed then unleashes his great discovery: "This was nothing less than the discovery of a French Limerick"—and quotes the following verse, which was first published in 1715:

> On s'étonne ici que Caliste,
> Ait pris l'habit de Moliniste,
>   Puisque cette jeune beauté
>   Ote à chacun sa liberté
> N'est-ce pas une Janseniste?[46]

Despite much labor in the literary vineyards laid down by old French chroniclers, Reed was able to turn up no more than a faint "suggestion" of a limerick in one other French verse. Nothing daunted, Reed simply *assumes* a French origin of the limerick verse form: "Assuming, then, that the Limerick is French in origin—how did it arrive in Limerick?"[47] He then creates a convoluted odyssey to get these limericks to Ireland to fit in with his earlier claim that limericks were sung in Ireland "about a century ago" (i.e., the 1820s). He suggests that soldiers in the Irish Brigade, who were attached to the French Army for a period of nearly one hundred years, from 1691, somehow learned the limerick verse form and brought it back "direct to Limerick." No tangible evidence whatsoever is offered for this idea, and most limerick scholars consider it a flight of fancy.

This French verse might have made some inroads into the consciousness of English readers, as it was included in a footnote of James Boswell's *Life of Johnson*, probably in the second edition of 1793 and then in subsequent editions. Boswell's book enjoyed considerable success, so the verse could conceivably have been known to the writers of what everyone agrees are books containing genuine limericks, which were published in the 1820s.

No limerick historian seems to have commented on this possibility.

Personally, I don't think it had any effect on the English limericks of the 1820s, because they were for children, and this French verse is really an epigram on free will.

I think this verse just happens to have a limerick-like layout. It certainly never gave rise to anything remotely resembling limericks in French. Limericks do exist in French. They are not of great antiquity and it is generally held that most were not written by French speakers. For example, Legman: "All limericks in French are actually in 'fractured French,' by English-speaking poets, and are usually terrible."[48]

America

The claim for an American origin of the limerick verse form depends on several mistaken ideas. And we all know that even *two* wrongs don't make a right.

In a 1935 book titled *Poetry and Its Forms*, the professor of English literature at the Pennsylvania State College tells us:

> The limerick is one of the few forms to have originated in America. In 1719 *Songs for the Nursery, or, Mother Goose Melodies for Children* made its appearance. In this publication the early forms and stages of the limerick are represented, from that of
>
> > Hickory, dickory, dock,
> > The mouse ran up the clock,
> > The clock struck one
> > The mouse ran down,
> > Hickory dickory dock!
>
> where the first line is repeated as the fifth, to the following where a new terminal line is introduced:
>
> > There was an old soldier of Bister
> > Went walking one day with his sister,
> > When a cow at one poke
> > Tossed her into an oak,
> > Before the old gentlemen missed her.
>
> The form of the limerick usually follows this latter arrangement.[49]

This viewpoint was still going strong in the 1938 reprint of the book.

Other writers certainly thought limericks came from Mother Goose, although none claimed American precedency. For example, a 1924 article in the *Atlantic Monthly*: "On the other hand, there can be no dispute that some of the earliest limericks come from the Mother Goose rhymes. Truly that is a noble birthplace, which no verse form should disdain."[50]

The idea that these "limericks" came from a 1719 American book may have originated in Clement Wood's 1926 little pocket book, in which he wrote: "My own theory has never been denied; perhaps because it has never been made public before. The first collection of Mother Goose rhymes was published in Pudding Lane, Boston, in 1719; and, since I have never seen a copy of its first edition, I am entirely without prejudice in stating that this edition contained the first limerick ever circulated."[51]

"Hickory Dickory Dock" is then given, along with several others. Wood repeated the claim in several subsequent books. Indeed, he even amplified it; for example, in his *Unabridged Rhyming Dictionary*[52] he explained that this Mother Goose book of 1719 contained the three stages in the development of the limerick. According to him these are, first, a nonsense sentence used in lines 1 and 5; next, a rhyming word in line 1 repeated in line 5; finally, a new rhyming word in the fifth line.

Let's examine the claim that limericks first appeared in an American book in 1719. I have three reservations.

Firstly, "Hickory Dickory Dock." There are certainly those who believe this is a limerick. Louis Untermeyer called it "a perfect limerick and probably one of the oldest."[53] Others had a quite different viewpoint. A review in *The Times* of Langford Reed's 1924 book commented: "[Reed] is inclined to see the first worthy example in the nursery jingle *Hickory Dickory Dock*. That, of course is a false Limerick, with the last line flatly repeating the first."[54]

I don't think it's a limerick because:

- the numbers of beats are 7-6-4-4-7. I am prepared to stretch things from the classical 9-9-6-6-9 for fabulous rhymes, wonderful images, metrical delights—but not for pedestrian text.
- the rhymes for lines 3 and 4—they don't. Maybe "one" and "down" did a couple of centuries ago.
- the first and the last lines are meaningless. So in reality the verse is a three-line poem. Little kids love the rhyme—I did when I was little. But I don't think it could ever be called a limerick.

Secondly, "The Old Soldier of Bister" [*sic*] did not make his first appearance in any Mother Goose book. He first appeared circa 1820 in *The Anecdotes and Adventures of Fifteen Gentlemen*, published in London.

Thirdly—and this trumps everything—there never was a Mother Goose book published in America in 1719. It is a literary hoax. The first claim that such a book had existed was made in 1860. One of the first people to investigate this claim was Mr. W.H. Whitmore, who published his findings in 1889. His trenchant opinion was made quite clear on the first page of his book: "I desire to dismiss, entirely, the idea that Mother Goose was a name which originated in Boston, Mass."[55]

After explaining why he believed the 1719 book never existed (and why people thought it did), Mr. Whitmore's book then reproduces *The Original Mother Goose's Medley*, as first issued by John Newbery, of London, circa 1760. This contains "Dickery dickery dock," a version of the well-known rhyme. It contains no limericks.

The general public, especially in America, was certainly told the 1719 book had never existed; for example, see items in *The New York Times* of 1899[56] and 1909.[57] For anyone interested in the story as to why the claim was ever made, the Opies clearly summarized the matter in 1951.[58] The internet shows some people still think the book was real.

Quoting from a nonexistent book: that's a skill I never learned as a scientist.

Chapter 2

Possible Limericks in English Prior to 1820

There are claims that limericks existed in English prior to 1820. A variant is that there were verses which, although not limericks themselves, developed into limericks.

I think the claimants fall into two broad groups. The first contains those who have actually plumbed the historical depths of literature in an attempt to try to find out the truth. Examples include Reed (1924), Morse (1948), Legman (1964 and later), Bibby (1978) and Belknap (1981). However, the style of their writing often leaves much—if not all—to be desired. Instead of just chronologically listing all the poems they have found, they jump from pillar to post, stick in extraneous limericks, and make irrelevant comments all over the place. I've also noticed that often just one stanza is given, not the whole poem. This stanza is usually the most "limerick-like" in the poem.

I sometimes wonder if this obfuscation is deliberate and designed to draw attention away from the poorness of the argument being put forward—which is that these verses are real limericks or, at the very least, proto-limericks. Reading such offerings is likely to result in a splitting headache, misaligned eyeballs and a sense of complete chronological bewilderment. It is not recommended.

The second broad group contains those who seem mainly interested in just compiling a book of limericks, but feel they need to pay lip service to the reader or the publisher by bunging in a few facts about the history of the verse. These "facts" would appear to have been lifted from more serious works. The lack of understanding about these original references can result in some absolute howling mistakes. Again, for a different reason this time, reading such chapters is not recommended.

Early Examples of Such Claims

Before we get to the big beasts of "ancient" limerick research, I'd like to look at a couple of early comments about when the oldest limericks might have been written or published.

I'm not really sure who first asked the question: "When were the earliest limericks written?" Mr. Tuer certainly asked in 1897 if there were any older than the children's books of the 1820s. (His letter to *Notes & Queries* is examined in the 1820s chapter; the answers to it mentioned only books published after the 1820s or earlier books which didn't actually contain limericks!)

In a short introduction to his 1908 book, Ralph A. Lyon casually stated that Robert Herrick (1591–1674) "wrote the following set of limericks" and then quoted "The Night-Piece (To Julia)." He followed this by saying that Thomas Moore, the famous Irish poet, "used the limerick form for several of his poems, both serious and humorous," and then gave the poem "I can no longer stifle."[1] A knowledgeable writer in *The New York Times* cited another Moore poem when reviewing Lyon's book: "The Time I've Lost in Wooing."[2]

The 1910 *Little Book of Limericks* by Wallace and Frances Rice stated:

> It will be further found that its rhyme and rhythm are inherent in the oldest Border Balladry. An apt illustration is the following stanza from *Lord Thomasine*, where the omission of a foot from the first verse and insertion of a rhyme gives
>
> > She called all her maids, I ween,
> > She clothed them all in green:
> >   And the very next borough
> >   She did come thorough
> > They thought it had been a great queen.[3]

The original first line read: "O then she called her merry maids all." The word "thorough" is used here in its obsolete sense of "through." We can note that the number of beats in this altered verse is 7-6-7-5-8.

The rest of the original poem, incidentally, has no rhymes in lines 3 and 4. It actually consists of four-line stanzas that rhyme ABCB—the Rices have changed the original third line into two lines. By no stretch of anyone's imagination did the original ballad have any limerick-like qualities.

What a pair of puddings the Rices were: rewriting verses so they became limerick-like—and then claiming the original verses *were* limericks. It's just not cricket. You might as well say that a dictionary is actually a proto-limerick book—because it contains all the words you'll ever find in a limerick.

However, that didn't stop the authors from proclaiming in another book a year later:

> Since it has not been noted elsewhere, it deserves to be set down here that the Limerick, of which this book contains a few examples, has not previously been traced back of the nineteenth century. Yet it owes its form to rare old Ben Jonson, who anticipated modernity in this as in the form of the stanza of *In Memoriam*. In Professor Edward Arber's *English Songs: Jonson and His Times* will be found the following perfect Limericks, written before the settlement of Boston:
>
>> To the old, long life and treasure!
>> To the young, all health and pleasure!
>> To the fair, their face
>> With eternal grace!
>> And the foul [*sic*], to be loved at leisure!
>
>> To the witty, all clear mirrors!
>> To the foolish, their dark errors!
>> To the loving sprite,
>> A secure delight!
>> To the jealous, their own false terrors![4]

I don't know how the settlement of Boston is going these days but I feel quite unsettled—because there is a misprint in the last line of the first verse; "foul" should be "soul." It changes the meaning somewhat!

Pre-1820 Verses Claimed to Be Limericks: In Chronological Order

Over the years other pre–1820 verses were suggested as being limericks, near-limericks, proto-limericks or pre-limericks. Learned articles have been written on such matters. Now, how can I summarize this whole field to make it easy for the reader to obtain a swift and accurate overview?

I think the only possible way is to list *all* the verses which have been suggested, in chronological order; cite the people who have suggested them; and give accurate information as to when and where they were first published. Rather than clutter up this section with fragments of poems and distracting references I have put this list as an Appendix, along with all necessary references and some comments which are hopefully helpful.

Pre-1820s Verses Not Previously Discussed in the Literature

During my own peregrinations along the highways and byways of long-forgotten literature, I have come across some verses which might be considered to be limericks and which do not seem to have been discussed in print by limerick scholars. I've also come across some references which state that such-and-such an early work contained limericks. Let's examine them in chronological order.

The Allison-Shelley Collection: Possible 17th- and 18th-Century Limericks

There are several electronic databases which catalogue the contents of individual libraries, or of groups of libraries. Some can be accessed by the public. WORLDCAT is one such, cataloguing mainly U.S. public and university libraries. Keen delvers into this will have spotted that the Allison-Shelley manuscript collection housed in the Rare Books and Manuscripts Section at Penn State University is titled "Limericks collection, ca 1650–1971." Part of this collection is said to consist of "17th and 18th century manuscript limericks."

Correspondence with the curator in charge of this collection has shown that most of the content in the folder marked "17th and 18th century manuscript limericks" is doggerel which is not even in five-line layout. Only one manuscript in the collection might be considered to be in limerick layout. This seems to be a narrative poem. The first page contains the title: *A Songe*. The next two pages contain 20 stanzas in a sloping copperplate hand. These do look as if they are in limerick layout. However, try as I might, I simply cannot read what the text actually says. It's a problem I have never encountered before. The bits I can read suggest the stanzas are not limericks.

There is no date on this document, and I can find no trace of it ever being published, so there's not much I can deduce from this reference. However, on the bright side, the collection does contain some interesting limericks, probably written in 1861, which we shall examine later.

1704–1706: Two English Periodicals

A 1930 book on English literary periodicals commented:

The *Diverting Post* of Henry Playford was designed for the entertainment of "those only, whose understanding and judgment have been refined, by liberal education and genteel conversation, from the heavy dross which clogs the reason of the vulgar; who take delight in the pleasing paths of poetry, not in the rugged ways of business; who had rather line their heads than their pockets..." He promised to publish all manuscripts sent in, provided they were free from scurrilous language and immodest reflections. In spite of the author's expressed aim, the *Diverting Post* had a rather brief and ignoble career

(October 28, 1704 to June 30, 1705, as a half-sheet weekly; then during January and February, 1706, as a ten-page monthly). It began well enough, filled with occasional verse, news matter, and dialogues. By January, 1705, the news matter had disappeared, as well as the dialogues. From this point on the *Diverting Post* was made up entirely of verse-prologues for Wilkes, Booth, and Betterton, riddles, limericks, and long poems. Like many of its predecessors, it became, as it progressed, more unequivocally indecent. Meanwhile, in January, such unpublished poems as had been found too concretely carnal for even the *Diverting Post*, were issued by Samuel Philips in the weekly *Poetical Courant*.[5]

Sitting down in the venerable Bodleian I looked forward to perusing these "concretely carnal" verses; a good description of a limerick if I ever heard one. Even the library catalogue number held out promise: Hopeful.102.

Alas; disappointment.

In the *Poetical Courant* there are no limerick-like verses. In the *Diverting Post* of April 14 to April 21, 1705, Mr. Sam Phillips gave us a four-stanza poem in limerick-like layout, titled "To Flavia." The last stanza will give you a flavor of Flavia:

IV
Our Bullets are amorous Kisses,
Our Field a fine soft downy Bed;
  Where I'll thunder, and plunder,
  (Unless you'll surrender)
Your delicate Maiden-head.

1717: John Tomlinson Diary Entry

John Tomlinson was an English clergyman known for his diary, kept from 1715 to 1722. Wikipedia, in a footnote to a short article on limericks, cites a diary entry as follows:

> An interesting and highly esoteric verse in limerick form is found in the diary of the Rev. John Thomlinson (1692–1761): "1717. Sept. 17th. One Dr. Bainbridge went from Cambridge to Oxon [Oxford] to be astronomy professor, and reading a lecture happened to say *de Polis et Axis*, instead of *Axibus*. Upon which one said, Dr. Bainbridge was sent from Cambridge,—to read lectures *de Polis et Axis*; but lett them that brought him hither, return him thither, and teach him his rules of syntaxis."

Well, let's try to put that into limerick layout:

Dr. Bainbridge was sent from Cambridge,—
to read lectures *de Polis et Axis*;
but lett them that brought him hither,
return him thither,
and teach him his rules of syntaxis.

Esoteric; yes. Interesting and/or a limerick: no. To my eye it is really a six-line verse, rhyming AABCCB, with "Bainbridge" rhyming with "Cambridge."

1718: Polyphemus's Song

Handel's *Acis and Galatea* was first performed in 1718, with words by John Gay. It contained an air sung by Polyphemus, which goes as follows:

> O ruddier than the cherry,
> O sweeter than the berry,
> O nymph more bright
> Than moonshine night,
> Like kidlings blithe and merry.
> Ripe as the melting cluster,
> No lily has such lustre;
> Yet hard to tame
> As raging flame,
> And fierce as storms that bluster!

A famous song, it can be listened to online as performed by various singers.

1786: Mrs. Thrale

A lady named Mrs. Thrale was a correspondent and friend of the famous Doctor Johnson. Later in life, when she was Signora Piozzi, she published her reminiscences. As one reference puts it: "She was infatuated with the vanity of acquainting the world that she had carried on a correspondence with Dr. Johnson."

Scotsman James Boswell was an intimate of Dr. Johnson and his subsequent biographer. In 1785 he published *Journal of a Tour to the Hebrides*, which described his trip with Johnson. The press obviously compared the two offerings, and an anonymous "Impromptu on two late publications relating to the late celebrated Dr. Johnson" appeared in the *General Evening Post* of May 4, 1786:

> The Ladies all cry—Pozz up—
> The Scotsmen all cry—Bozz up—
> They do not contest,
> Of the two which is best,
> But cry, which is worst is a—toss up.

(Without an explanation the verse makes little sense today. When I first found it I was certainly puzzled.)

1806: Mrs. Thrale (Again)

In the thrillingly titled *Thraliana, The Diary of Mrs. Hester Lynch Thrale (later Mrs. Piozzi)*, an entry for May 1806 reads:

> Another Death! nothing else indeed I think—the pleasant Bishop of Limerick; gay, gallant, chearful Creature that he was—when known by name of Barnard Dean of Derry: Friend & Companion to dear little Goldsmith Reynolds, Burke, Johnson; all the old Coterie of the Turks head: where after Supper he used to sing the Song of Polypheme in Acis & Galatea;—Can one then *help* exclaiming
>
>> Has then the Dean of Derry
>> Past o'er the darksome Ferry?
>> Who once more bright
>> Than Torch by Night
>> Shone forth 'mong wits so merry!
>>
>> He to the Grape's ripe Cluster
>> Could lend Convivial Lustre;
>> When blythe & gay
>> In Garrick's Day
>> Sweet Mirth her Friends did muster.
>>
>> But since the Dean of Derry
>> Has cross'd the Stygian Ferry;
>> Wit Sense and Worth
>> Shall join with Mirth
>> And cry We are griev'd,—*ay Very!*[6]

Her acquaintance with that capital man of letters, Dr. Johnson, doesn't seem to have taught her much about Capital Letters. The poem, incidentally, was first published in the *St. James's Chronicle* in April 1806, and a clipping sent to Mrs. Thrale.[7]

I'm surprised this verse hasn't been paraded as the origin of everything limerickal—after all, it is actually about the Bishop of Limerick. Doubtless it will be when it becomes better known.

Readers familiar with Polyphemus's song (see 1718 above) will no doubt recognize that this poem is a pretty fair parody of that air; which, as stated in the clipping, was one of the late Bishop's favorite songs.

Pre-1820 Verses Claimed to Be Limericks: Some Informed Comment

The reader, having had the opportunity to consider every pre-1820 poem cited as being in limerick form, may be interested in reading what others have said about these verses.

Dr. Bibby started a chapter of his 1978 book: "'The pre-history of the Limerick,' Gershon Legman has assured us, 'is remarkably easy to trace.' Well, maybe. Perhaps it is—provided that one is not too particular about precisely what constitutes a limerick, and provided also that one does not examine too critically some of the claims which have been made about so-called early examples."[8]

In his 1981 article titled "The History of the Limerick," George N. Belknap examined claims that limericks had existed prior to the 1820s:

> In the 1970 Introduction to *The Limerick*, expanding a first try in *The Horn Book*, Legman claims to have settled the question of the origin of the limerick once for all. On first reading his case is impressive though flavored with crochets and dogmas in his usual manner. He argues that the limerick is a distinctly English verse form, with roots in English literature as early as the fourteenth century, and documents his case with quotations of early prototypes and citations of other examples. He maintains that, "The pre-history of the limerick is remarkably easy to trace," but then drops the cautious term "prehistory" and repeatedly uses such phrases as "limerick form," "limerick meter," "in limerick," "limerick stanza," "true limerick," and "full limerick rhythm" to characterize examples he quotes from the 14th through the 17th century.
>
> Legman's examples fall conspicuously short of the form that became standard in the nineteenth century.[9]

Later Belknap says (my emphasis): "The examples from the seventeenth century and earlier are for the most part ballads, love lyrics, drinking songs, and bawdy songs or fragments of examples of these genres—together with several verses on tobacco. *Conspicuously absent are the nonsense, playful wit, irony, and satire characteristic of the fully developed limerick at its best.*"[10]

In three articles published in 1996–7, Marco Graziosi examined the claims of Legman, Bibby, and others about the origin of the limerick.[11] The articles are reproduced on his website. In essence he found little which could be described as a limerick or a limerick precursor. One comment he made is telling. Legman makes a big play of claiming that the original limericks were all dirty[12]; Signor Graziosi considers that few, if any, of Legman's "early" examples fit the bill of being dirty and of being a limerick.

In 2015 Dr. Jenni Nuttall came across an article which suggested that limericks dated back to at least the 11th century. As a lecturer at Oxford and an expert on Middle English poetic form, she wondered how she could have possibly missed such verses and promptly set about rectifying the matter by doing a little research (her emphasis):

> But, of course, *there aren't eleventh-century limericks*: it didn't take me long to work that out. Various bits of early verse, either by coincidence or because of

their musical form, are somewhat similar in form to the modern limerick we know and love. There seems to be an almost irresistible temptation to find the supposed origin of the limerick. And that temptation raises the question of what defines a form. If an early bit of verse (or a bit of an early verse) meets the criteria by which we recognize a current verse form, should it be called a "limerick"? I don't think so, and here's why.

Dr. Nuttall goes on to give a succinct and refreshingly accurate summary of some early English poems touted as limericks.[13]

Conclusion

1. After considering every verse in English I know of which has been suggested as a pre–1820 limerick, I think that there were no real limericks written or printed prior to 1820, though there are a couple of close misses.

2. Did any of these verses lead on to the modern limerick, as exemplified by the children's verse of the 1820s, or to any other sort of limerick? I can see no evidence that they did.

3. I can discern no trend whereby verses changed over time toward becoming limericks, so that the next verses in this sequence would be the limericks in the children's books of the 1820s. The only possible contender would be "Hickory Dickory Dock"—but since this spent at least three-quarters of a century generating precisely nothing, we can hardly regard it as a trendsetter.

4. My own opinion can be expressed in limerick form, by rewriting an old favorite:

>Thus spake an exposer of SHAM;
>"For pre-limericks I don't give a damn.
>You may think it odd o' me,
>I like 'em writ properly.
>You may call me a pedant—I am."
>—*Bob Turvey*

Chapter 3

Possible Irish Origins Prior to 1820

The claim that limericks originated in Ireland is based on the suggestion that they were originally composed in Gaelic and that these gave rise to limericks in English which then became immensely popular. Let's examine the evidence for this idea.

The Maigue Poets

The main claim for an Irish origin of the limerick verse form is that a school of poets originating from Croom in County Limerick in the mid-1700s wrote Gaelic poems and that some of these poems were limericks. The members of this group were called the Maigue poets, after the river Maigue which flows through Croom.

The main problem with this claim is that the English versions of these poems were not published until 1849. The "translations" were made by someone with little knowledge of Gaelic, from prose translations. There is considerable doubt that the original verses were actually in any form of limerick layout. Another unexplained and problematic matter: how did they give rise to English limericks?

Spread of the Idea

The first claim that the Maigue poets wrote limericks seems to have been made by Robert Herbert, librarian in the Limerick City Library, and a historian. He wrote a column in the local newspaper, *The Limerick Leader*, called "Worthies of Thomond." This began on July 10, 1943, and continued for several years. (Thomond was one of the Kingdoms of Ireland before the Norman invasion. Essentially it is North Munster, and it includes County Limerick.)

Chapter 3. Possible Irish Origins Prior to 1820

The column for August 21, 1943, started off by describing John O'Tuomy, a publican and Gaelic poet who was born at Croom in 1706. The middle part of the column read:

> O'Tuomy and his friend, Andrew McGrath, "the merry peddler," had many a wordy battle. In one of these O'Tuomy wrote to Andrew in the well known five-lined verse, with the third and fourth lines short, now known as a limerick. McGrath replied in the same meter. It is probable that this was the origin of the term "limerick" for such verses. O'Tuomy wrote:
>
>> I sell the best brandy and sherry
>> To make my good customers merry;
>> But at times their finances,
>> Run short as it chances.
>> And then I feel very sad, very.
>
> And McGrath replied:
>
>> O'Tuomy, you boast yourself handy
>> At selling good ale and bright brandy
>> But the fact is your liquor
>> Makes everyone sicker,
>> I tell you that, I, your friend Andy.

Nowhere did Herbert explain where these English versions had come from. Three pamphlets were subsequently produced, which contained collections of the columns produced by Herbert. The first of these was a two-shilling offering titled *Worthies of Thomond: Being a Compendium of Short Lives of the Most Famous Men and Women of Limerick and Clare to the Present Day*. This was reviewed by the *Times Literary Supplement*[1] in April 1944, which commented that it was an example of local piety which deserved to be commended, not least because there were several odd and a few important characters on the list. The review ended: "Of some interest too is John O'Tuomy who has claims to be the originator of the 'Limerick' form of verse."

This was picked up by *The New York Times*,[2] which quoted the last sentence of the *TLS* review. The *New York Times* went on to question this assertion, asking what else O'Tuomy had going for him other than geography. It then asked readers if anyone knew when the word "limerick" had come into being, and who had fathered it. One reply[3] was printed a fortnight later, but added little.

Later in 1943, *The Limerick Leader* printed an article[4] by Robert Herbert in which he expanded his thoughts on where limericks originated from, and why they were called limericks. Much was as before, but this time he commented: "Here is one verse from O'Tuomy's original drinking song, written in Irish, and part of James Clarence Mangan's translation of Andrew Magrath's answer. The translation was made about the year 1840 and was first published in 1849." A Gaelic stanza was then given. Lines 3 & 4 do not look as if they rhyme. Five stanzas in English then followed. (A version of this article was printed in the same newspaper in 1955,[5] and a condensed version in a 1957 magazine.[6])

In late 1946 two articles on limericks were printed in *The New York Times Magazine*.[7] These somehow attracted the attention of one Harold Collins, in Dublin, who started off his letter[8] to the editor as follows: "I wish to contradict the statement that no one knows when or how the limerick got its name." The Maigue poets were then described.

Shortly after this, a letter[9] in *American Notes & Queries* opined:

> One of the first limericks? The role of the Maigue poets in popularizing the Limerick form should be noted. The group of poets, lead [*sic*] by Sean O'Tuama and Andrew McGrath, flourished in County Limerick, Ireland, in the 1750's. Much of their verse, written in Irish, was in the form of Limericks. Harold Collins, of Dublin, writing to the Editor of *The New York Times Magazine*, May 4, 1947, states that it scarcely takes the imagination to assume that there might be a close relation between the word "limerick" and the name of the county where that type of poetry was very much in vogue before people were composing such poems in English.
>
> Collins quotes a Limerick by O'Tuama:
> > Dob ait liomsa ceol na dteampan
> > Dob ait liomsa spoirt is amhrain
> > Dob ait liom an gloine
> > Ag Muireann da lionadh
> > As cuideachta saoithe gan meabhrain.
>
> This he translates roughly as: "He was fond of good company, fun and music…"
>
> —J. Lynch

In 1947 Kathleen Hoagland edited a book titled *1000 Years of Irish Poetry*.[10] This included John O'Tuomy's "Drinking Song" in four English stanzas and Andrew Magrath's reply to this in ten English stanzas. At the end of both poems, Miss Hoagland included the comment: "Version by James Clarence Mangan from the literal English of John O'Daly." An endnote gave a brief description of Mangan, and commented that "Mangan knew little Irish, but many of his lyrical versions from the literal translations of O'Donovan, O'Curry and O'Daly are true and exquisite."

In a 1965 article[11] in *The New York Times Book Review*, Morris Bishop stated that in Miss Hoagland's book he had "found some perfect limericks, translated from the Irish." He then quoted the first stanza of O'Tuomy's poem. Baring-Gould quoted Bishop's comments in 1967.

When Mr. Chaim Bermant wondered, in the *Observer* newspaper in 1967[12], "why Ireland's holiest city should have given its name to the most profane form of verse?" Dr. Hanrahan[13] of Dublin was on hand to state

Chapter 3. Possible Irish Origins Prior to 1820

that the question which intrigued Mr. Bermant had not been answered conclusively, but "it was surely more than a coincidence that the Filí na Máighe school should have made extensive use of this verse form."

Extensive, eh? Fourteen possible stanzas. And the example given contains a mistake, replacing "your liquor" with "good liquor"—which throws the whole sense of the verse out of whack.

This mistake notwithstanding, Vivien Noakes referred to Dr. Hanrahan's letter in her 1969 book[14] as describing a *possible* origin of the limerick verse form. This then became a much more likely source in Dr. Noakes's later books[15]: "Many ideas have been put forward as to its origin; the most convincing is that it was used extensively by the poetic school, Filí na Máighe, which flourished in County Limerick in the mid-eighteenth century."

In 1976 Jean Harrowven published a book titled *The Limerick Makers*. After a cursory look at a few supposed early limericks in English, in a chapter accurately titled "Fragments," she turns her attention to the Croom poets. A chapter describes their history. She elects to spell the name of Séan ó Tuama as John O'Toumy; most other writers use O'Tuomy. All of the English version "limericks" in Kathleen Hoagland's book are given, along with two stanzas in Gaelic. The rhyme scheme of these originals is stated to be AABBA; as we shall see, it is not.

Mrs. Harrowven then gives two possible explanations of how the Maigue "limericks" became the models for subsequent English limericks (more of that anon). She does, however, comment: "But still the Irish limericks as translated by Mangan were unheard of in England at that time. In fact it is only in recent years that news of the traditional Irish verses has come to light in England at all."

Two years later Bibby[16] cited Harrowven and quoted six of the English translations.

A 2002 article[17] in the prestigious *Smithsonian* magazine describes the author's long-standing interest in limericks. He then tells us that he journeyed to Ireland to "settle the matter" of whether limericks originated in Limerick or not. Part of this research consisted of meeting a couple of local scholars in a pub in Croom. We are not made privy to exactly what was said at this meeting, but we are told that "the five-line verse probably originated from the limerick-makers of Croom, known as the Maigue poets, who flourished in the 18th century." A short description of them follows.

At least one person wrote to the magazine to complain about the ideas presented. The letter[18] started: "After twenty years of studying the limerick and its origins, I never fail to get a chuckle at the Maigue Poets fable." Its main complaint was that the original verses were not in limerick form and that the translator spoke little Irish and relied on prose translations.

An entry in the 2006 *Historical Encyclopedia of Celtic Culture*[19] simply states as fact that "Ó Tuama, Seán, (1707/8–1775) was one of the most famous of the poets of the Maigue, who invented the limerick."

Attempts to Link the Verse to the City or County

Attempts have been made to link the verse form to the city or county, possibly for commercial reasons or to attract tourists. A communication[20] was sent in 1995 by the Shannon Development Company to the editor of an American magazine for limerick enthusiasts. It stated that the Maigue poets had written their poetry in the swinging meter of the "Limerick," and that the continuous connection the area had had with the verse form should be acknowledged. The organization was apparently "progressing the idea" of having a center in Limerick City "to feature this verse form."

An article in *The New York Times* in 1998[21] described how the city of Limerick was trying to pull itself out of economic depression. It concluded with the following:

> The verse limerick was recently promoted, as a tourist attraction, with the first international limerick contest. Each entry had to begin "In Limerick where once I did stay."
>
> The winner among 1,500 entries, by Marian Gormley, of Drogheda, County Louth, started that way and ended with a McCourt reference, "From 'Ashes' they've come a long way."
>
> Shannon Development officials, who sponsored the contest, produced research purporting to prove that Limerick was really the birthplace of the limerick, that Gaelic-speaking poets learned the form in France in the 16th century and came here to develop it in pubs. They brushed off the statements in reference books that the origin of the form is unknown and that it first appeared in print in England in 1820.
>
> Maeve Kelly, the author of two novels, who was chief judge, said in an interview: "It doesn't matter whether it originated in Limerick. It was popularized here."

A press release from 2005 recorded that "Deutsche Welle TV from Berlin, Germany are in Limerick at the moment and along with MKP they are trying to establish the real origin of the 'Limerick'—the short rhyming poem ... we went to Croom in County Limerick to visit the birthplace of the Maigue Poets who used the Limerick a great deal. All this will end up as a four minute segment on DW TV which broadcasts all over Europe."[22]

This apparently caught the attention of the then mayor of Limerick: "Referring to his campaign to reclaim the limerick verse form for Limerick

Chapter 3. Possible Irish Origins Prior to 1820

[Mayor Diarmuid Scully] said that the origin of the idea came about as a result of the German TV crew who visited Limerick last year to make a documentary on the origin of the limerick and based themselves at the White House. He hoped to announce the winner of his recent competition for limericks to adorn every street plaque in the city next month."

Those interested in limericks on plaques in streets in Limerick can read more in a *Limerick Leader* article[23] titled: "The limerick finds its way home."

In early 2013, limerick enthusiasts were excited by the announcement of a competition to be held to find "the best limerick in the world 2013." The University of Limerick played host to a literary event called "Limerick Gathering Fest—Bring Your Limericks to Limerick Competition." There were 620 entries from 16 different countries. The "rules" stated that the title and the 1,000 euros prize money could only be given to those who actually traveled at their own expense to Limerick in August and declaimed their verse. Despite the fact that this automatically made it impossible for most of the entrants to win the contest, it went ahead anyway.

Of far greater interest to historians of the limerick verse form were claims on the website:

> As part of the Tailteann Nua festival which will take place over the August bank holiday weekend from 2–5 August the University of Limerick in association with The Limerick Writers Centre plan to bring the five line famous "Limerick" verse home to Limerick.... Coinciding with the competition and festival The Limerick Writers Centre have commissioned local historian Matthew Potter to write a history of the "Limerick" and its association with the area.

Comments on Dr. Potter's website read: "Historical consultant with 'Bringing Limericks to Limerick,' a project for the 2013 Gathering based on the connection between the limerick poetic form and Limerick City and County."

We waited with bated breath. Would we be overwhelmed by evidence that the Maigue poets did invent limericks—or would we be able to point out all the logical flaws in the evidence presented?

The book[24] duly appeared and the launch was blessed by the mayor of Limerick, who stated: "Dr. Potter has set out to associate an established literary form with Limerick in the same way as Shakespeare is associated with Stratford, Joyce is linked with Dublin and satirical comedy is occasionally coupled with Irish politics."

The back cover announced: "One of the principal aim [sic] of this book is to create an awareness of the connection between the place and the poem so that Limerick can establish itself as one of the few places that gave its name to a literary form."

Part of that is certainly true. The place did give its name to a literary form. But what is the connection between the place and the poem?

Alas. In a book heavily padded with extraneous matter, it is not until page 53 that the Maigue poets are even discussed. Little new information is given. Then the next chapter starts off with the statement: "The first and most obvious point to make is that Limerick is not the birthplace of the limerick."

Despite all this, the mayor of Limerick comments in her Foreword: "However, the Maigue poets are also given extensive coverage and Dr. Potter has done a great service in restoring them to their rightful place at the center of the limerick story."

What that means is anyone's guess. The second edition of Dr. Potter's book in 2017 contained no new information about the Maigue poets.

Other Gaelic Verses

A few other Gaelic verses have been mentioned in print as having a limerick-like layout. Harrowven mentions a couple.[25] William Mahon[26] describes eight stanzas, taken from two poems written before 1756, and gives both the original verses and English translations. These resemble the Maigue poems in layout.

Even Earlier Gaelic Verses

In 1955, the daughter of Langford Reed wrote a letter to the mayor of Limerick. On his behalf, the city manager wrote a letter summarizing her request to the editor of *The Limerick Leader*. The editor printed this in the newspaper.[27] The lady was planning a new edition of her late father's *Complete Limerick Book*. She explained that it would contain a history of the limerick, and would, like the original, be dedicated to the city of Limerick. She said that her father, after much research in the British Museum and elsewhere, had come to the conclusion that the limerick verse form had been brought direct to Limerick by the returned veterans of the Irish Brigade, which had been attached to the French Army for nearly one hundred years, from 1691. Something like a million men served in the Brigade, and the verse form which had become so popular in France became equally popular among her Irish allies. (We have examined this idea earlier.) The city manager finished his letter by saying the mayor would be glad to hear from any person who had any theory as to the origin of the use of the word "limerick" to indicate the verse form.

Chapter 3. Possible Irish Origins Prior to 1820

This prompted Robert Herbert to write to the newspaper. In his excitement he seemed to confuse Reed's daughter with Reed's wife, and the mayor with the town clerk. His letter began:

> In Mrs. Langford Reed's letter to the Town Clerk, she suggests "the 'limerick' form of verse was brought direct to Limerick by the returned veterans of the Irish Brigade, which was attached to the French Army for a period of nearly one hundred years from 1691."
> There is little proof that few, if any of these veterans ever returned to Limerick: and I would, therefore, go one further than Mrs. Reed, and suggest that the French copied an old Irish form of verse which the Jacobites brought with them into France, and that the French form in turn found its way back to Limerick, via the English language.
> In proof I submit the following.[28]

Alas; no Jacobite limericks were given; the rest of the letter consisted of a modified version of Herbert's article on the Maigue poets which had been published in the same newspaper in 1943.

Quite how Jacobite Irish verse became French verse which became English verse which ended up in Limerick is beyond my comprehension. And how did it get there if no one came back from France? Where did the one million "returning" Irish Brigade members go?

Mr. Herbert wrote no more on this matter; he drowned the following year on a fishing trip.

Hearsay: Sounds Like a Limerick

George Thomson was an English classical scholar who made himself fluent in Gaelic and lived in Ireland. In a 1949 book[29] he wrote: "In Ireland, early in the last century, the Limerick school of poets used to forgather in the same way, improvising stanzas on a fixed pattern which one has only to hear to recognize the origin of the limerick (Dinneen FM). In Cambridge during my student days similar symposia were held annually, but improvisation bred impropriety, and they have been banned."

For a while I thought Dinneen FM was a Gaelic radio station, but it actually refers to Father Patrick Dinneen's 1906 book *Filidhe na Máighe*, which described the poems and poets of the Maigue school.

Jean Harrowven describes a stanza from an eighth-century Irish poem in Gaelic called "Ronan's Lament." When the Limerick librarian read this out to her, she "could clearly define the meter, which had an internal rhyme scheme."

One comment: any verse in a limerick-like layout will probably sound like a limerick when spoken. For example, a verse in which each beat is represented by the word *da* will sound like a limerick when "spoken." But it is the way the content is written that determines if it is a limerick.

What Gaelic Scholars Think

I don't speak Gaelic, but I know several people who do. Two scholarly articles have been published which explore whether limericks really were written in Gaelic; few, if any, writers on matters limerickal seem to have heard of them.

Analysis of the Bunting collection of music and songs

In 1927 the *Journal of the Irish Folk Song Society* (based of course in London) published an in-depth examination of the Bunting collection of Irish folk music and songs. Songs and texts were translated and edited from original manuscripts by D.J. O'Sullivan. One 1796 song, called "Giolla Na Sgríob," had a limerick-like layout. An English translation of the stanzas shows little limerick-like layout or content, although the last line of stanza V remains tantalizingly untranslated—because it was "unsuitable for printing."

The editor then considers several early English songs, which he says are limericks. (We have seen them all earlier; see Appendix.) These are then compared to various Irish songs, including the limerick-like poems of the Maigue poets.

The most interesting part of the article then appears. The "Limerick Form in Irish and English Verse" is discussed. The author suggests that Gaelic verses which have limerick-like attributes can be split into two classes. The first is the "Giolla Na Sgríob" type, which resemble English ones in their arrangement of rhymes (AABBA), but have a Gaelic rhythm in the line-ends. (This Gaelic end rhyme is a double rhyme, such as strong beard/long feared/song cheered.)

The second type is Gaelic in both rhyme and end-rhythm. The first verse of Séan Ó Tuama's "Drinking Song" is given as an example, along with the same verse rendered into English in the same rhyme and end-rhythm manner:

> Is duine mé dhíolas leann lá,
> Is do chuireas mo bhuidhean chum rangcáis.
> Muna mbeidh duine im' chuidecht dhíolfas,
> Mise bheas thíos leis I n-antráth!

Or, in English,

> In my house you may tipple and swill, sirs,
> And I serve my good ale with a will, sirs.
> But if you don't pay I am put on my mettle
> And then I must settle the bill, sirs!

The rhyming of the mettle/settle words is a feature of this type of verse. In the original Gaelic there is a further internal rhyme in line three (*duine / chuid*echt) which was not put into the English translation.

After further discussion a summary is given as follows: "We may accordingly sum up our conclusions thus: that the Irish and English varieties of the limerick verse-form occurred independently, neither being modelled on the other; that the English form is the older; and that both were composed to be sung to a dance tune of Irish origin."

Dr. Colm Ó Baoill

A 1994 presentation[30] to the Gaelic Society of Inverness, titled "The Limerick and Gaelic Song," was printed in the society's journal in 1995. In this 26-page work the author examines many aspects of Gaelic poems and tunes, including verses by the Maigue poets. However, it seems to me that little is added to the conclusions of the earlier analysis by D.J. O'Sullivan vis-à-vis the relationship of Gaelic limerick-like verses and English limericks. I think the author also thinks this, since he concludes the work as follows: "Having discussed some Gaelic metrical forms which look, to varying degrees, like English limericks, all I can now say in conclusion is that I have done so. Nothing has been proved. Nothing much has been added to our knowledge of Gaelic song. Possibly a little has been added to our knowledge of the limerick, if it is accepted that both the limerick and the Gaelic verses have a common ancestor in the old songs of Europe, which includes both Britain and Ireland."

Comments by George N. Belknap

Mr. Belknap held several posts at Oregon University, lecturing in Greek, Latin and philosophy. He was university editor and director of the University of Oregon Books, which published academic works. In 1968 he published the definitive work of all material printed in Oregon from 1845 until 1870.

In 1981 he explored the "History of the Limerick" in a 32-page article[31] in *The Papers of the Bibliographical Society of America*. In one section of this he considered the Maigue poets. After giving a couple of English translations, he comments on Mangan's lack of understanding of the Irish language, and then writes:

They were first published in Mangan's *The Poets and Poetry of Munster* in 1849, shortly after his death. In this and later editions Mangan's verses are accompanied, on facing pages, by Irish texts—five-line stanzas that parallel the three-two-foot requirement of the limerick but lack the equally essential meter and rhyme requirements. The Irish meter is a mixture of trochees and dactyls and the line-end echoes are assonance, not ordinary rhyme. I am indebted to several Irish scholars for this information, which I hope I am reporting correctly; an insuperable language barrier prevents me from directly understanding what they tell me. At any rate, unless I have misunderstood my information, Mangan's verses owe little, in form, to the Irish language.

How Did Gaelic Verse Give Rise to English Limericks?

Ignoring for a moment the question whether they were actually limericks or not, claims that certain Gaelic verses gave rise to English limericks have one main problem: *how* did they give rise to them?

One suggestion was made in 1970 when a festival was held in Croom to celebrate the bicentenary of the Maigue poets. The prizewinner in the English limericks competition at this meeting was Dr. Wyse Jackson, who stated in a lecture: "Séan Ó Tuama kept a tavern in Mungret Street, in Limerick city, in the 1750s, and all the visiting actors from London at the nearby theatre heard these Gaelic witty verses in Ó Tuama's tavern and when they copied the style in England, they called them limericks."

This appeared in a 1975 pamphlet[32] which was printed so that German tourists to Limerick city could be furnished with "information on Limerick's links with the limerick verse form." It was referred to in Harrowven's 1976 book.[33]

Mrs. Harrowven[34] also suggested that Irish verses traveled to England because an Irishman such as Thomas Moore "wrote occasionally using the limerick meter, and may have easily obtained ideas for this form from the works of the Maigue poets." Well, did Moore speak Gaelic? I don't know. We have already considered his English verses in an earlier chapter.

Perhaps the most extensive attempt to establish how the Irish limerick was exported to England and became the English limerick is to be found in a 210-page work by Críostóir Ó Floinn, a bilingual poet, playwright and teacher. In his 2018 book[35] *The Irish Origins of the "Limerick,"* he describes early Irish poets at length, paying special attention to Uilliam English, Tadhg Gaelach and Donncha Rua, natives of the Limerick area, and to the Maigue poets. He believes these bilingual men were *not* responsible for creating the limerick, but were responsible for refining it to a high peak of perfection. He claims that the word "limerick" was applied to their verses because of where they came from.

He suggests that the word "limerick" was then taken to England "orally" by persons unknown, "long before the year 1800." He attempts to flesh out this statement by considering the movement from Ireland to England of poets and bilingual people, who, it is suggested, took examples of the verse in English with them.

Critique

I have several problems with the idea that Gaelic verses gave rise to English limericks.

1. The first is that the number of original Irish verses which could be said to be actual limericks, even as judged by a kindly soul, is vanishingly small. Ó Floinn is scathing of Mangan's "translations" of the Maigue poets and supplies his own. While certainly in limerick layout, they seem to me to lack the fizz and vigor that real limericks have.

One verse which could possibly be judged as a limerick is Ó Floinn's translation of a Uilliam English verse from 1757—Fonn Fáil is a poetic way to say Ireland:

> All ye in Fonn Fáil can take pride
> In George vanquished, of succor denied,
> The state of his britches
> Has me in stitches
> And the tide wouldn't clean his backside.

How close, though, is the above to the original? The verse of which this is a translation is little known in limerick scholarship. It has been described as follows:

In 1757, Uilliam English, a member of the Augustinian community in Cork city, celebrated Austrian victories over Frederick II of Prussia, a British ally, by directing scatological abuse at George II in a Jacobite song:

> An eol díbhse 'dhaoine i bhFonn Fáil
> Seoirse go cloíte 's i lomghá?
> Aiteas mo chroí 'stigh
> mar theagmhaigh a bhríste,
> 's ná glanfadh an taoide a thiompán.

(Do you know, O people in the land of Ireland, that George is crushed and in dire need? It's a joy to my heart within, what happened to his breeches, and the tide wouldn't clean his fundament!)[36]

2. The second problem I have is that it is all very well to say "it is reasonable to suggest that the word limerick was used to describe the verses." Saying so does not make it true. It is all very well to suggest that the verse made its way to London, orally carried by persons unknown. Saying so does not make it true. It is all very well saying that there is no written evidence because very little was written down or printed at the time in Irish. It can be pointed out that things were written down and printed extensively in English at the time—and the word limerick does not appear in print until well after 1860.

3. If limericks were being recited and spoken of in England as being limericks before 1800 (Ó Floinn's date)—why were these supposedly catchy and memorable verses not written down or printed somewhere?

4. Limericks were demonstrably printed in English from the 1820s onward. Why were they not called limericks by someone in England—in a private letter, newspaper or book? If they really were known as such, where is the proof?

Vice Versa?

If Irish poets could have taken limerick-like verses from Ireland to England the converse is also possible. To quote from D.J. O'Sullivan's 1927 paper: "It is quite historically possible, owing to the enormous vogue of *The Beggar's Opera* [1728, which contained limerick-like verses], that the tune was introduced into Ireland."

The Elephant in the Room

If Irish verses along the lines of those produced by the Maigue poets in the 1750s were so clever, witty, inventive and memorable (all features of the limerick as we know it)—why were no more of them created in Gaelic until the bicentennial celebrations of 1970?

Conclusion

There are three questions a seeker after truth would ask about a possible Irish origin of the limerick verse form:

1. Were there any verses in Irish prior to 1820 which had the same layout and rhyme scheme as modern limericks?

Chapter 3. Possible Irish Origins Prior to 1820

2. If any such verses existed, did the content have that mysterious spark that real limericks have?

3. Is there a clear path that shows these verses gave rise to English limericks?

After considering everything I can find about Irish verses my answers are:

1. Nearly all do not conform to the classical rhyme scheme. Their apparent limerick-like layout comes from translations by a non–Gaelic speaker who was quite possibly influenced by the then current English limericks.

2. The Irish verses in a limerick-like layout are just pedestrian texts. They no more contain the "spark" that real limericks contain than the early English "limerick-like" verses. And anyway the English ones came first.

3. There is no evidence that Gaelic verses had any influence whatsoever on the creation and development of the English limerick. They didn't even have any influence on the development of the Gaelic limerick. Which, of course, means that the answers to questions (1) and (2) are academic and only of interest to Gaelic scholars.

So: did the Irish invent the limerick?

In my opinion, no.

PART II

Limericks from 1820 to 1920

Previous chapters have explored claims that some limericks were created prior to 1820. I believe that an unbiased and reasonable person would conclude that very few—if any—of these verses could be said to be real limericks. Others have held the same opinion. Iona and Peter Opie, in *A Nursery Companion* (Oxford University Press, 1980, page 125), concluding a short but remarkably comprehensive summary of early limerick-like verses, stated: "Yet 'the fact must be faced' (as the old woman of Epping declared) that no true limerick—that is to say no example of that infectious type of verse which a hearer cannot resist trying to imitate or improve upon—has been found before 1820; while after 1820 such verses became endemic."

The old woman of Epping, incidentally, seems to be a character lost in the mists of time; I know nothing about her.

Even if it is considered that one or two of the pre–1820 verses are real limericks, there is no evidence that these verses had any effect on the subsequent development of the limerick. In other words, if such "limericks" existed, they were one-offs that excited no particular interest in the literary community, and because of this they fathered no descendants.

I can find no evidence of other verse forms changing into limericks. The limericks that were published in children's books in the 1820s seem to have arrived on the scene fully formed and functioning. Of course, their authors could have been influenced by verses they had read, but we will never know. Down that road of speculation lies only madness.

It is simpler to apply Occam's razor as follows: someone, somewhere, invented limericks. Original copies of these 1820s children's books exist to this day. These books can be shown to have given rise to the subsequent development of the limerick verse form. So the accolade of producing the first limericks goes to their authors.

This part of the book traces the development of the limerick through the years from 1820 to 1920. Each decade is examined in a separate chapter.

Chapter 4

The 1820s
At Last—Limericks!

In my opinion the accolade for creating the first limericks goes to the authors of the five books of limericks published in London in the 1820s. Or, to be pedantic, to the author of the first of those books to be published. Before we can attempt to identify him or her, let's introduce the books.

1820s Children's Books which Contain Limericks

Most researchers, literary and limerick, consider these books to have been published in the following order:

circa 1820: *The History of Sixteen Wonderful Old Women.*
  (Pub: John Harris. Contained 16 limericks.)
circa 1821: *Anecdotes and Adventures of Fifteen Gentlemen.*
  (Pub: John Marshall. Contained 15 limericks.)
circa 1822: *Anecdotes and Adventures of Fifteen Young Ladies.*
  (Pub: John Marshall. Contained 15 limericks.)
circa 1823: *Little Rhymes for Little Folks: or, a Present for Fanny's Library.*
  (Pub: John Harris. Contained one limerick and 14 other rhymes.)
circa 1824: *A Peep at the Geography of Europe.*
  (Pub: John Marshall. Contained 15 limericks.)

Each book is an illustrated book written for children. Each limerick is printed in a five-line layout and stands underneath a picture.

Which book actually came first?

There is some disagreement about the position of the first three books. It would, of course, be simple if we could go to a source such as *The English*

Catalogue of Books 1801–1836[1] and just read the publication date. Unfortunately, children's books were not rated highly at the time, and most were not included in such catalogues. Even such authorities as the Opies, who amassed an amazing collection of early children's books, do not seem to have come across the *Young Ladies* or the *Geography of Europe*.

There are two main reasons for considering that one of the *Fifteen* books could have been the first one published. Firstly, some eminent literary scholars have said so. For example, *The Cambridge History of English Literature*, 1914, contains a chapter by F.J. Harvey Darton, an Oxford don. His grandfather was Darton the publisher. In the text he comments that "*Sixteen Old Women* (1821) contains the first instance of the metrical form commonly called a limerick." However, the bibliography to this chapter gives 1820 for *Sixteen Old Women* and contains an entry which reads:

> Anecdotes and Adventures of Fifteen Young Ladies. n.d. [before 1820]. [The first "Limericks."][2]

Interestingly, later books written by Mr. Darton omit the reference to *Fifteen Young Ladies*.[3] Make of all that what you will.

Secondly, some scholars have thought along the same lines as Gershon Legman. In a 1984 letter to Dr. Arthur Deex he wrote: "I should mention that I hardly believe the Harris volume (*Sixteen Old Women*) could have been the first of the group; since Sharpe and his publisher Marshall could have hardly been competing with an existing sixteen title, by dropping back to fifteen. The logic of it is that the *Fifteen Gentlemen* (and maybe the *Fifteen Young Ladies* too) came first, and that Harris now tried to top the fad with sixteen Old Women."[4]

Amplifying this line of thought, George Belknap wrote:

> *Gentlemen*, which shows no year of publication, is usually dated c.1822, apparently on the assumption that *Gentlemen* was an imitation, the production of which would have required about a year. This involves the further assumption that John Marshall, publisher of *Gentlemen*, could be expected to imitate Harris, but not the other way round. I have, however, been informed by Judith St. John, Osborne Collection librarian, that there is evidence that Harris sometimes imitated Marshall. The conjectured date of *Gentlemen* should be c.1820, as it is in Philip James, *Children's Books of Yesterday* (1933).[5]

So any one of three books could have been the first book of limericks ever published. *Sixteen Old Women* has no known author. The *Fifteen* books are generally believed to have been written by Richard Scrafton Sharpe (c.1775–1852), who was a Bishopsgate grocer, and illustrated by George Cruikshank's elder brother, Robert.

The accolade would therefore appear to go to one of two people. Perhaps *Anon.* is the most deserving recipient; after all, he did write most of the truly great limericks of all time, and he has had a most diverting biography[6] written about him.

Some comments

Whether the author of *Fifteen Gentlemen* was the first writer of limericks or not, there is a strong case to consider him the most important limerick writer in this 1820s group. He introduced new rhymes in the last line and told stories of greater complexity than are evident in *Sixteen Old Women*. He also wrote several limericks which did not begin: "There was a...." His characters are not merely "old people," but real people with a personality:

> There was an old soldier of Bicester
> Was walking one day with his sister;
> A bull, with one poke,
> Tossed her into an oak,
> Before the old gentleman missed her.

The books of the 1820s set the style for many subsequent books. The layout was five lines. All but one limerick had lines 3 and 4 indented as compared to the other lines. A picture stood above the limerick.

Although *Little Rhymes* contains only one limerick, that limerick is about a dog, not a person.

The most important limerick in these books

There is a case to be made that the sick man of Tobago is the most important limerick ever written. It appears in *Fifteen Gentlemen* and Edward Lear specifically states that this was the verse which inspired him to write his own limericks. It is arguable that this inspiration resulted in the limerick becoming what it is today, as we shall see in the 1860s chapter.

> There was a sick man of Tobago,
> Liv'd long on rice-gruel and sago;
> But at last to his bliss,
> The physician said this —
> "To a roast leg of mutton you may go."

Scholarly interest in these books

Questions asking when the first limericks were written appeared in print as early as 1897. A publisher named Andrew White Tuer asked in *Notes & Queries*:

NONSENSE VERSES.—A London evening paper has incorrectly claimed for the late Edward Lear the invention of nonsense verses of the type of that commencing "There was a Tom-cat in the City." I should like to know whether there is anything earlier in this way than the *History of Sixteen Wonderful Old Women, illustrated by as many Engravings exhibiting their principal Eccentricities and Amusements*; London. Printed for Harris and Son, Corner of St. Paul's Churchyard, 1821, which forms No. 15 of Harris' *Cabinet of Amusement and Instruction*, twenty-six in the set. This little book, published by Newbery's successors, is an extremely rare one, with colored illustrations of the drollest. Perhaps space may be spared for a verse taking one back to the days when lotteries were not illegal:

> There was an Old Woman of Ealing
> Who jump'd till her head touch'd the ceiling,
> When 2 1 6 4
> Was announced at her door,
> As a prize to th' Old Woman of Ealing.
> —ANDREW W. TUER.
> The Leadenhall Press, E.C.[7]

Answers came there several, but none of the suggested books actually predated *Sixteen Old Women*. One correspondent managed to show an interest in the verse form while at the same time seeming to dislike it.

> I do not know the exact age of the "Old Man of Tobago," but he has been so long familiar to my ancestors and myself that he can hardly be any younger than the *Sixteen Wonderful Old Women*. However, I hope we are not to be flooded with these compositions.
> —C.F.S. WARREN, M.A.
> Longford, Coventry.

Interest in this subject was not confined to the English side of the Atlantic. *The New York Times*[8] and other American newspapers[9] reprinted Tuer's letter.

Tuer subsequently included some illustrated limericks in his 1898–9 book, *Pages and Pictures from Forgotten Children's Books*. They came from *Old Women* and *Fifteen Ladies*. Tuer mentioned Mr. F. Hockcliffe in the preface, so it is likely that he used books owned by him. The Hockcliffe collection can nowadays be viewed online.

Other Possible Early Limerick-Containing Books

Some other books of this era have been cited as containing limericks. Let's examine them briefly.

The sick man of Tobago. *Anecdotes and Adventures of Fifteen Gentlemen*, believed to be Richard Scrafton Sharpe (author) and Robert Cruikshank (illustrator), John Marshall, London, circa 1821.

Gammer Gurton

Several respondents to Tuer's letter discussed *Gammer Gurton* as an earlier source of limericks than *Sixteen Old Women*:

> A gentleman of great literary experience remarked that such nonsense verses were as old as *Gammer Gurton*, and that the "man from Tobago" was to be found therein. I cannot remember that he said *Gammer Gurton's Needle*. But I had never heard of another *Gammer Gurton*, and was surprised to hear of the occurrence in that celebrated old comedy of any verses other than those in praise of ale which form a prelude to the second act. I should think the Tobago rhyme is more likely to be found in some part of *Gammer Gurton's Garland*, a collection of nursery rhymes which I am informed […] was published in 1784.
>
> KILLIGREW.

> I cannot find the "man from Tobago" in *Gammer Gurton's Garland*, 1810, of which little book I have a copy.
>
> W.F. PRIDEAUX.

> "The old man of Tobago" is in the *Arundines Cami*, which was published in the year 1841, and is said there to have been taken from *Gammer Gurton*. Col. Prideaux has pointed out that *Gammer Gurton's Garland* appeared first in 1784, and afterwards, with additions, in 1810.
>
> E. YARDLEY.

Arundines Cami (The Reeds of the Cam) was a collection of hymns, songs, limericks and shanties translated by Cambridge scholars into Latin and Greek. It certainly contains the Old [sic] Man of Tobago and the verse stands above the words *Gammer Gurton*. The verse is translated into Latin, Greek, French and Italian, but, alas, not into a limerick layout.

There were two books called *Gammer Gurton*—the *Nedle* or *Needle*, and the *Garland*. I have read all the editions of both that I could find. There are no limericks in any of them.

Gammer Gurton is a good example of how well-meaning people with faulty memories waste the researcher's time. Ditto incorrect secondary references.

It is also an excellent example of the truth of the adage: Always verify your references. Relying on secondary references can lead you astray.

The Old Woman and Her Three Sons

Readers of Melvyl (the catalogue of the University of California libraries) and WORLDCAT may be excited to be told that this 1815 (probably 1819) book contains "Fate and fatalism; Juvenile poetry: Limericks." Copies of this book can be read online; alas, there are no limericks in it.

Dame Trott?

In the first edition of his 1924 *Complete Limerick Book*, Langford Reed wrote: "The author has discovered many poor Limericks in old 'Chap Books' published in 1820."

In a 1925 American magazine article, written to advertise his *Complete Limerick Book*, Reed wrote: "Limericks were in vogue a good many years before *The Book of Nonsense* first saw the light of day in 1846, for during recent research I have discovered a whole string of them in a chapbook published by the Yorkshire Publishing Company of Otley, in 1824. They deal with the adventures of Dame Trott and other legendary figures of the nursery."[10]

In both cases Reed goes on to talk about "Dickory Dickory Dock." So "limericks" in the chapbooks may or may not be real limericks at all. Finding the 1824 chapbook has proved impossible. I can find little about the Yorkshire Publishing Company, except that a company called the Yorkshire Joint Stock Publishing and Stationery Company Ltd. of Otley seems to have existed around the right time. Where Reed was doing his research is unclear; he certainly worked in the British Museum[11]; however, no UK library I know of has anything resembling such a publication.

Searching on "Otley Chapbooks" located a set of 16 chapbooks, one of which was titled *The Renowned History of Dame Trot and her Cat*. This, however, contains no limericks.

The Beauties of Shakspeare [sic]

A 2021 article mentions a booklet for children and quotes a limerick from it.[12] No publication date appears in the work,[13] but the publisher was active at the stated address possibly between 1819 and 1847. The article suggests the booklet was an imitation of *Sixteen Wonderful Old Women*.

Conclusion

The earliest known books containing limericks are the five listed above. It is uncertain which of three possible candidates was published first, and if the date of publication of that book was a year or two earlier than 1820.

At the end of the 1820s there were at least 62 limericks in existence. All were written to amuse children and were illustrated.

CHAPTER 5

The 1830s
Little Progress—On the Surface

As regards the publication of limericks, things were quite quiet. But underneath the surface, Edward Lear had started to create the limericks which would transform the verse form. As he did so, the Houses of Parliament burned down. There was probably no connection between these two events. Let's examine firstly what entered the public domain.

Anecdotes of Seven Curious Old Couple [sic] *of England*: 1830–32?

WORLDCAT is a U.S.-based system which catalogues books contained in many libraries worldwide. It has a particular knowledge of U.S. college and public libraries. Books included in the database typically have their contents described in a few words and short phrases. The descriptor for *Anecdotes of Seven Curious Old Couple of England* reads: "Nonsense verses, English. Limericks, Juvenile. Children's poetry, English." Further notes for the book state: "Each leaf bears a half-page illustration above a limerick."

No previous book or article describing the history of the limerick verse form has mentioned this book. It exists in a seemingly unique copy in the Princeton library, which is a second edition. It was written by one S.S.W. and published by Carvalho of London. I had high hopes for this book, wondering if the first edition could have been published in the 1820s.

Alas; after a great deal of effort to find out what was actually in the book, the contents turned out to be merely illustrated children's verses which were not limericks.

Leigh Hunt: 1830

An article titled "The Limerick" appeared in an issue of the *Atlantic* magazine in 1924. At one point Leigh Hunt is discussed. The author remarks:

"Hunt also wrote in 1830 a series of humorous limericks on the poet Galt, but they are not nearly so worthy of quotation as the 'Song to Ceres.'"[1]

It took me several years to run these four "unworthy humorous limericks" to ground:

THE "CARTILAGINOUS" AUTHOR

Lord! what a dish without salt!
What a terrible morsel is GALT!
All "cartilaginous,"
No oleaginous,
Not to be swallow'd is GALT.

In vain we take Rhenish or malt,
Or rum, which doth valour exalt;
There's no getting down,
Though in liquor we drown,
This vile cartilaginous GALT.

Oh Colburn, how thumping the fault,
To mix up poor Byron with GALT!
There's a grill in the bard
But 'tis devilish hard
To make it a garnish for GALT.

No, no, there's no swallowing GALT,
Horrible hazy old GALT;
'tis past all defining
The horror of dining
On tough, cartilaginous GALT.[2]

The Young Man at St. Kitts: 1834

Toward the end of 1900 and in the beginning of 1901, *The Globe* newspaper of London published several limericks, along with readers' comments on matters limerickal. A March 1901 text read:

In answer to our enquiry, a correspondent guarantees the Limerick to have flourished, at any rate in the reign of William IV. This is one of the several he remembers as current at his public school in 1834:

There was a young man at St. Kitts
Who was very much troubled with fits:
The eclipse of the moon
Threw him into a swoon,
When he tumbled and broke into bits.[3]

Carolyn Wells was an American writer of detective stories and one of the stalwarts of limerick lore and legend. She wrote many famous limericks, published several articles and books containing them, and knew other writers of the verse form, for example Oliver Herford.

In a 1902 book published in the U.S., she wrote: "This type of stanza, known as the 'Limerick,' is said by a gentleman who speaks with authority to have flourished in the reign of William IV. This is one of several he remembers as current at his public school in 1834."[4] The limerick quoted earlier is then given.

This comment subsequently appeared in a variety of articles and books; most authors (including Miss Wells) seemed to have no idea where the verse came from. The limerick is actually one of the *Fifteen Gentlemen*, published circa 1821. The comment by the "gentleman" shows that such verses had obviously become popular in the nursery and had then been taken into schools. It also shows how limericks mutate as they are passed around by word of mouth, since the original limerick went:

> There was a young man at St. Kitts
> Who was very much troubled with fits;
> An eclipse of the moon
> Threw him into a swoon,
> Alas! Poor young man of St. Kitts.

The gentleman's comment also neatly illustrates a perennial problem for the limerick researcher. People just can't seem to remember things correctly and can't be bothered to check their sources, or else they seem to deliberately rewrite texts to make them sound better. For example, a 1908 article mentions the gentleman and his limerick, and precedes it with the "information" that the limerick verse form "is said by good authorities to date back to the time of William IV and to have been very popular at the court of this monarch."[5] As regards King William IV, I'm pretty sure he used to send text messages on his cell phone along the lines of "Billy 4 limericks LOL" to all his courtly circle.

A 1924 article tells us: "The next limerick really begins the history of the form as we generally know it. That is the well-known 'There was a young man of St. Kitts,' which had a wide circulation in the English university circles about 1834."[6]

Conclusion

The most important event in the 1830s was one that did not become public knowledge until the next decade. Edward Lear had become acquainted with limericks via one or more of the 1820s children's books and had started writing and illustrating his own verses. He recited them to the children of the Earl of Derby; publication would have to wait until 1846.

Chapter 6

The 1840s
Some Progress Comes to Light

Limericks were spreading in the 1840s. They appeared in magazines. Both famous and non-famous people took to writing them. A book containing 73 illustrated limericks was published by Edward Lear. Let's look at how events unfolded.

Arundines Cami: 1841 Onward

A book containing a collection of rhymes, songs, poems and hymns, translated into Latin, Greek and other languages, would fall dead off the presses if published today. However, the past is a different country and this book ran to a total of six editions; 1841, 1843, 1846, 1851, 1860 and 1865.

Not only that, but some reviewers waxed lyrical over it, as we shall see later in this chapter and at the beginning of the next. Of immediate concern to us is that this book contained one limerick: the old man of Tobago. Quite possibly this book condemned several generations of public schoolboys to offer their own classical translations of the limerick.

James Orchard Halliwell: 1842 Onward

Halliwell's *The Nursery Rhymes of England* enjoyed great success in the 1840s. The first edition of 1842 contained two limericks (Leeds, Norwich).

The second edition of 1843 added one more (Tobago), and the third (1844) and fourth editions (1846) added three more (Surrey, Reigate, Bombay). All these are from *Sixteen Wonderful Women* or *Fifteen Gentlemen*. None is attributed. A few exhibit the usual changes caused by oral transmission.

Some comments made by Halliwell in his preface were misconstrued by Langford Reed—probably deliberately—as suggesting that these limericks had an origin going back to the Stuarts. Other limerick historians have repeated the claim. Belknap (page 19) calls this "the strangest example of the irresponsibility of limerick scholarship."

William Makepeace Thackeray: Mid-1840s

The Victoria & Albert Museum owns a card on which a sketch was drawn by Thackeray circa 1844.[1] A limerick is written underneath:

> Theres [sic] a wealthy old man of Tabreez
> With a maudlin affection for fleas,
>   He'll grin with delight
>   When they scratch him and bite
> —Perverted old man of Tabreez!

On the other side a second drawing stands over another limerick:

> This gay and light hearted old Persian
> Used to punish his wives by immersion;
>   Said his daughter, "Tis cruel!"
>   —"Perhaps so, my jewel,"
> (Quoth he)—"but tis pretty diversion!"

One of the frustrations facing the limerick historian is when he comes across a limerick which is demonstrably early—and is therefore important in showing the development of the verse form—but which has no date associated with it. Thackeray is known to have written at least two limericks about his friend James Spedding (1808–1881). He was a confirmed bachelor and Francis Bacon scholar whose enormous forehead and bald head was an object of much fun for his friends. When the limericks were written is uncertain, but Thackeray died December 24, 1863. One of them is included in a book which described Thackeray's life from his birth until 1846. The author had access to Thackeray's papers and family archives and the verse is included in a section discussing the mid-1840s, so it was possibly written then[2]:

> I would have you know, my dear Spedding
> In case you are thinking of wedding
> That a babe at the breast, disturbs the night's rest
> And occasionally moistens the bedding.

Poor old Spedding; such a conscientious man, too.

Chapter 6. The 1840s

The second limerick by Thackeray on Spedding will be considered in the 1870s chapter, as an example of how limericks were spread. Access to the Thackeray papers might solve the date problem.

Punch Magazine: 1845

Just before Christmas, 1845, *Punch* magazine[3] stunned its readers by announcing that limericks had been banned from the nursery of Queen Victoria's children. It didn't actually use the word limerick, but explained that "recently we have heard that our old friends the Man of Tobago, the Sailor [sic] of Bister [sic] &c., &c., have been excluded from the most Gracious School-room to make room for an entirely new class of picture book containing short-rhymed lessons in history, taste and morality, calculated to instruct as well as amuse the Royal Infants, and forming altogether a Juvenile Library, on a most successful plan."

The sick man of Tobago was printed at the bottom of the page to remind those who had "forgotten these friends of their youth." (We can note he was now an old man who lived on rice, sugar and sago and was tended by a mere doctor.)

Punch also provided six limericks as examples "of these excellent Didactic Poems" which the royal infants would apparently enjoy in place of the *Anecdotes and Adventures of Fifteen Gentlemen*. Presumably written by Mr. Punch himself, they all seem to refer to the good and the great of the time. The first one contains what seems to be a pun on a person's name:

> There was an old broom of St. Stephen's.
> That set all at sixes and sevens;
>   And to sweep from the room
>   The convictions of BROUGHAM
> Was the work of this Broom of St. Stephen's.

Langford Reed[4] identified Henry Lord Brougham as the Lord Chancellor of England, who played a leading part in carrying through the Reform Bill of 1832. Dr. Bibby[5] further explained that in 1832 Parliament sat in St. Stephen's chapel in the old Palace of Westminster.

The last limericks show a freedom in rhyming and dispense with the last line being a repeat of the first; for example:

> There was an old Singer of Avon,
> Who, Aunty Bess thought, was a brave one;
> But Mamma doesn't care
> For this stupid Swan's air,
> Any more than the croak of a raven.

The lucky recipients of this new style of teaching were Queen Victoria's four eldest children, one of whom was Bertie, aged four. He subsequently became the Prince of Wales before ascending the throne in 1901 as King Edward VII.

I've often thought that deprivation as a child can result in overindulgence as an adult. The legendary Frank Harris described in his memoirs[6] one occasion in 1889 when he was talking to the Prince of Wales in Monte Carlo. The Prince apparently could not get enough of his jokes. Harris then says:

> It was the limericks he seemed to like most; one in especial pleased him so much that he tried to learn it by heart. Here it is.
>
> There was a young lady at sea
> Who said, "God, how it hurts me to pee."
> "I see," said the Mate,
> "That accounts for the state
> Of the captain, the purser and me."

Edward Lear: 1846

Edward Lear is a pivotal player in the history and development of the limerick verse form. He took his inspiration from two of the children's books of limericks published in the 1820s.

The first book containing limericks by Edward Lear was published by Thomas McLean of London on February 10, 1846, in two volumes, selling at 3s 6d each. In today's money that's perhaps £15 each. However, anyone lucky enough to actually own a first edition could sell it today for substantially more. In 2016 a newly discovered copy, containing the two volumes bound as one, went on sale for $75,000.[7]

Each of the 73 limericks was accompanied by one of Lear's childlike sketches. Some critics have suggested that the books sold because of these pictures, rather than the verses. It is interesting that the sketches are quite crude, in most marked contrast to the draftsmanship displayed in his flora and fauna paintings, and the landscape paintings of his later years.

The number of books in the first edition was probably between 250 and 500. Most of Lear's limericks start off along the lines "There was an old someone…" and most finish with a variant of the first line. In his 1846 book the text was italic capitals, and most verses were in a three-line layout.[8] For example:

> *THERE WAS AN OLD PERSON OF HURST,*
> *WHO DRANK WHEN HE WAS NOT ATHIRST;*

WHEN THEY SAID, 'YOU'LL GROW FATTER,'
HE ANSWERED, 'WHAT MATTER?'
THAT GLOBULAR PERSON OF HURST.

Some of Lear's 1846 limericks were certainly known to others at the time; one was published in 1850 and two others in 1851 in a college magazine.[9] At this point in its life the school in question trained 16–18-year-olds to administer India.

Despite the limited print run of Lear's first book of limericks, it may possibly have influenced other writers in the 1840s, as we shall see in the next sections.

Lewis Carroll: 1846

In 1845 13-year-old Charles Dodgson created a magazine called *Useful and Instructive Poetry* for his younger siblings. Some of the poems for this magazine were written in 1846.[10] Four were limericks. Were they inspired by Lear? Some think so: "probably created as a result of reading Edward Lear's book."[11] Some think not: "these limericks may well have preceded Lear's, or were at least contemporaneous with Lear's first book of nonsense in 1846."[12]

As to their place in limerick history, they were unknown to the general public before they were published in 1954[13] and would have had no effect on the development of the verse form. They can be found on websites; at least two are worth reading:

> There was once a young man of Oporta
> Who daily got shorter and shorter
> The reason he said,
> Was the hod on his head,
> Which was filled with the heaviest mortar.

> His sister named Lucy O'Finner,
> Grew constantly thinner and thinner;
> The reason was plain
> She slept out in the rain,
> And was never allowed any dinner.

Bishop How and Cuthbert Bede: Circa 1846

In 1999 Christie's sold a manuscript book whose contents were described as "a collection of 25 original autograph limericks." The author was William Walsham How, a little-known stalwart of the church and a prolific hymn-writer. An inscription in the book read: "The illustrations in this book are originals by Edward Bradley, better known by his nom de plume of 'Cuthbert Bede,' who did them for me, I giving him the rhymes, about the year 1846. W.W.H."

Walsham How was the rector of St. Andrew Undershaft and bishop suffragan of Bedford between 1879 and 1888. He then became the first Bishop of Wakefield.

The Rev. Ernest Bradley was most famous for his novel about university life, titled *The Adventures of Mr. Verdant Green*, which he wrote to occupy his time before becoming ordained—he was too young to take holy orders after graduating from Durham University.

How studied at Wadham College, Oxford, prior to going to University College, Durham, where both he and Bradley matriculated on October 25, 1845.[14]

Whether the verses were written as a result of either man reading Lear's book will probably never be known, but the Christie's catalogue described them as being "contemporary with, and clearly influenced by, the work of Edward Lear." Having seen some of the verses I agree with this comment.

As I write, this book is for sale by a well-known antiquarian bookseller. It can easily be yours if you have £2,500 to spare. Interestingly, it seems to have lost a verse, being described as "a Collection of 24 Manuscript Limericks, each with a laid down original ink illustration by Cuthbert Bede."

The Reverend Abraham Calovius Simpson, LL.D.: 1848

In 1867 a sketch of the life and character of the Reverend Simpson was published anonymously in *The British Quarterly Review*.[15] It later appeared in book form.[16] The article contained the following quotation from one of his letters, describing breakfast with his younger children:

> Sutton, June 26, 1848.—In one of the magazines you sent, I came suddenly, at breakfast-time, on some nursery nonsensical verses about sixteen old women of different towns. As I read them, I slipped in an extemporaneous one, which went off like the others, and the girls do not know it was a fudge:
>
> > There was an old woman of Sutton,
> > A goggle-eyed, riotous glutton;
> > Toads, hedgehogs and owls
> > Were dainty as fowls
> > To the hungry old woman of Sutton.

This is an interesting letter for two reasons. It shows that limericks were being published in magazines, and it shows that "ordinary" members of the public were quite happy to have a go at creating similar verses.

It is also interesting because it shows that this is where the real history of the limerick is to be found, in that most difficult of all things to find—private letters and diaries.

The Belfast Comet: 1849

"A Belfast Journal of Fun, Frolic and Literature"—as *The Comet* described itself—contained an odd article in 1849.[17] Headed "A Spectre Bridegroom," it described an apparition which apparently recited poetry, dressed in kilts and was a rabid debater in political circles. It then tells us:

> It is said that a Miss M., of the Lodge Road, was so haunted by the apparition that she was compelled to leave for America in consequence. Since her departure, it been observed gliding about St. Ann's Buildings, but more particularly on the roofs of the houses of North Street Place, where it rants "Richard," and composes such verse as this:
>
>> My name is tall Kilty M ' G.
>> And I will be a something you see:
>> My future abode
>> Will be up the Fall's Road,
>> Where apartments are ready for me.

Presumably the whole thing was a dig at a local character. Or maybe the Guinness was stronger in the old days.

A couple of months later,[18] *The Comet* published a poem of 20 stanzas in limerick layout—except that each stanza had a sixth and seventh line, which actually didn't add much or affect the poem. However, it is not in strict limerick form—so out with it. A pity though; the title is "The Inauguration of Larry's New Pole." It's probably not quite what you thought it was about; Larry was a barber.

Limericks in North America

When limericks first became widely known in America is a difficult question to answer. It is quite likely that copies of early limerick books were imported. An argument in favor of this is that the Frothingham family of Montreal had a hand-created copy of the *Sixteen Old Women*.

Another way Americans became aware of limericks was by reading reviews of books which contained them. For example, *The Southern*

Quarterly Review, which was published in Charleston, South Carolina, published a review of *Arundines Cami* in 1842.[19] The reviewer explained that he had enjoyed the poems contained in the book, and was "anxious that our readers should partake of the same gratification." The old man of Tobago was then given in Greek, followed by the original in English.

I don't have a list of subscribers to *Punch* magazine, but it would not surprise me if copies circulated in the New World in the 1840s.

The earliest book I know of which was printed in America and which contained limericks was the wonderfully titled *The Book of Nursery Rhymes Complete. From the Creation of the World to the Present Time.*[20] This was published in Philadelphia in 1846 and contained six limericks, all from *Sixteen Old Women* and *Fifteen Gentlemen*. None were attributed; they were probably stolen from Halliwell, since the illustration for the old man of Bombay is the same in both books. Incidentally, I could find no poems which actually date from the creation of the world. Typical American braggadocio.

Conclusion

Limericks came on apace in the 1840s. Lear's first book was published. It is interesting that private documents such as letters, diaries, homemade creations and handwritten cards with drawings can tell us much about the development of the verse form among the general population. It is a great pity that such ephemera were often destroyed, and that those that remain are so difficult to find.

Chapter 7

The 1850s
The Calm before the Storm

Arundines Cami: 1851

In 1851 the fourth edition of this book was published in the UK. In 1856 perusers of an excitingly titled American book[1]—*Dealings with the Dead, Volume 2, by a sexton of the old school*—would have been able to read a review of *Arundines Cami*. It was described as "a very bijou of a book," and the author had "never seen a more beautiful specimen of typography." The old man of Tobago was included, along with his un-limerick-like Greek translation.

The Haileybury Observer: 1851

Set up by an Act of Parliament and subsequently closed by an Act of Parliament, the Honorable East India College was initially sited in Hertford Castle and then relocated to nearby Haileybury House. Here, 16–18-year-old youths were trained to become civil servants to work in India to "qualify them to governing themselves." They were not, perhaps, the best examples of English gentlemen. The school was once described as "the disgrace of England," and tales exist of pupils stoning unpopular masters and beating up college servants with cudgels. Thomas Malthus, among others, was one of the masters who tried to keep them under control.

When not engaged in this sort of behavior, pupils danced and fenced in order to acquire social graces. They also produced a magazine called *The Haileybury Observer*. As we saw in the preceding chapter, the students were familiar with several limericks which had appeared in Edward Lear's 1846 book. It seems that such verses were mainly used to provide text to hone Latin translation skills. One William Waterfield, however, seems to have either written his own limerick or found a non–Lear one. The translation is in a more limerick-like layout than some:

> There was an old man of Barbadoes,
> Who was blown quite in two by tornadoes;
> So roughly it blew him,
> His dinner fell through him,
> Which grieved that old man of Barbadoes.

SENEX BARBATENSIS

> Senex quidam est Barbatæ,
> Plane ruptus tempestate:
> Flatu vente violente
> Cœna medium perlabente
> Mœstus hic restabat mente.—G.A.[2]

The Bridle Roads of Spain: 1853

The donkey is not a popular mode of travel these days, but it was obviously de rigueur in 1853. In a work titled *Las Alforjas*,[3] which, "as any fule kno," means "saddlebags" in Castilian, our lovesick hero pens a six-limerick sequence to his beloved. He comments that it expresses his feelings better than any serious verse. The sequence stands under the descriptive title of "Mabblings and Babblings." The heroine is one Mabel, whose name is rhymed many times with consummate ease. Our hero also manages to rhyme "saddle, he" with "badly." This gem can be read online. I doubt if it gave rise to later limericks which describe various athletic activities of a lady called Mabel, but you never know.

Burton and Its Bitter Beer: 1853

Dr. John Stevenson Bushnan inadvertently started the Great Pale Ale Controversy of 1852 by printing in his medical journal a report from a French chemist which claimed that Burton beer owed its bitterness to the strychnine which was being added to it. Apparently, he honestly believed this to be true, despite the fact that the amount of strychnine involved would have killed the entire population of India in one year.

As a sort of apologia for this libel, he then wrote a treatise on the historical, chemical, economic and social aspects of beer-drinking. This book, published in 1853, waxed lyrical on the benefits of the liquid; quite literally in several instances. One poem was a five-stanza verse, the last part of each stanza arguably being a stand-alone limerick. Indeed, after giving the whole poem, the good doctor used the last "limerick" to muse philosophically about the adulteration of a fine product:

> There is much philosophy in this humorous and clever lyric, the moral of which is—that the adulteration of any of the necessities or luxuries of life has physically an unhealthy, and mentally demoralizing effect. To meet his expenses, the unjust publican adulterates his beer; and the mechanic, when he finds it unpalatable, or, in more vernacular language, "summut so queer," that he cannot relish it, takes to gin, which soon deadens the power of thought, excites the passions, and prompts to acts of brutal violence. Hence we may understand how
>
> > The want of a drop of good beer
> > Drives lots to tipples more dear;
> > And they licks their wives,
> > And destroys their lives,
> > Which they wouldn't have done upon beer.[4]

A plea then followed for a reduction in duty upon this socially uplifting amber nectar.

Ridiculous Things, Scraps and Oddities, Some with, and Many without Any Meanings: 1854

This is the title of what can only be described as the work of a peculiar but very creative mind. Published in 1854, the author was John Orlando Parry, an Englishman of Welsh extraction and an actor, pianist, artist, comedian and singer. Of the 32 plates in the book, one is titled "Stray Leaves from *A Book of Nonsense*." This consists of nine limericks, all of which are illustrated.

One Parry verse contains an example of a rhyming trick sometimes used in later limericks, the Procrustean method:

> There was an old Duchess of Como,
> Who sent for her doctor, (a Homo-
>   -pathic Professor,
>   Also Hair-dresser,)
> Who "brushed up" the Duchess of Como.

Of the nine limericks two do not start with "There was somebody…" five do not end "That something someone of," and most have some sort of action going on.

One explosive illustration contains a good rhyme for Swansea and is an early example of the obsession that some limerick writers have with ladies who blow themselves apart.

Illustration from *Ridiculous Things, Scraps and Oddities, Some with, and Many without any meanings*, **John Orlando Parry, Thos. McLean, London, 1854.**

I have no idea if Parry was influenced by Lear, but the two men had some things in common. Parry's publisher was the same as Lear's—Thomas McLean. Lear's limericks were created to amuse Lord Derby's children: "The Late Lord Derby was a special lover of children, and he wrote at least one book designed for their special use. It may not be so generally known that some of the designs in Mr. John Parry's folio guinea book, *Ridiculous Things, Scraps and Oddities*, were originally drawn by him, at Lord Derby's request, for the amusement of his family."[5]

Edward Lear Again: 1855

In 1855 Edward Lear published a new edition of his 1846 book. He had new lithographic stones made of the illustrations in his first book. He also set out the text in the "standard" five-line format rather than the three-line layout he had mainly used earlier. The font was more conventional. Apart from these visual changes this second edition contained exactly the same limericks as the first edition.

William Makepeace Thackeray: Circa 1855?

Limericks hidden in prose are extremely rare—and it takes an eagle eye to spot them. The oldest one I know of is undated but is almost certainly from the 1850s and is contained in a humorous letter from Thackeray to his friend Synge.[6]

For those who have trouble reading copperplate I append the text:

> SIR I am desired by Lord Palmerston to say
> that Perhaps you have heard of Miss Simons?
> She dines at a twopenny Pieman's
> But when she goes out to a ball or
> a Rout Her stomach is covered with
> di'monds. I have the honor to be, Sir;
> Your obedient Servt.
> W M Tomkins.

J.W. Churton: Mid-1850s?

Consider the following limerick from Reed's 1924 book:

> There was a young man at the War Office,
> Whose head was an absolute store office.
> Each warning severe
> Went in at one ear,
> And out of the opposite orifice.
> —*J.W. Churton*

Reed identifies the author in a footnote: "The late J.W. Churton was the uncle of Dean Inge."

I assume someone wrote to Reed about this verse since the 1926 edition gives the second line as "Whose head was an absolute store of vice," and the footnote is amplified with the comment: "The [author] composed the above Limerick when a schoolboy at Charterhouse."

The verse still makes the occasional appearance in print.[7] No one seems to have ever identified when it was written. Efforts to find out which version was the original and when the verse was written bore fruit when two newspaper references were found. A 1921 reference reported:

> Dean Inge—"the Gloomy Dean," as some critics style him—has been doing something that should induce re-consideration of the description. He has been writing about games to sharpen the wits of young people and indulging in comments upon Limericks. And, as if to prove that he comes from a strain that possesses humor, he has stated that an uncle of his, then a public school-boy, made one of the most ingenious rhymes he has ever seen:—

> There was a young man at the War Office,
> Whose head was an absolute store of vice.
> Each warning severe
> Went in at one ear,
> And out at the opposite orifice.[8]

I have not yet been able to find Dean Inge's writing on Limericks. Possibly this was Reed's source for the verse and the attribution to J.W. Churton.

In 1953 the *Yorkshire Evening Post* received a letter from the then 93-year-old Dean. He was inspired by a photograph of the village where he was born which had appeared in the paper, commenting: "The changes in education, now that children are sent to school at five, are remarkable. I was taught at home, and very well taught, too, till three months before I went to Eton at 14. There was much reading aloud and, as a treat, round games, Nouns and Questions or Limericks. One of these perhaps deserves to live."[9] The same version Inge had given in 1921 was then printed.

Research showed that Joshua Watson Churton was an old Carthusian who matriculated at University College, Oxford, on March 21, 1857, aged 18, but died before taking his degree.[10] Since Inge stated he wrote the limerick while at school this would probably put its composition sometime between 1850 and 1857, most likely at the end of this period.

I find this an interesting limerick for several reasons:

- Dean Inge's mother was Susanna Churton (born 1833), so she either remembered her brother reciting the verse or it had been written down.
- Inge (himself a writer of limericks) commented that he thought the rhyme one of the most ingenious he had ever seen.
- Inge remembered this limerick until his death.
- Inge went to Eton circa 1874, so recitation of limericks as a treat was happening in his home before then.

Two possibly relevant comments. The expression used in the limerick was apparently not uncommon around the composition date; for example, an 1865 newspaper records: "The Commissioner censured him for his absence, but this censure went in at one ear—and whether it stopped within or passed out at the opposite orifice did not appear."[11]

The War Office was the main government department responsible for the British Army from the 17th century until 1964. Britain's military governance received a severe shake-up in 1855 as a result of its perceived poor performance during the Crimean War; one example was that the Board of Ordnance was abolished.

Lewis Carroll: 1856

> There was a Greek Reader named [Stokes]
> Who indulged in the mildest of jokes:
> But they had not a bit
> Of the genuine wit,
> So he had to enforce them with pokes.[12]

The above is one of four recently discovered personal limericks written by Lewis Carroll about Oxford contemporaries. The verses were found in the back of an unpublished journal kept by Thomas Vere Bayne, a lifelong friend and colleague of Carroll's at Christ Church.

All four limericks are quoted in an article published in 2022. The surnames were "tactfully omitted in the original." However, the author identifies and describes Carroll's "Christ Church contemporaries."

Old Nurse's Book of Rhymes, Jingles and Ditties: 1858

Our old friends the soldier of Bister [*sic*] and the fat man of Bombay, whom we first met in *Fifteen Gentlemen*, reappeared in this 1858 book. This time the fat man had his pipe stolen by a snipe that was almost as big as he was.[13]

Cuthbert Bede, as Both Writer and Artist: 1858

The year 1858 saw the publication of a work titled *Funny Figures*, by A. Funnyman. The title page gave the author's name as Cuthbert Bede. This was the nom de plume of Edward Bradley, the reverend gentleman whom we met in the 1840s chapter. Subtitled "One shilling plain, two shillings colored," it contained 24 illustrations and 24 verses for the delectation of small children. Twenty of the verses were limericks. None are of any great moment, a typical one being:

> There was a young lady of Sparta,
> Who never would wear any garter,
> Her stockings came down,
> As she walk'd through the town,
> Which quite shock'd the good people of Sparta.[14]

The University of Cambridge: 1858

It is often said that the great universities contain enormous amounts of knowledge because each undergraduate brings a little with him when he enters the place, and no graduate ever takes any away when he leaves. This is not a new idea; a verse that dates back to at least 1789[15] puts it this way:

> No wonder that Oxford and Cambridge profound
> In learning and science so greatly abound
> Since some carry thither a little each day
> And we meet with so few who bring any away.

The oldest limericks I currently know which emanated from a university and which were printed for public consumption were two published in a Cambridge undergraduate magazine in 1858.[16] Edited by an old Harrovian, this is perhaps an example of how universities accumulate knowledge, in this case by importing limericks. Standing under the title "Nursery Rhymes," the first reads:

> There once was a freshman of Caius
> Who was partial to sermons and teas:
> But, shocking to say,
> He soon fell away,
> And now reads *Bell's Life* at his ease.

For those unfamiliar with the reading habits of mid-19th-century students, *Bell's Life* was a sporting weekly with a special interest in horses and pugilists.

Mr. Richard Hutton: 1858?

Mr. Hutton's limerick is almost impossible to date—I include it mainly to show the problems the limerick historian faces. A biography of Walter Bagehot was written by his sister-in-law Mrs. Russell Barrington, née Emilie Isabel Wilson. In it, a letter written by Bagehot on January 15, 1858, describes how a friend, Mr. W.R. Greg, "has gone into captivity to an over-fascinating woman." She was a widow; how long the relationship lasted is unknown; Mr. Greg married the authoress's sister in 1874.

To Bagehot's letter dated January 17, 1858, a footnote about the lady (her name is not recorded in the book) reads:

> This poor lady who Walter criticized so severely, was treated in like manner by his friend Mr. Hutton, as well as by Arthur Clough. Mr. Hutton wrote a nonsense verse about her which I illustrated:

> There was an old lady of Putney,
>   Who looked as if she would butt me;
> She came with a rush and a passionate gush,
>   That ecstatic old lady of Putney.

This aversion was a typical example of an inveterate antipathy which Mr. Hutton, Mr. Clough, Walter Bagehot and other men of their set entertained towards a certain flashy form of insincerity.

I can only assume that the limerick was written around the time of the meeting or while the relationship was still going on; why would Mr. Hutton write a verse about the lady when she had presumably disappeared from their social circle?

The problem for the limerick historian is that this verse could have been written at any time between 1858 and 1874. The authoress was a writer and artist; born October 18, 1841, she was 16 and a quarter at the start of 1858.

As I said, I include the limerick to show the problem it raises. Since it has a definite Learian feel it would not surprise me to date it a little after publication of Lear's 1861 book, which we shall encounter shortly. Perhaps a more knowledgeable historian can tell me the date of composition and illustration.

Conclusion

The 1850s gave us a story sequence in limerick stanzas, a limerick hidden in prose, a Procrustean rhyme, some innovative rhymes and storylines, and more evidence that the common man was prepared to have a go at composing limericks.

The limericks created don't always start "There was a somebody," and they don't always end with the same rhyme word. Some have a bit of fizz to them in that the characters involved do something quite active.

Chapter 8

The 1860s
The Limerick Explodes

At the beginning of the 1860s, America was on the brink of a bloody civil war, with the possibility of splitting into two weak nations. The limerick was a little-known children's verse form, possibly on the brink of fading into obscurity.

At the end of the 1860s, the United States of America was taking its first steps to becoming a dominant world power. The limerick was well on its way to becoming a permanent presence in world literature and arguably the dominant humorous verse form—for adults. There is of course no causal relationship between the two events, as far as I know, but it is interesting that the limerick was active during the American Civil War—and only on the Union side, as far as I know.

Punch: 1860

Punch started the decade rolling by reprinting a variant of the Old Soldier of Bicester—he had turned into an old tailor and the bull had somehow transmogrified into a jay.[1] Two other limericks appeared in *Punch* before the year was out: one[2] mocked Mr. Gladstone's introduction of the Ten-Penny Income-Tax, and the other[3] summarized Irish opinion toward comments made in the *Times* about the Irish Brigade.

Lucy Cavendish: August 1860

Lucy Caroline Lyttelton (1841–1925), sometime lady-in-waiting to Queen Victoria, married Lord Frederick Cavendish in 1864. After his assassination in 1882 she became active in promoting women's education. Lucy Cavendish College, Cambridge, was named for her in 1965.

Sir Stephen Richard Glynne was her uncle. He was a Welsh landowner

Chapter 8. The 1860s

who was an MP for many years but never spoke in Parliament due to shyness. During one parliamentary campaign he started libel proceedings against a local newspaper for alleging he was homosexual. He never married, possibly on account of visiting over five and a half thousand churches and making copious notes about them.

The National Library of Wales contains a large number of documents relating to the Glynne family. Among them are two items of interest to us. The first is a letter from Lucy to her uncle,[4] which begins:

> Hagley
>
> Aug. 25.1860.
>
> My dear Uncle Stephen,
>
> It was thanks to your letter's correct date that I remembered the Saint's Day at all! so it was of great use.
>
> How charming of you to send me such excellent examples of Old Persons. I can hardly doubt that I am right in supposing you to be the author? especially of the Old Persons of Cheedle [sic], of Calcutta, of Parma, of Kildare, & the young lady of Bute. Here are three we were incited to compose after the perusal of yours.
>
> > There was an Old Woman of Broom,
> > Who lived in the dowdiest room!
> > The chairs were decay'd—
> > The dust was ne'er laid—
> > O! scrubly Old Woman of Broom!
> >
> > There was an Old Woman of Frome,
> > Who wore a superb ostrich plume;
> > In a habit of green,
> > On a war-horse was seen
> > This rampant Old Woman of Frome.
> >
> > There was an Old Doctor of Churchill,
> > His physic made poor Mr. Birch ill—
> > Of arsenic his potions:
> > Of strychnine his lotions:
> > This criminal Doctor of Churchill.

The "we" probably refers to her elder sister Meriel, who is mentioned later in the letter as being with her.

This is an interesting letter for several reasons. The first is obviously that we have a dated letter which contains three Lear-like limericks written by a young lady of almost 19 and her companion.

The second reason is that her uncle had obviously sent her several examples of "Old Persons." What these were we don't know. It is interesting that Lucy assumes her uncle wrote them; presumably she would only have thought that if he had earlier written such verses for her, or if she had heard him declaiming such verses.

(We can note that Edward Lear's 1846 and 1855 books both contained limericks about:

- an Old Person of Cheadle
- an Old Man of Calcutta
- a Young Lady of Parma
- an Old Man of Kildare and
- a Young Lady of Bute.)

A second "document" in the archives consists of nine pages.[5] These contain some 28 full limericks, very much in the style of Lear. There are in three different handwriting styles, suggesting three different authors. To my untrained eye none seem to be the hand of Miss Lucy. Eight of the verses are identical to limericks in Lear's 1846 and 1855 books or are slight variants of them. Of the rest some are really quite good, employing unexpected rhymes and creating unusual storylines.

These limericks have been ascribed to Lucy Cavendish. However, this assertion is seemingly based on the fact that Lucy refers to "Old Persons" in her letter—and these pages contain examples of such poems. It could just as well be argued that some of these pages came from Sir Stephen. The main problem for me is that the pages are undated. They may well all date from 1860, but unless firm evidence comes to light I can do no more than refer to them in passing.

Lucy Cavendish kept diaries for many years and after her death they were published in an abridged and annotated two-volume work.[6] The fifth volume of her diaries (covering the end of 1859 and most of 1860) was lost almost as soon as it was written, so we have no information about what Lucy was doing when she wrote the letter to her uncle. Also, alas, it means that any comments she might have made in the diary about the "Old Persons" have been lost. A trawl through both volumes of the annotated work failed to find any references to Old Persons, Old Women, etc.

Cuthbert Bede: 1861

Cuthbert Bede included a limerick in his 1861 book[7] about Scotland. The preface is dated June, so the verse predates that:

> There certainly must be occasional personal discomforts attendant upon the wearing of the kilt; for, what says the poet?
>
> > There was a short-kilted North Briton
> > Who promiscuously sat on a kitten;
> > The kitten had claws—
> > The immediate cause
> > Of much pain to the short-kilted Briton.

Whether Bede wrote the limerick or was just quoting a current verse I don't know. What I do know is that the fifth Earl of Dartmouth was impressed by the verse—and that his son most certainly was not. After Reed's limerick book was published in 1924, the sixth Earl wrote to Reed, enclosing three limericks and commenting on them. Reed included the limericks and the Earl's comments in his 1926 second edition. Part of the letter read: "About the same time [mid-1850s] my father found the [North Briton limerick] in an old Scottish book, and to my annoyance made me learn it by heart and repeat it when called upon."

Limericks in the Allison-Shelley Collection: 1861

Keen students of library catalogues will doubtless have come across a reference to a unique collection housed in Pennsylvania State University. A list of its contents includes the following: "nursery rhymes (fifty-one limericks, 1861); 17th and 18th century manuscript limericks."

Extensive communication with Sandra Stelts, curator of rare books and manuscripts at Penn State, showed that, alas, there are no 17th- and 18th-century limericks in the collection. However, there is one item of considerable interest—the collection of 51 limericks. This is a small booklet which contains some eight pages loosely held inside front and back covers. A handwritten title reads *Nursery Rhymes 1861*; examination shows that the paper bears a watermark date of 1859.

On each side of these pages, and inside the back cover, there are 51 handwritten limericks. One comes from *Sixteen Wonderful Old Women*; one comes from *Fifteen Gentlemen*; and 30 come from Lear's *Book of Nonsense*. All of the Lear limericks appeared in the 1846, 1855 and 1861 editions—except the Old Man of New York, who only appeared in the first two. While none of the 43 limericks published for the first time in Lear's 1861 edition are given, we can't say for certain that the writer was copying from an 1846 or 1855 edition; perhaps he or she copied from an 1861 UK edition and simply remembered the Old Man of New York.

The remaining 19 have never appeared in print, as far as I know, with one exception. That limerick throws up a "neat" pun:

> A juggler who lives at S. Neots
> Threw up eggs, among other strange feats;
> But do what he can
> He is beat by a man
> Who throws up whatever he eats.

The town is presumably St. Neots in Cambridgeshire.

The only other appearance I know of this limerick is in a 1934 privately published book,[8] which does not say where it was collected from.

The limericks use place names mainly from the UK. Obviously anyone with a map or gazetteer can write limericks about anywhere on earth, but the author includes towns and areas which would probably not be familiar to a non–UK resident, such as Clovelly, Streatham, Holloway and St. Neots. Also, a detailed knowledge of London hairdressers seems evident:

> A bald headed man of May Fair
> Thought he'd try to recover his hair;
> So he said, "Mr. True-
> Fitt, how do you do?
> Pray sell me some grease from the bear."

Presumably Mayfair is being referred to. Truefitt's, in St. James's Street, London, opened for business in 1805. As Truefitt & Hill it is currently the world's oldest barber shop. Mr. Truefitt's was described by Charles Dickens in *The Uncommercial Traveller* as an "excellent hairdresser's."

Bear grease was thought to be a cure for baldness; for example, the second book of Kings, Chapter Two, tells us the prophet Elisha tried to cure baldness by applying bear grease to his head. It retained its popularity over the years; for example, in 1858's *The History of Pendennis, vol. 2*, by William Makepeace Thackeray, we read: "'Stuff!' growled the other, 'you fancied you were getting bald the other day, and bragged about it, as you do about every thing. But you began to use the bear's-grease pot directly the hair-dresser told you; and are scented like a barber ever since.'"

(Whether Mr. Truefitt ever sold bear grease or not I don't know.)

This is the second example of a Procrustean rhyme in limericks, both of which involve hairdressers. Perhaps they are a cut above the average man.

Judging by the contents of this booklet, I think it was probably written in England in 1861. Exactly what inspired its creation and who actually wrote it we may never know, but at least we can appreciate the 19 new limericks it contains.

Edward Lear—*The Book of Nonsense*: November 1861

Introduction and overview

In their autobiography the celebrated engravers George and Edward Dalziel recorded:

Chapter 8. The 1860s

Early in the Sixties we made the acquaintance of Edward Lear, who was a landscape painter of great distinction, a naturalist, a man of high culture, and a most kind and courteous gentleman. He came to us bringing an original chromo-lithographic copy of his *Book of Nonsense*—published some years before by McLean of the Haymarket. His desire was to publish a new and cheaper edition. With this view he proposed having the entire set of designs redrawn on wood, and he commissioned us to do this, also to engrave the blocks, print, and produce the book for him. When the work was nearly completed, he said he would sell his rights in the production to us for £100. We did not accept his offer, but proposed to find a publisher who would undertake it. We laid the matter before Messrs. Routledge & Warne. They declined to buy, but were willing to publish it for him on commission, which they did. The first edition sold immediately. Messrs. Routledge then wished to purchase the copyright, but Mr. Lear said, "Now it is a success they must pay me more than I asked at first." The price was then fixed at £120, a very modest advance considering the mark the book had made. It has since gone through many editions in the hands of F. Warne & Co.[9]

The amount of money Lear received for selling the copyright varies from source to source. Lear himself records both £125 and £200.[10] The Dalziels suggest £120 (see quotation above). Based on simple purchasing power calculations, £125 would be 10 to 15 thousand pounds today.

This edition of *The Book of Nonsense* was published in time for Christmas 1861. December newspapers[11] advertised it at 3s. 6d a copy, perhaps 15 pounds today. One paper[12] briefly reviewed the book. In January 1862, a newspaper reproduced two limericks with their illustrations, stating they were from *The Book of Nonsense*.[13]

Compared to previous editions it contained 43 new limericks. It omitted three "rather fierce ones"[14] which were in the first two editions. This gave a total of 113 illustrated verses in the new edition. For the first time, Lear's name was on the cover.

Lear's book was ready on October 28, 1861, and on November 2 Lear asked Dalziel to print 1,000 copies.[15] By June 1862, 6,000 copies had been printed and 4,000 of these had been sold.[16] A trade advertisement[17] in December 1865 stated "eighteenth thousand," presumably the number of copies printed to that date. In other ads[18] the publishers claimed it was "the most successful Child's Book of the Year."

The Book of Nonsense went on to appear in many editions and has never been out of print.[19] For anyone not familiar with Lear's limericks, his books can be read at many sites online, with colored or with plain illustrations.

Most limerick historians believe that this book somehow caused the reading and writing of limericks to become massively popular with the general public. Limericks then changed from being mildly amusing verses for children, morphing into a whole range of verse styles enjoyed mainly by adults. By doing so they became the verse form we know and love today.

The Book of Nonsense is therefore arguably both the most important and the best-selling book of limericks ever published. Why it became so popular and so influential is difficult to understand at this remove in time. In the past 50-odd years there have been many in-depth analyses of Lear's limericks. The ideas put forward range from thought-provoking to completely nonsensical (which in this context is not a good thing). However, none, as far as I can see, address the question: Why did this particular book become so popular and give rise to a whole raft of limerick creation?

In children's books, illustrations specifically related to the text were coming into vogue around the time Lear was writing his limericks. Lear's illustrations of his limericks have been examined in their historical context.[20] Perhaps the illustrations somehow really appealed to children. But if that's so, why didn't the previous editions take off? Fewer pictures and more expensive?

The previous two editions had been published by a print-seller. Maybe the book was pushed harder by the new publisher—Routledge and Warne were initially selling the book on commission, then they bought the copyright on November 1, 1862. Routledge and Warne were publishers of children's books; maybe they had more market savvy. But that still doesn't explain why an avalanche of limerick-writing seems to have been created by this book.

Maybe it was simply that indefinable thing—the timing was just right. There's probably a PhD in this one matter alone for some keen young historian.

Ann C. Colley has commented that "the pleasure of [Lear's] limericks is that their hyperbolic and parodic modes exaggerate and widen the spaces the metaphor admits and let the reader play safely among them." She concludes: "The power of the limerick seems, finally, to derive from the spaces provided by the metaphoric vehicle."[21]

We'll probably never know if that's what people thought in the 1860s. I'll probably never know what these comments actually mean.

Reactions to Lear's Book

We may not be able to understand why the book affected people, but we can look at the effect it had. Let's look at what contemporaries and near contemporaries said about it. The following is in as chronological an order as I can make it.

The earliest review was probably the long and largely positive description which appeared on page 18 of *The Spectator* on November 9, 1861, only a few days after Lear signed the agreement on November 5 for Routledge to publish the book on commission.[22] In February 1862, an Australian newspaper[23] reprinted this review. Several limericks were quoted.

In December 1861, *The Spectator*[24] reviewed an almanac by one Zadkie Tao-Sze. The vagueness of his prophecies was discussed and he was said to resemble:

> in this respect a remarkable woman in our children's nonsense book:
>
>> There was a young lady of Prague,
>> Whose mind was excessively vague;
>> If you asked, "Are these caps?"
>> She answered "Perhaps,"
>> That oracular lady of Prague.

The use of "our" to describe Lear's book shows a touching adoption of the work. Either that, or it simply refers to the book belonging to the writer's children. (The lady of Prague was present in all three editions of Lear's book, so the reviewer could have been quoting from any, but I think it's most likely it was the new edition.)

In April 1862, Mr. Punch opined[25]:

> Then came the Budget for 1862. Its features are mild, not to say inexpensive, and when MR. GLADSTONE, after talking pleasantly through three columns, came to the statement that the probable revenue for next year would be £70,190,000, against an expenditure of £70,010,000, the Commons began, as he said, to Buzz. As the *Book of Nonsense* has it:
>
>> There was a great person called G.,
>> He was bored by the rude H. of C.,
>>   When folk said, "Does it buzz?"
>>   He replied, "Yes, it does,
>> And its meaning's a riddle to me."

Ah, the good old days when government budgets actually balanced. European Union—take note. (The limerick parodied here first appeared in 1861, so Mr. Punch is referring to the third edition.)

In June 1862, Australian newspapers[26] reprinted a description of Lear's book that had appeared in a UK paper. It shows how far knowledge of the book had spread, and that people were copying Lear's style and writing their own limericks:

> Nonsense Verses.—There is nothing so delightful as nonsense at the right time. We have just been looking through *A Book of Nonsense*, by Mr. Edward Lear, an artist of some celebrity. It is a series of deliciously ridiculous drawings, illustrating doggrel verses no less ridiculous. Thus—

> There was a young lady of Norway,
> Who casually sat in a doorway:
> When the door squeezed her flat,
> She exclaimed, "What of that!"
> This courageous lady of Norway.

We cannot pretend to describe the expression of this Norwegian young lady's countenance, as she suffers her squeeze, in the drawing. As Homeric translation has lately been fashionable, perhaps Professor Arnold and his rivals may be interested in the following:

> There was an old person of Cromer,
> Who stood on one leg to read Homer;
> When he found he grew stiff,
> He jumped over the cliff,
> Which concluded that person of Cromer.

Now we desire to draw attention to the fine spirit of nonsense in these rhymes. The book caught our eye in a pleasant country residence not very far down the South-Western Line; and one evening we all set to work to make imitative rhymes about the stations on that railway, which a young caricaturist in petticoats, ten years old, incontinently illustrated. Somebody began at Waterloo—

> There was an old party at Waterloo,
> Who gave eighteenpence to his daughter Loo;
> But she ran away,
> And went to the play,
> Which grieved that old party at Waterloo.

One more only—

> There was an old lady at Staines,
> Who got in the way of the trains,
> Which cut her in half.
> And caused her to laugh.
> That funny old lady of Staines.
>
> —*Literary Budget*.[27]

A biography of the American writer Nathaniel Hawthorne by his son commented that "the Nonsense Verses were coming into vogue at this epoch, and everyone was trying his own hand at producing them." A poor example of a limerick is given.[28] The date is difficult to determine; either autumn 1862 or 1863. Hawthorne died in May 1864.

Fun magazine, in a September 1863 issue, contained a limerick said to have been written by the author of *A Book of Nonsense*. It wasn't. In November 1864, 13 limericks were given under the heading: "Omitted from the Book of Nonsense." They hadn't been. Between December 1864 and February 1865, the magazine printed three sets of six limericks, all about Oxford colleges, under the heading: "Contributions to the Book of Nonsense." They weren't accepted.

American writer and poet Bayard Taylor led an interesting life, translating Goethe's *Faust*, traveling widely, and at one point living in Russia

He wrote what has been called American's first gay novel. A biographer records how Taylor and his friends reacted to Lear's book[29]: "When Edward Lear's *Book of Nonsense* was young, verses of like character were made by the New York triumvirate after they wearied of parody."

An article in an 1866 American newspaper also commented that as a result of the popularity of Lear's book, the limerick verse form had become widely known and composed[30]:

> Then came *The Book of Nonsense*, appearing in England in 1860 [sic], and at once becoming popular, but not reaching us in America until about a year ago. The meter of this was in its favor, and the tang of it—the note, as Matthew Arnold would say; but the poems of the original *Book of Nonsense* were such rubbish—without fun or point—that the feeblest imitators have surpassed their model. Private circles have been delighted with the "thick-coming fancies" which take form in that fortunate meter; conceited people have been gracefully "taken down a peg"; "toad-eating little cities" or communities have been properly characterized and quizzed, as the *Nonsense Book* showed how.

The above reviewer was quite forthright in his opinion that Lear's poems "were such rubbish—without fun or point." He wasn't the only one. In an 1866 article in the *Era* a reviewer described *Lear's Shilling Book of Nonsense*, which contained Lear's limericks in three separate volumes. After getting somewhat irate about the whole matter he concluded by remarking: "That a man should fancy himself so overcharged with genius as to hope to find a publisher for his rubbish is by no means surprising; but it certainly is marvelous in these days of close dealing and competition to find a publisher supporting such unmitigated and pointless trash."

Pointless or not, there was something about the verse form that made all sorts of people copy it. The poet Rossetti wrote hundreds of limericks[31]: "The habit of making satirical rhymes like these was an outcome of the appearance of Lear's *Book of Nonsense*. D.G.R. began the habit with us, the difficulty of finding a rhyme for the name being often the sole inducement. Swinburne assisted him and all of us; and every day for a year or two they used to fly about. The dearest friends and most intimate acquaintances came in for the severest treatment; but as truth was the last thing intended though sometimes slyly implied nobody minded."

An article[32] describing Rossetti's limericks mentions that he presented Oliver Madox Brown with a volume of Lear's *Nonsense Verses*, which had the following limerick written on the fly-leaf:

> There was a young rascal called Nolly,
> Whose habits, though dirty, were jolly,
> And when this book comes
> To be marked with his thumbs
> You may know that its owner is Nolly.

Hall Caine described Rossetti creating limericks[33] "at the making of which nobody who ever attempted the form of amusement has been able to match him."

(Hall Caine was probably the only person who could write in all seriousness[34]: "My intercourse with Rossetti, epistolary and personal, extended over a period of between three and four years.")

Having read those limericks which are still extant, I agree with Langford Reed: "On the whole they are surprisingly poor, for a poet of the caliber of Rossetti."[35]

In 1866 a London magazine[36] advised its readers on how to be funny at the dinner table in society:

> If you can't remember any "widdles," or have exhausted your four puns, go in for paraphrases of Mr. Lear's book of nonsense. Flights of fancy, such as
>
>> There was a young lady of Chester,
>> Who swallow'd a patent digester
>> Till her uncle and aunt
>> Said, "Really we can't"
>> In this course suicidal arrest her.
>
>> There was a young lady of Hull,
>> Ran away with a Scotchman from Mull,
>> But ruthless Sir Cresswell,
>> (Whom all ought to bless well)
>> Declared that the marriage was null,
>
> are sure to convulse the company. Troll them out *da capo*, and never mind if you halt for a rhyme. People are sure to laugh heartily all the same.

Some reviewers expressed huge enthusiasm for the limericks. In January 1867, the journal *Once a Week*[37]—apart from describing the author as "Edwin" Lear—called the book "very remarkable" and said that it "has made more children laugh than any other [book] of modern date."

An American visiting the Paris Expo of 1867 described various hotel guest books he had encountered on his peregrinations round Europe[38]:

> In the album on the top of the Brevent, near Chamonix,—which is eight thousand five hundred feet high, and offers a noble view of Mont Blanc,—where a neat little inn is kept for the "rectification of the frontiers" of dilapidated tourists, I saw a very spirited drawing intended to illustrate the misfortunes of one of a party who had found the ascent disagree with him. The sufferings of the exhausted victim, the ministrations of his friends, and his recovery were portrayed very cleverly in a series of expressive figures, and under the whole were these lines:
>
>> There was a young man of Geneva
>> That was took very bad with a fever;
>> When they brought him a pill,

Chapter 8. The 1860s

He said, I'm not ill,
This mendacious young man of Geneva.

Hopefully, while rectifying the frontier, dilapidated tourists were cheered up by this Lear-like limerick.

Travelers round Europe at this time were happily using the names of local places to create limericks. Anthony Trollope's brother[39] recorded a trip in the autumn of 1867: "Perhaps some people may yet remember, that about the time I am writing of, there had arisen a sudden whim for making doggerel rhymes on the names of places in imitation of Lear's celebrated *Book of Nonsense*, as thus: There was an old Lady of Prague.... Well, we took it into our heads to fall in with the fashion as a mode of commemorating the progress of our journey ... every place on our route was recorded in [these effusions]."

Australian newspapers in 1869[40] and 1870[41] described various literary pastimes, one of which was the creation of:

NONSENSE VERSES.

This game was suggested by the immense success in England a few years ago of *The Book of Nonsense*, which contained quaint rhymes, with names of many well-known English towns, all in a uniform rhythm. Some of the "Rhymes for the 'Riddler'" published in the *Observer* a few months ago, strictly followed this model. It makes an amusing game to take the name of some Australian township, and let each player write one or more verses on the theme so given out. The following samples will suffice to illustrate the idea:

ADELAIDE.

There was a policeman of Adelaide,
His hands on an innocent lad he laid.
 Then took him to gaol
 And allowed him no bail,
That stupid old peeler of Adelaide.

Fifteen other limericks then follow.

All sorts of people played such games. A guest[42] at Coventry Patmore's house in the early 1870s recalled:

One evening we played at impromptus in the manner of Lear's nonsense verses. The poet sat reading. After a while someone gave out the word "Cadiz," and with a smile he looked over his paper and said:

There was an old fellow of Cadiz
Who lived in a place where no shade is;
So he lighted his cloak, and sat under the smoke,
That clever old fellow of Cadiz.

After that he often made nonsense verses, which, alas! I have forgotten.

Alexander William Kinglake was a travel writer and historian. His magnum opus was an eight-volume epic about the Crimean War. Kinglake met a lady named Madame Novikoff at Lady Holland's in 1870, and mutual liking ripened rapidly into close friendship. Then, as his biographer tells us[43]:

> At the time when a certain kind of nonsense verse was popular, he, with Sir Noel Paton and others, added not a few facetious sonnets to Edward Lear's book, which lay on Madame Novikoff's table. His authorship is betrayed by the introduction of familiar Somersetshire names, Taunton, Wellington, Curry Rivel, Creech, Trull, Wilton:
>
> > There was a young lady of Wilton,
> > Who read all the poems of Milton:
> > And, when she had done,
> > She said, "What bad fun!"
> > This prosaic young lady of Wilton.
>
> There were many more, but this will perhaps suffice; *ex ungue leonem*.

More domestic moggy than literary lion, if you ask me.

Reviewing Lear's 1876 book, *The Examiner*[44] commented on his earlier *Book of Nonsense*: "We all know what followed upon the publication of this volume. It was in vain that the serious-minded members of every family publicly sneered at these picturesque little quintains; they were invariably discovered laughing in private over what they openly mocked at. The metrical discovery was so simple, so obvious, that everyone adopted it."

Others loved the rhymes; an 1887 newspaper commented[45]: "As for Mr. Lear's rhymes of the same kind [limericks], their name is legion and their quality excellent, being both milk for babies and strong meat for grown men."

When Lear died in 1888, his obituary in the *Times*[46] began: "Among the persons of note who passed away last week was Mr. Edward Lear, the popular and humorous author and artist, who achieved a very wide celebrity as the originator of the 'nonsense verses' which, some years ago, were in everyone's mouth."

Limericks Which Appeared Shortly After Publication of Lear's Book but Which Are Not Recorded as Being Directly Inspired by It

The preceding section listed contemporary comments on Lear's book and cited limericks which seem to have been directly inspired by it. Many other limericks were created following publication of Lear's book. Whether they were inspired by the book or not is impossible to say, but I suspect most were. Let's examine some.

Chapter 8. The 1860s 95

The Langham Sketching Club: Circa 1862

The Langham Sketching Club started life in 1838. Every Friday night at seven, from October to May, members would draw for two hours on a chosen topic. The resulting drawings would then be pinned up and discussed. At nine thirty a cold supper of bread, cheese and unlimited beer would be served. Members were mainly professional artists or those wishing to associate with them.

(In 1898 an argument broke out between younger members who wished to have hot suppers and the old guard who wished to retain the cold collations. The upshot was that the "hots" broke away and formed the London Sketch Club. Both clubs are still in existence.)

Princeton University owns a unique copy of a handwritten book containing limericks. The library catalogue entry reads:

> Synge, William Webb Follett. Famous People of Famous Places. ca. 1860. UK. Manuscript. 80. Album of 170 limericks, each with a pen-and-ink drawing, written by or attributed to Follet Synge, Lord Tenterden, Horatio Lucas, W. Owen, Sir Villiers Leslie, W.M. Thackeray, and Thackeray's two daughters, Mrs. Stephens and Lady Ritchie, probably members of the Langham Sketching Club (London). ca. 1860. 1 v. (80 leaves).

The "long view" catalogue entry says this was owned by W.W. Follett Synge, then Sir John Leslie. It seems to have been bought in 1949 in Cheltenham by Shane Leslie, who took it to Glaslough in Ireland. New York book dealer Justin G. Schiller then owned it, apparently selling it to Robert H. Taylor, in whose collection in Princeton it now resides.

The album definitely contains limericks. Some have a Learian feel—the last line repeating the first with an unusual adjective to describe the protagonist:

> There was a proud Chieftain of Fife
> Who sought many years for a wife,
>   But when he had found her
>   He took and he drowned her;
> Incongruous Chieftain of Fife!

It is difficult to judge when such a volume could have been written and/or compiled, but perhaps we can put some parameters on individual contributions. The *DNB* tells us that Synge returned from a long period in the U.S. to work in London on February 28, 1860. He was appointed commissioner and consul-general for the Sandwich Islands on December 27, 1861. Assuming he went abroad shortly afterward, he could have been in physical contact with the other contributors to the album for most of 1860, all of 1861, and perhaps a short time in 1862. He seemingly did not return for several years. Thackeray died on December 24, 1863. So, if the album required all contributors to be in physical contact, 1860–1862 seems to be the only time-slot available.

My *guess* would be that *if* the album dates from one single drawing session, it would be late 1861 or early 1862, and that the limericks plus drawings were created "in response" to Lear's book. The records of the Langham Sketching Club were recently donated to the V&A, but I have not got very far in trying to find out if such a session ever took place.

Thackeray—The First Known Dirty Limerick: March 1862

Punch magazine staff held weekly editorial meetings. Between 1858 and 1870 one participant made notes about some of the topics discussed. That man was Henry Silver, and his writings have become known as the Silver diary. This long remained the property of *Punch* magazine, but when *Punch* closed its doors the diary was sold to the British Library, where it currently resides. The diary has been consulted by various writers, typically those interested in the history of the magazine or in participants of the meetings, in particular Thackeray. Quotations from the diary have appeared in print.

A couple of attempts have been made to transcribe the diary, but neither is accurate nor available to the general public. Dr. Patrick Leary is currently attempting to produce a version which will be both. He has kindly mined his extensive notes on my behalf. The entry for March 12, 1862, reads:

> Present are Frederick Evans, John Leech, Henry Silver, John Tenniel, Mark Lemon, Percival Leigh, Shirley Brooks, W.M. Thackeray.
> E[vans] mentions case of lady who had her bladder taken out and sewn up. And W.M.T. improvises: There was a poor lady grown sadder, By having disease of the bladder. They put her to bed and sewed it with thread, And then the Chirurgeon had her!—Only fancy the brutal chirurgeon taking mean advantage of her helplessness.

This limerick seems to have escaped the attention of the professional limerick hunter, although it has appeared in several books.[47]

Fun Magazine: July 1862

Fun magazine started in 1861; W.S. Gilbert contributed to it for the first ten years. A rival to *Punch*, it contained quite a few limericks before its demise in 1901. Early issues contained the odd limerick-like verse, but the first real limerick probably appeared in July 1862. Like many limericks which the magazine subsequently printed, it was a description of a current news event.

Tom Hood became editor in 1865. The magazine was purchased by the Dalziel Brothers in the following wonderful way: "In 1870—Mr. Wylam wishing to devote his entire attention to the development of 'Spratt's Dog Biscuits,' the patent for which he had recently purchased—we became the sole proprietors of the publication, paying for the goodwill and copyright the sum of £6,000, Hood continuing editor until his death."

Sir William Ewart Gladstone: September 1862

"The four-time Prime Minister of England was dedicated to self-flagellation both to punish himself for impure thoughts and to achieve a pleasure from the act, which he then repented."[48]

Whether he repented the writing of limericks is unknown, but write them he did. He called them Penmaenmawrs, which was the name of the North Wales resort he was visiting at the time. They obviously follow the Edward Lear model and they aren't very good—but they are limericks. For example, the following is one of two recorded in his diary on September 10, 1862[49]:

> There was an old woman of Broughton
> Whose deeds were too bad to be thought on;
> She poisoned her brother
> And throttled another
> This flagitious old woman of Broughton.

Contemporaries said that Gladstone was devoid of humor; perhaps they were right. But at least he knew that "flagitious" meant extremely wicked; a word, incidentally, this devout Anglican might have applied to his sister, who converted to Roman Catholicism, went mad, and then used tracts written by Protestant theologians as toilet paper.[50]

Mrs. Sivret of Boston: November 1862[51]

Thomas Wentworth Higginson was famous in his day as a minister, author, abolitionist and soldier. He held particularly strong views on the abolition of slavery. One of his books contains passages where he admires the physiques of Negro soldiers bathing.⁵² The twice married Higginson's male friendships were at the limit of what was socially acceptable at the time.⁵³ He was "preceptor" and encourager of the poet Emily Dickinson.

In November 1862, he was considering whether to take command of the first ever regiment formed of freed slaves in South Carolina. His views were well known to the public, so, as the good colonel wrote in his autobiography⁵⁴:

> There came into vogue about that time a "nonsense verse," so called, bearing upon my humble self, and vivacious enough to be widely quoted in the newspapers. It was composed, I believe, by Mrs. Sivret, of Boston, and ran as follows:
>
> > There was a young curate of Worcester
> > Who could have a command if he'd choose ter.
> > But he said each recruit
> > Must be blacker than soot,
> > Or else he'd go preach where he used ter.
>
> As a matter of fact it came no nearer the truth than the famous definition of a crab by Cuvier's pupil, since I had never been a curate, had already left the pulpit for literature before the war, and was so far from stipulating for a colored regiment that I had just been commissioned in a white one; nevertheless the hit was palpable, and deserved its popularity.

Interestingly, I have scoured many databases containing American newspapers and magazines for the 1860s and I have not found a single printed example of the limerick. However, it was certainly public knowledge at the time; a letter exists dated a year later in which a lady writes to her husband and includes the limerick.⁵⁵ Who Mrs. Sivret was and where the limerick first appeared I have never been able to find out.

Those interested in the definition of a crab can easily find it online. It appeared in several U.S. magazines in the 1850s and is still told today in a variety of guises. In essence members of the French Academy were said to have written the dictionary definition of a crab as follows: it is a small red fish which walks backward. The great naturalist Cuvier was then asked in a letter for his opinion. His reply was that it wasn't a fish, it wasn't red, and it didn't walk backward; however, with these exceptions the definition was excellent. Quite how Cuvier's pupil got substituted for the Academy members isn't clear.

Mr. Punch: December 1862

Mr. Punch got all jingoistic at the end of 1862 and in an 18-verse sequence in limerick layout berated that "Triumph of Military Tailoring"—the cutting down of the Indian war expenses by four million.⁵⁶ This might have helped Mr. Gladstone balance his budget earlier in the year. I leave the reader to decide whether the verses are really limericks.

Mr. Punch; or, to Be Precise, Mr. Shirley Brooks: 1862–1863

Charles William Shirley Brooks (April 29, 1815[57]–February 23, 1874) was on the staff at *Punch* magazine for many years. He joined in 1851 and became editor in 1870. He has been described thus: "First, there was Shirley Brooks, the journalist. Secondly, there was Shirley Brooks, the serial-writer. Thirdly, there was Shirley Brooks, the versifier and rhymester. And the greatest of these three was the last."[58]

When he died he was famous enough to merit an obituary in the *Times*[59] and to have Charles Dickens as a mourner at his funeral.[60]

Whether Mr. Brooks was influenced by Edward Lear's book we may never know, but for the *Punch Almanac* of 1863—published on December 17, 1862—he wrote six limericks.[61] As well as being available via *Punch* itself, these verses were widely reprinted in the UK in late 1862, although the source was not always acknowledged. Examples can be found in Bristol,[62] Belfast,[63] Exeter,[64] Nottingham[65] and Southampton[66] newspapers. In January 1863, three of these limericks appeared in an American paper,[67] hopefully providing some amusement amid descriptions of what was happening in the Civil War.

The first issues of *Punch* in 1863 contained a series of limericks by Shirley Brooks which also traveled round the world. A biographer of Brooks describes the events[68]:

> At the beginning of 1869 [*sic*] Shirley began contributing to *Punch* a series of "Nursery Rhymes," now better known as "Limericks." Many of these were charmingly illustrated by Charles Keene and du Maurier. They were, according to a note appended to the title, "to be continued until every town in the kingdom had been immortalized" but, although he showed by choosing such difficult names as Carshalton, Cirencester, and such like that no rhyme was difficult enough to daunt his ingenuity, they did not run to a greater number than thirty-eight. The following, which has point in more senses than one, may be given as a good example:
>
> > There was a young lady of Cheadle,
> > Who was deeply beloved by the beadle,
> > But she scoffed at his prayer,
> > Left her work on his chair
> > And the beadle sat down on the needle!

Like the preceding *Almanac* limericks, this series of limericks was also widely reprinted in the UK press.[69] And, specifically citing *Punch's* lead, newspapers as far afield as Canada[70] and Australia[71] produced limericks using the names of their own towns.

One Welsh reader was so outraged that *Punch* had stopped producing limericks before his local towns had been "immortalized" that he wrote a stiff letter to the *Carmarthen Chronicle*[72] enclosing ten limericks. None were particularly good.

Great limericks can certainly be written about Welsh towns. *Punch* published one[73] a week before our Carmarthen firebrand's letter appeared in print:

> There was a Young Lady of Denbigh,
> Who wrote to her *confidante*, "N.B.
> I don't mean to try
> To be married, not I,
> But where can the eyes of the men be?"

This limerick has an interesting history. In 1872 *Punch* reprinted a slightly modified version and changed the name to another Welsh town—Tenby[74]—under the title "Sweet Innocent"! Not so sweet or innocent was the person who then stole the limerick to enter a newspaper competition for *original* limericks—and win a three-guinea prize with it. Mr. Langford Reed spotted this deception, apprised the editor, and the miscreant was made to pay back the cash.[75]

This series of verses has given rise to several mistaken ideas. It was never "a competition"—as stated by those[76] who blindly copy a claim made by Legman.[77] How could it possibly have been when one man was writing all the verses? In addition, the simplest perusal of *Punch* magazine of the time will show that no one was ever invited to submit any verses, and there was no mention of any prize or contest.

There is also no evidence that the series ground to a halt because the great British public swamped *Punch* with "a disconcerting number of bawdy and sacrilegious limericks being submitted anonymously." That's another claim made initially by Legman and regurgitated by others.[78] The public certainly sent in uninvited verses; that's the reason Mr. Punch gave on March 7, 1863, as to why he stopped printing this series of limericks.

However, we don't know what sort they were. Some may have been dirty, but most *Punch* readers would have been astute enough to realize that only clean verses stood any chance of publication.

While we're on the subject of mistakes, Baring-Gould states that 33 limericks were published in Mr. Punch's 1863 series.[79] There were actually 38, plus Mr. Punch's goodbye verse. Possibly he missed the initial five on January 3. Dr. Bibby certainly missed these—he states that Mr. Punch's project started on January 10, 1863.[80]

THE LAST NURSERY RHYME.

THERE was a good-natured Old Chap,
Who made rhymes for a child in his lap,
But volunteer bards
Sent their nonsense in yards,
Till he cried, "I SHALL TURN OFF THE TAP."

N.B. To the above *Mr. Punch* begs to add, that he sent for SIR GEORGE GREY, and proposed to make, in honour of PRINCESS ALEXANDRA, a bonfire, on the 7th March, out of the mountain of Rhymes which have been coming in upon him since he playfully issued the first. SIR GEORGE said that it was not for him to oppose *Mr. Punch* (we should think not), but humbly suggested, that if the plan were carried out, London would infallibly be burned down. Upon which *Mr. Punch*, always open to reason, smote SIR GEORGE affably on the head, sold the poems to the butter-men, and laid out the money in a fine estate near that of his young friends, the Prince and Princess, at Sandringham. Any of the poets, on calling there, and showing their original MS., will receive a fourpenny piece and a glass of beer.
                                                            PUNCH.

Cartoon from *Punch* magazine, March 7, 1863, page 91.

Mr. Godfrey Morgan—Another Dirty Limerick: January 1863

Dr. Leary has alerted me to an entry in Silver's diary for January 14, 1863, which records: "S[hirley] B[rooks] asks for rhymes (which H.S. sends on Friday)—quote Godfrey Morgan's There was a young fellow at Bicester

Who determined to b. his sister So he thought the best plan before he began was to wipe out her a. with a gly.."

The last word is presumably glyster, an archaic variety of "clyster," which is itself pretty archaic. Who Godfrey Morgan was and how he fits into the grand scheme of things I have no idea at all. We shall, however, come across this limerick later, in *The Pearl* magazine of 1879.

Bishop Colenso: January 1863

John William Colenso was an undergraduate in the 1830s at St. John's College, Cambridge. Visitors to his rooms were often startled by pet snakes skedaddling away if a chair was moved.[81] After graduating as Second Wrangler (receiving second place in the math finals), Colenso wrote several textbooks on mathematics. In 1852 he became Bishop of Natal. He quickly learned the Zulu language and created a grammar and a dictionary. However, as a story told by Bertrand Russell illustrates,[82] he didn't know the language as well as he thought he did. Instead of saying "God is Love," he said "God is Butter." Since Zulus were very fond of butter, this converted them in droves.

Working with interpreters, Colenso translated the bible into Zulu. One assistant in particular, William Ngidi, is said to have asked many questions about the literal accuracy of the bible. For instance, Leviticus 11:6 says the hare chews its cud—and the Zulus proved to him that it didn't by giving him a hare to watch.[83] (This matter is still discussed on rabid Christian websites, all intent on proving the Bible is, in fact, correct.)

In 1855 he published *Remarks on the Proper Treatment of Polygamy*, in which he argued that Christians should be tolerant of the practice. An 1861 book explained why he could not accept that the heathen ancestors of the Zulus were condemned to eternal damnation.

Things really came to a head when Colenso began to question the accuracy of the Pentateuch, the first five books of the Bible. These are often called Mosaic books, following a belief that Moses wrote them. In early 1862 Colenso wrote the first volume of a work titled *The Pentateuch and Book of Joshua Critically Examined*. In this he argued that Moses couldn't have been the author and, moreover, that most of what was written was factually wrong. He backed up his claim with strong arguments. Some were based on the numbers of men being assembled for battles and the like, which Colenso showed were impossible. He also included comments such as "a Universal Deluge, such as the Bible manifestly speaks of, could not possibly have taken place in the way described in the Book of Genesis," and backed that opinion up with factual argument as well.

Chapter 8. The 1860s

After publication in South Africa the book was published in England on October 29, 1862.[84] The prevailing idea at the time was that the Bible was the literal word of God, and as such was correct in every aspect. As a standard work for ministerial students put it: "The BIBLE is none other than the Voice of Him that sitteth upon the Throne!"

The ordure, predictably, hit the revolving vanes.

People rushed to defend the Bible. For example, in the snappily titled *The Pentateuch Vindicated from the Aspersions of Bishop Colenso*, the author declared in a preface dated February 1863 that "for Scholars no refutation is needed.... THE FOUNDATION OF GOD STANDETH SECURE." Other attempted refutations bore titles like *Moses Right and Bishop Colenso Wrong* and *The Pretensions of Bishop Colenso to Impeach the Wisdom and Veracity of the Compilers of the Holy Scriptures considered*. (All of these, as well as Colenso's book, can be read online.)

Parodists and joke-smiths trotted out all sorts of comments on the ideas that were rocking the Church. Many were in limerick form. In a letter to his Cambridge mathematician friend, dated January 19, 1863, Alexander Macmillan wrote[85]:

> To Rev. Barnard Smith.... Here's the last:
>> There was a wise Bishop Colenso,
>> Who counted from one up to ten so,
>> That the writings Levitical
>> He found were uncritical
>> And went out to tell the black men so.

The above has been claimed to have been written by Macmillan.[86]

A version was given in a letter of virtually the same time[87]:

> I may add that Robin [George Meredith[88]] was in wild spirits when he was not squeamish, and he composed numerous extempore verses on the voyage [this was taken January 12–18, 1863]. One was composed about Swinburne, a wild, red-haired poet, who lives with Rossetti. Le voici!
>> There was a young poet of Chelsea
>> Who never was able to spell "sea."
>> With "C." he....
>> But it always came....
>> "That'll do!" said the poet of Chelsea.
>
> I met W.G. Clarke, the Public Orator, the other night in the club, and he told me the new rhyme, in the same meter as the preceding, on Bishop Colenso:-
>> There was a wise Bishop Colenso,
>> Who could just count from one up to ten, so
>> He thought books Levitical
>> Not arithmetical;
>> And he went and told the black men so!

(Quite what the original middle line rhymes were in the Swinburne limerick are beyond me. Presumably they were rude as the biographer missed them out. Maybe "With 'C' he put front / But it always came cunt." Or: "With 'C' he would start, but it always came fart." The original letter may still exist.)

Another version appeared in an 1892 letter[89] to *Notes and Queries*. Perhaps it illustrates how limericks change with memory; perhaps it was the original:

> Many people have, since the appearance of Lear's book, been pestered with nonsense verses, in which obscenity is far in advance of wit. One, however, which dates from the period when Bishop Colenso startled the orthodox world by his conclusions as to the Pentateuch, seems good enough to merit preservation:
>
>> There was a Lord Bishop Colenso,
>> Who counted from one up to ten, so
>>   That the numbers Levitical
>>   Proved un-arithmetical,
>> And he went out and taught the black men so. URBAN.

A diarist with the wonderful name of the Right Hon. Sir Mountstuart Elphinstone Duff Grant met Colenso in London in February 1863 and commented[90]: "Met Bishop Colenso at breakfast, and walked across the Park with him. He is full of vigor, and would have made a good grenadier."

Some years later, on hearing some rhymes, the same diarist recorded[91]:

> They seem to me as good as those which were so much repeated in London at the time of the rage for Lear's *Nonsense Verses*, and which were attributed to the late Bishop of Oxford:—
>
>> There once was a Bishop of Natal,
>> Whose doubts on the deluge were fatal;
>> Said the infidel Zulu,
>> D'you believe this—you fool, you?
>> No, I don't, said the Bishop of Natal!

Some one whom I know—I think Lord Houghton—once repeated these last verses to Thackeray, who instantly replied:

>> This is the bold Bishop Colenso
>> Whose heresies seem to offend so.
>> Quoth Sam of the Soap,
>> Bring fagot and rope,
>> For we know he a'nt got no friends oh!

Variants exist of when and where Thackeray "capped the rhyme" of Soapy Sam, Bishop Samuel Wilberforce[92], but the limericks quoted are the same.

The Musical World of February 21, 1863, was seemingly worried that the fabric of society might come unraveled if nobody sorted Colenso out:

Chapter 8. The 1860s

VOICE FROM THE WEST.

There was an old Bishop of London
Who said, "Why the Church will be undone;
And, by some one that's learn'd
If the tables aint turn'd
On Colenso—Oh! we're every one done!"

A March 1863 magazine[93] opined:

There was a wise Bishop, Colenso,
Who was bothered among the black men so,
That he thought such a pen as his
Might overset Genesis:
Still, Moses *may* outlive Colenso.

Fun magazine of April 11, 1863, offered a sequence of five limericks to be sung by bishops in convocation to persuade Colenso to mend his ways.

By June 1863, even children in California were seemingly concerned. Bret Harte wrote several poems on the matter under the heading "Colenso Rhymes for Orthodox Children." Two were limericks[94]:

A SMART man was Bishop Colenso
'Twere better he never had been so
He said, "A queer book
Is that same Pentateuch!"
Said the clergy, "You musn't tell men so."

There once was a Bishop of Natal
Who made this admission most fatal;
He said: "Between us
I fear *Exodus*
Is a pretty tough yarn for Port Natal."

I'm not sure when the following was written; it has been claimed that the *Natal Witness* newspaper printed it in 1863 but I can't verify that.[95] It was certainly in print in 1868[96]:

THE BISHOP AND THE ZULU.

There was an old Bishop of Natal,
Who had a Zulu for a pal—
Says this Caffre, "Look here—
Ain't this Pentateuch queer?"
Which perverted that Bishop of Natal.

A limerick first published in 1894[97] presumably originated around the time of the controversies; after all, why would anyone write such a verse long after the leading protagonist is dead?

> There once was a bishop, Colenso,
> The Pentateuch smashed, *in extenso*.
> He said: "See what comes
> Of Rule of Three sums,—
> Though I'd not an idea it would end so."

As late as 1923 people were interested in limericks about Colenso. A whole raft of them appeared in *The Sunday Times* letters column.[98] One correspondent, Sir Frederick Fison, asked—seemingly in vain—if anyone remembered a set of limericks created in the 1860s, of which he could only recall three.

Colenso was excommunicated and relieved of his bishopric. Those in power elected another in his place. His friends supported him morally and financially. After complaining to Queen Victoria that his dismissal was illegal, the Privy Council reinstated him, so there were effectively two Bishops of Natal. He published six more volumes of his critique of the Bible. Today he is a forgotten man; his ideas are mainstream Christianity.

Poema Militare: April 1863

The first of April 1863 was probably as good a day as any to create a book with the title:

> ***Poema Militare***
> Seu
> Equitum Auratorum
> Cohortis Secundae
> Historia
> Pseudo-Comica Nec Non
> Veracissima
> Carminibus Caninis Reddita

The book contains 29 limericks in English about past and present members of the Second Regiment of the Life Guards, then quartered at Regent's Park. In the Bodleian copy someone, probably the editor, has handwritten a further six limericks on men already lampooned. Some printed limericks stand opposite the handwritten name of the man described; for example, Captain G.J.F. Berkeley:

> There was a young man they call GINGER,
> With his fist he's a regular swinger;
> His whiskers are red,
> And so is his head,
> And that's all we know about Ginger.

The limericks aren't brilliant, but they do have a roar and a rhythm to them, and a personal touch. The endpaper states:

> Written at the Barracks near
> the Styx (i.e., the Canal)
> at London, approved of by all April 1. 1863
> VIVAT REGINA

This book is an excellent example of people in the 1860s making limericks about friends. It has never been discussed by limerick historians; this may be because there are only two known copies.[99] Perhaps the lads got together in the mess, sank a few, joshed their mates, then thought their efforts worth preserving for posterity. Or, being English, perhaps it was afternoon tea and cucumber sandwiches on the veranda. Exactly when the book was printed is unclear, since the Bodleian copy records a handwritten dedication: "For little naughty, from the Editor—15/3/63."

Abraham Lincoln's Cabinet: April 1863

In the middle of April 1863, *The New York World* published 10 limericks, each purporting to describe the supposed characteristics of the commander in chief and members of his cabinet.[100] These subsequently appeared in several contemporary American newspapers and in a collection of popular songs of the time.[101] Standing under the heading "Cabinet Pictures. [After *Punch*.]"—they were obviously inspired by something in *Punch* magazine, most likely the series of limericks written by Shirley Brooks in 1862/3 which has been mentioned earlier.

Rummical Rhymes: May 1863

The *Oxford English Dictionary*, that fount of all wordy [sic] knowledge, fails to record *rummical*. Perhaps it comes from rum, meaning queer. Perhaps it has another source. Whatever it means, the word seems to have appeared once, and once only, on the world stage. In the extravagantly named *RUMMICAL RHYMES; With PICTURES to match, Set forth in fayre prospect ALPHABETICALLY & Geographically*, 26 limericks are accompanied by 24 red and black illustrations. Each picture contains a letter, and this is the initial letter of the place name of the accompanying limerick.

For those wondering how 26 letters can be accommodated in 24 pictures—I and J share one, as do U and V. Talking about the illustrations, it has been commented that a couple of the characters strongly resemble those drawn by Tenniel in *Alice in Wonderland* (written 1862–4; published 1865).[102]

As a small example of the problems of literary research, two prestigious library catalogues[103] suggest that this book was first published in 1862 in New York by Hurd & Houghton. Although this date has been used by others, it is incorrect. The first U.S. edition of the book was published on September 15, 1864,[104] a fact that took me years to find. It was advertised in the national press shortly afterward.[105] The U.S. publisher also reprinted the text and illustrations in a book[106] published at the end of 1866.[107] Anyone hoping to learn the alphabet from this latter work might have been a little puzzled, because in my copy the limericks and illustrations are all there—"but not necessarily in the right order"—as Eric Morecambe once said about another matter entirely.[108]

Rummical Rhymes was created in London. It was first published in 1863, probably in May. The U.S. version is either a legal edition printed after the initial UK publication, or a plagiarism (*vide* Dickens's books). Plagiarism is certainly a possibility, since the illustrations in the abovementioned reprint are fractionally different from the UK published ones, and the initials JVB are missing from all the American illustrations. Alternatively it could just be that it was easier to copy pictures and text from a book rather than send woodcuts and plates to America.

Most of the place names are English; some are quite obscure. Few references credit either an author or artist. The artist can be identified from initials in the pictures as J.V. Barret, who worked with Dean and Son of London on several books around this time.[109] The Bodleian library catalogue suggests Charles Henry Ross was the author. Ross was a Londoner who created Ally Sloper and wrote penny dreadfuls. He is credited with writing another of the three books in the series created by Dean & Son published at the same time (see below).

Whoever the creators were, the book was a great success. Discussing Dean and Son's publications in a December 1863 issue,[110] a London trade magazine stated:

> A step higher brings us to three most original and really very funny books for children. These are severally known as *Ye Comical Rhymes of Ancient Times*, *Rummical Rhymes*, and *Ye Booke of Pictures Painted by Ancient People*. The "rhymes" are, however, simply accompaniments to quaint and curious pictures admirably printed in red and black, so arranged as to present a variety of tints. These books have deservedly obtained immense popularity, for they are witty and irresistibly comic—the fun, indeed, which children understand, because in it there is not a particle of satire, and not the remotest allusion to politics, the heathen mythology, or the events of the day; nothing, in short, of the comedy which delights adults.

A later review in a New York newspaper[111] described the book in such glowing terms that the U.S. publishers used it as advertising.[112] By doing so they were seemingly happy to acknowledge that it had been inspired by Lear's book:

> The best result of the *Nonsense Book* so far is *Rummical Rhymes with Pictures to Match, set forth in fayre prospect, alphabetically and geographically*. The pictures to this—admirable caricatures of medievalism, cleverly designed for printing in red and black—are so unusually good that worse verses would be endurable, but the verses are good too; *exempli gratia*, take the third one—
>
> > There was a young lady of Cork,
> > Who, declining to eat with a fork,
> > Her fingers would use
> > And the feelings abuse
> > Of the delicate people of Cork.
>
> The title of the above is "Contrary to etiquette." Now that we have written the stanza, we see how much it lacks in lacking the illustration. Until to-day we have met no rhyme and picture book so good as *Rummical Rhymes*. —*The Nation*.

Observant readers will have noticed small numbers on the back cover of the UK edition, at the bottom left, which often vary from book to book. Some cataloguers suggest the initial figure records the print run and the latter figure the date of printing. The following are the numbers I have found on some extant copies:

3000–5,63	Bodleian Library copy
6000–6,63	Copy once seen for sale online
1590–8,63	My own copy
4000–10,63	Bodleian Library copy
3000–1,64	NLS copy (last two numbers are faint)
3000–4,64	University of Nottingham copy. Osborne Collection copy in Toronto Public Library. Harvard University copy. University of Florida copy (can be read online. Note: Z is missing).

If the figures do indicate print runs, then tens of thousands of copies were printed, if not many more. The book was advertised in the UK, America and Australia.[113] Presumably this book was read by lots of people in lots of places: today, few even know it ever existed.

This book seems to have been created entirely for children, containing little of interest for the adult reader. Only a handful of copies exist today. The reason is probably the usual one of children reading them to destruction. I'm surprised it was so popular, but different times have different tastes.

The Musical World: 1863

The Musical World was a long-running London paper which reported on concerts, singers, songs, instruments and the latest developments in matters musical in the UK and the wider world. During 1863, for some unknown reason, following no precedent within its pages whatsoever, it published over 400 limericks. In the main they were humorous pen-pictures mocking someone or something. Subjects included composers, musicians, singers, playwrights, theater owners, critics, lawyers, judges, authors, newspapers, magazines, noblemen, actors, painters, MPs, politicians, famous folk, the odd expansionist French dictator—

> There was an old Louis Napoleon,
> Whose ideas invasions ran wholly on,
>   He look'd into some lexicons,
>   And found the word "Mexicans"—
> "Here's at 'em!" cried Louis Napoleon.

—and such oddities as smoking, subscribers, owls, wayward compositors and the source of the Nile.

Six of these were in French, one in German, one in Italian, and half of one was in Latin. They seem to have been composed by a variety of hands. Few were what you might call memorable, but some showed a fearless approach to rhyming, content, puns and repetitive alliteration. For example:

> There was an M.P., Monckton Milnes,
> Who's many more pounds than I've shill'ns.
> No Havelock nor Napier
> Appearing, they a peer
> Have made of this old Monckton Milnes.

"Pounds/shillings—Napier/appear/a peer"—not bad!

Richard Monckton Milnes apparently appreciated literary merit in others and actively fostered it. Where were you, Dick, when I needed you?

In 1864 the number of limericks printed in *The Musical World* dropped to a tenth of its 1863 output, and after that they only appeared spasmodically. However, its rival, *The Musical Standard*, seems to have produced only one limerick[114] during this time.

Many of the limericks in *The Musical World* seem to have been written by one indefatigable writer who gave himself the nom de plume of Dilettante Curtainlifter, often shortened to D.C. I believe he was "that master of limericks, Charles Lamb Kenney."[115] Another writer used the odd nom de plume of Zamiel's Owl. He was our old *Punch* friend, Shirley Brooks.[116]

Nursery Rhymes for the Army: May 1863

Wilkes' Spirit of the Times was a New York newspaper with Unionist sympathies. The issue of May 2, 1863, contained 23 limericks.[117] Titled "Nursery Rhymes for the Army," they stood above the cryptic letters L.L.D. All featured young men, usually from places or incidents associated with military actions. They often included the names of prominent commanders. All ended in a Learian fashion, with the young man being described with an adjective in the last line; for example:

> There was a young man of Antietam,
> Who knew if he followed he'd beat 'em,
>   So he called for a spade,
>   And a truce there he made,
> This considerate young man of Antietam.

It has been suggested that the author was Charles Godfrey Leland,[118] since the letters of his surname with the vowels removed are LLD. Leland certainly wrote limericks, but the style of the ones in *Ye Book of Copperheads*, which he is known to have written, is quite different from these. I suspect another hand.

The above is a good example of the difficulty of running some references to ground. Although it has been cited by Legman and others,[119] finding a copy of the newspaper was difficult. The New York Public Library has one; in 2004 it cost me $21 in postage and photocopying fees to get a copy. Afterward, as these things so often happen, I found out that not only are all these limericks available in a book,[120] but the book can be read online! Mind you, it is a book so unknown to limerick historians that it has never been referred to as far as I know. The book is anonymous and library catalogues contain no information about the author.

Interestingly, there is an extra limerick in the book as compared to the newspaper, and the majority have slight changes made to them. For example:

In the newspaper	In the book

XXI
There was a young man of Winchester,
Who loved a segar and siesta,
   With wife, baby and maid,
   Very long there he staid,
This luxurious young man of Winchester.
	XXII
	A young man en route to *Winchester,*
	Loved his cigar and Siesta—
	   With wife, baby and maid,
	   Very long there he staid,
	Uxurious young man of Winchester.

Lear's Book in America: May/June 1863

Copies of Lear's 1861 edition doubtless made their way from England to America. In May 1863, the *American Publishers' Circular and Literary Gazette* carried an advertisement[121] in a section devoted to publications by Willis P. Hazard of Philadelphia:

> Very Nearly Ready.
> THE BOOK OF NONSENSE. BY EDWARD LEAR.
> From the Tenth London Edition.
>
> With many New Pictures and Verses. Oblong 8vo. With one Hundred and Twelve full-page Engravings in the most Comic Style. Price, $1.00; or, finely colored $1.50.
>
> This is a fac-simile in every respect of the London edition, at a much lower price, of one of the most comic books ever published. Its merits have created a sale of ten editions in a very short time.

This first American edition was definitely on sale in June 1863.[122] M. Doolady of New York issued an edition[123] at the same time as Hazard. Two other New York publishers also published the book shortly afterward: John Bradburn in 1865[124] and James Miller in 1870.[125] It became popular in America and new editions appeared regularly.

Abraham Lincoln and other eminent Americans certainly read Lear's book[126]:

> There was popular, many years ago, a pictorial book of nonsense to which Lincoln once referred in my presence. He said he had seen such a book, and recited from it this rime as illustrating his idea that the best method of allaying anger was to adopt a conciliatory attitude. The picture shown, he said, was that of a maiden seated on a stile smiling at an angry cow near-by in the field, and saying:
>
> > I will sit on this stile
> > And continue to smile,
> > Which may soften the heart of that cow.
>
> A few months later, after Lincoln's death and the capture of Jefferson Davis, the latter and some of his party, including his private secretary, Col. Burton N. Harrison, were brought to Fort Monroe, their baggage and official papers being forwarded to Washington.... In examining the satchel of Colonel Harrison, I came across a copy of the old book of nonsense above mentioned. Years afterward, having business relations with Harrison, I told him of the coincidence, and he explained that the volume had been put into his satchel by the captain of the gunboat on which he was brought to Fort Monroe, and that it had served to while away many idle hours.

Chapter 8. The 1860s

The limerick quoted made its first appearance in the 1861 edition of Lear's book. Not all generals agreed with their commander in chief as to the benefits of conciliation:

> **Conciliatory Mesmerism.**
> General Garfield aptly illustrated, by the following quotation from an old English nursery rhyme, the policy of those extra-bleached and super-superior patriots who sought to put down the rebellion with conciliatory mesmerism:
>> There was an old man who said, how
>> Shall I flee from this horrible cow?
>> I will sit on the stile
>> And continue to smile,
>> Which may soften the heart of this cow.

This comes from a book of anecdotes of the Civil War, published in 1866.[127] Quite what is being referred to is unclear. It's a good example of a reference which puzzles more than enlightens. However, the diligent scholar can run the source to earth. It is from Garfield's first major speech to Congress, delivered on January 28, 1864. Shorn of a few highfalutin words presumably added by a newspaper reporter or the collector of anecdotes, the future president actually said[128]:

> I have lately seen a stanza from the nursery rhymes of England, which I commend to those gentle-hearted patriots who propose to put down the rebellion with soft words and paper resolutions: (the limerick is given). I tell you, gentlemen, the heart of this great rebellion cannot be softened by smiles.

Another Union General was also keen on what appear to be Learian limericks. Describing General Warren in the latter part of 1863 or early 1864, his aide-de-camp records[129]:

> It may have accounted, however, for the manifestation of what seemed to me a queer sense of humor, namely, his laughing and laughing again while alone in his tent over a small volume of "limericks," the first to appear, as I remember, in this country. He would repeat them at almost every meal, and, I think, with wonder that they did not seem nearly so amusing to others as they did to him. I am satisfied that it takes a transverse kind of humor to enjoy limericks.

"A transverse kind of humor…." That's one way to put it, I suppose.

Ye Book of Copperheads: June (?) 1863

Copperheads, referring to an American poisonous snake, was a derisory term used by the Unionists to describe a group in the North who wanted an immediate cessation of the American Civil War and a return to the way things had been. Clement Vallandigham was their leader, and he was ridiculed in a limerick.

Not one of the world's great limericks to be sure, but an early example of coping with a difficult-to-rhyme word.

The book contained 24 illustrated limericks, five pages of un-illustrated poems and a quote from a newspaper. Of the un-illustrated poems, 18 are limericks. It was probably first published in June 1863. Although published anonymously, we know who wrote it: in his biography[130] Charles Godfrey Leland recorded that "I was very busy during the first six months of 1863 ... I also wrote and illustrated, with the aid of my brother, a very eccentric pamphlet, *The Book of Copperheads*."

The book was reprinted in 1864 and used, along with other pamphlets, as propaganda to rally support for Lincoln in the election of that year. In a biography[131] of Lincoln, Leland wrote:

> After Abraham Lincoln's assassination, two comic works, both well thumbed, indicating that they had been much read, were found in his desk. One was the *Nasby Letters*, and the other, *The Book of Copperheads*, written and illustrated by myself and my brother, the late Henry P. Leland. This was kindly lent to me by Mr. M'Pherson, Clerk of the House of Representatives, that I might see how thoroughly Mr. Lincoln had read it. Both of these works were satires on that party in the North which sympathized with the South.

Leland enlisted in the Union Army and fought at Gettysburg. He was a scholar and folklorist who wrote books on English Romani and Italian witches. He has been called the originator of neo–Paganism. In his 1889 book[132] of cant and slang he used a limerick to define the word "beak." Legman described him as a "sedulous-ape."

Ye Book of Sense: December 1863

The seaside resort of Torquay is not often suspected of being a hotbed of limerick production, but an illustrated book containing 40 limericks was published there in 1863.[133] I know of eight extant copies.

An early review of the book was not promising. Actually, it was worse than that; *The Morning Post* of December 18[134] gave it an absolute pasting. After giving us the undoubted wisdom of his thoughts on the morality of what is right and wrong to give to children at Yuletide, the reviewer then pitches into this festive offering:

> It is hardly fair to make the nursery the vehicle, or rather the excuse, for the production of books having neither reason nor common sense to recommend them; for assuredly that which older and wiser heads would almost disdain to laugh at, can hardly be said to be profitable or beneficial to the young. These remarks are suggested by a publication which has just appeared under the title of *Ye Book of Sense*, which professes to deal out a profusion of those

Chapter 8. The 1860s

"One of those who worship dirty gods."—*Cymbeline*, III. 6.

There once was a chap named Vallandigham, whom the Copperheads chose for commanding 'em;
But a trip to the South soon silenced his mouth,
And the world as a *Tory* is branding him.

7

Ye Book of Copperheads, Charles Godfrey Leland, Frederick Leypoldt, Philadelphia, 1863, page 7.

newly-revived nursery rhymes, beginning with, "There was a young lady of," &c., or "There was an old woman of," &c., or "There was an old man of," &c. It need hardly be said that this highly poetic form of rhyming has been exhausted lately, and if anything new is to be written in the like strain it should be good at the same time. But with every desire to view these little publications simply as amusement for the passing hour, the most indulgent parent or guardian is apt to cry out, "The force of nonsense must no further go"; and this must unavoidably be said by the reader of the present book long ere he can arrive at the final page. With excusable irony it is called *Ye Book of Sense*, but one is hardly prepared to find the exact reverse, carried to its utmost limits of extravagant absurdity, nor is the absurdity redeemed, except in a very few instances, by that which is calculated to raise a laugh, The rhymes are meagre and meaningless in the extreme, and it would seem a pity that the artist, who has obviously a natural taste for caricaturing, should not have deferred his task until his crude sketches could be better matured, and the descriptive part rendered less likely to destroy the patience of the reader. It is to be regretted that this emanation from as genial, if not inspiring, a climate as Torquay should not be entitled to higher encouragement than is here given.

In passing we can note how widespread limericks had become by this date: "It need hardly be said that this highly poetic form of rhyming has been exhausted lately, and if anything new is to be written in the like strain it should be good at the same time."

My opinion about *Ye Book of Sense* is the exact opposite of the reviewer's. I think it's a great book of limericks for children—and especially

"Is it true, think you?"
Winter's Tale.

E. Croydon, Printer & Publisher, Royal Library, Torquay.
London, Whittaker & Co Ave Maria Lane.

Title page of UK edition of *Ye Book of Sense*, Anon., E. Croydon, Torquay, 1863.

for adults. I think the quality of the limericks is significantly better than Lear's, and better than much of what had gone before. Consider for example the delightful silliness of:

> There was an old man who said—"Oh!
> That spider has trod on my toe!
>   I was asked to a ball,
>   In Free Mason's Hall,
> And now I'm so lame I can't go."

And the pensive philosophical quality of:

> There was an old man who said—What
> An uncommonly beautiful spot!
>   Now really, this view—
>   Is too good to be true—
> I would rather have seen it than not.

Several have appeared in later compilations,[135] for example:

> There was an old man who said—"Do
> Tell me how I'm to add two and two?
>   I'm not very sure
>   That it doesn't make four;
> But, I fear that is almost too few."

Naturally this one has "gone forth and multiplied" in a mathematical sense[136]:

> There was an old man who said, "Gee!
> I can't multiply seven by three!
>   Though fourteen seems plenty,
>   It might come to twenty—
> I haven't the slightest idee!"

And also in a biological sense:

> There was an old man who said—"Cor;
> Working out one plus one is a chore.
>   I don't know about you
>   But I usually get two;
> Tho' with rabbits I get a lot more."
> —Bob Turvey

Speaking of examples which have been rewritten by less-than-pure minds, I am sure readers know the fate of this one[137]:

> There was an old man who said—"Why
> Can't I put my own chin in my eye?
>   If I give my mind to it,
>   I think I could do it,
> But no one can tell, till they try."

How widely this book was read is unknown. Ads for it certainly appeared in Australia.[138] An American edition was also published. In this the limericks appeared in a different sequence compared to the UK edition and there were seven fewer limericks. There were some differences in the text, the typography was different, and there were observable differences in the pictures.

The U.S. title page was quite different, with extra text suggesting a relationship to Edward Lear's book.

It is, however, quite clear that the two books are intimately related. Because neither edition has a date of publication, it has taken considerable effort to sort out what the relationship is.[139] The U.S. edition is a copy of the UK book; it could have been plagiarized, or it could have been copied legally. It was probably published in 1871.[140] There are perhaps nine extant copies. One can be seen online at nonsenselit.com; one at the University of Florida website. Note: this last copy has two cards stuck in the front bearing much later verses, a fact which seems to have eluded at least one limerick historian.[141]

A Surfeit of Riches: 1864–1870

During 30 years of study I unearthed enough references to double the length of this chapter. However, we already know that Lear's 1861 book

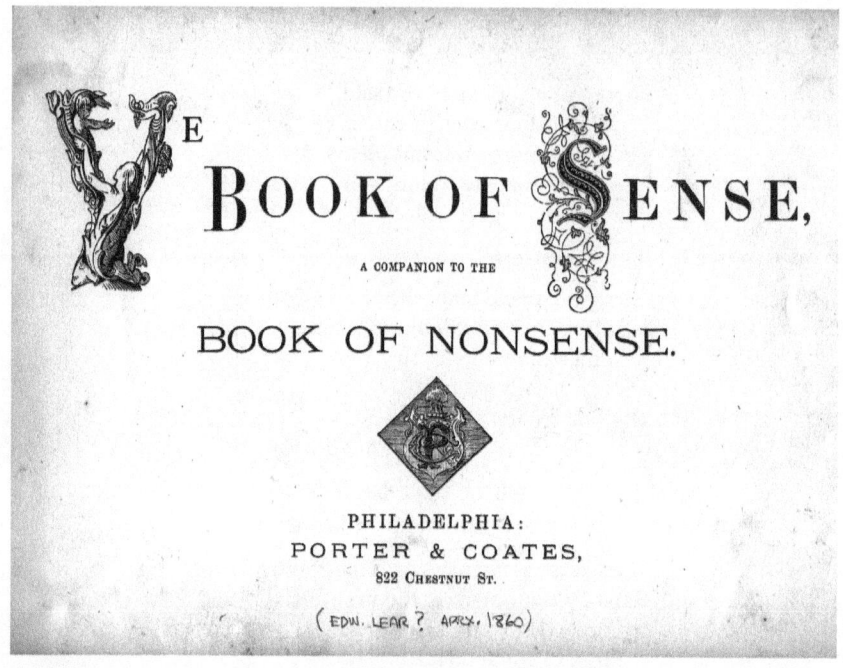

Title page of U.S. edition of *Ye Book of Sense*, Anon., Porter & Coates, Philadelphia, 1871.

started a deluge of limerick-writing and we have an overview of some of the activity that immediately followed it. Rather than bore the reader with what could be considered "more of the same," I will select just a handful to complete this decade.

The Book of Bubbles: March 1864

After the outbreak of the American Civil War, civilian philanthropists created the Sanitary Commission in 1861 to provide medical aid, food, books, clothing, support, etc., for wounded Union soldiers. It was based on the British Sanitary Commission established during the Crimean War. At first Abraham Lincoln did not think it would be of much use, likening it to the fifth wheel of a coach. He changed his mind when he saw the good work it did, especially that done by women members. One way the commission raised funds for its work was by holding fairs in the larger cities. The first was in Chicago from October 27 to November 7, 1863. Another was in New York between April 5 and April 23, 1864. A minor contribution to the coffers of this fair came from the sale of a book of limericks hastily created for the occasion. At least two copies can be read online.

The Diary of Sidney George Fisher: 1865

At the time of interest to us the lawyer and writer Mr. Fisher was a Maryland peach farmer. In his diary he recorded personal limericks he had written about his neighbors.[142] One did not take too kindly to the depiction and wrote his own verse in retaliation. Mrs. Fisher objected to the "profanity" in her neighbor's verse and rewrote the limerick to remove it. It is interesting to note how these personal limericks were spread round the community in written or printed form, and by personal recitation.

Judy Magazine: October 1867

There was a young lady of Bray,
Who went riding out every day,
But one day it rained
And she was so pained,
That she patted her horse, and said, "Neigh."[143]

The Young Lady of Rio: February 1868

Readers keen to improve themselves spiritually will no doubt be aware of a magazine called *The Monthly Packet of Evening Readings for Members of the English Church*. The February 1868 issue contained the second part of a story called "The Summer Vacation." Mum, Dad and a variety of precious children have gone on holiday to Yorkshire and, apart from the odd child nearly dying of a fever, are entertaining themselves in the time-honored way that respected members of the English Church did in those days—writing stories with morals in them and reading them aloud. One "child" is Edward. We met him in a story a year earlier, when he managed to win a mathematics scholarship at the imaginary Oxford College of St. Cuthbert's. His mother seems astonished that an Oxford man could write a story:

> After Johnny's story had been freely discussed and laughed at (in which Johnny heartily joined), Edward said—
> "I, too, have written a story, if you would like to hear it."
> "You, Edward! Is it possible you have written a story? Let us hear it by all means."
> Then Edward produced a little book, the thinnest that ever was seen, and said—

"Mamma, my feelings being too many for me, will you read my book?"

Mrs. Grey took the little volume and opened it. On the first page was written very beautifully, "The Young Lady of Rio."

"That, I suppose, is your heroine? And now let us hear.

> There was a young lady of Rio,
> Who tried to play Hummel's grand trio;
> But her skill was so scanty,
> She played it Andante,
> Instead of Allegro con brio."

I'm afraid I must conclude this reference with the not-too-surprising revelation that years later *Anon.* got his grubby hands on this verse, with predictable results:

> A young violinist in Rio,
> Was seduced by a lady named Cleo.
> As she took off her panties
> She said, "No *andantes*—
> I want this *allegro con brio*."

There are several variants of the above, but the general thrust is always the same. One thing I think we can be sure of: even those of us with no musical ability whatsoever will now always know that *andante* means slowly, while *allegro con brio* means with fire, energy and brilliance. So, if for nothing else, thanks for that, *Anon.*

Three More Dirty Limericks: August 1868

Another entry in the Silver diary for August 12, 1868, was sent to me by Dr. Leary:

Present are William Bradbury, George DuMaurier, Henry Silver, Shirley Brooks, Fred Evans, Horace Mayhew, R.F. Sketchley, Tom Taylor.

> New rhymes: There was a young princess called Dagmar,
> Who sd I shd much like a shagma,
> So I think if I speaks to the King of the Greeks,
> He will lend me his tally wagma.

> There was a young lady of Glo'ster
> Whose relations all thought they had lost her:
> Till they found on the grass the print of her—
> And the knees of the man who had crost her.

> There was an old lady of Putney,
> Who was sadly addicted to Glut'ney:
> Twas her custom to pass her thumb up her—
> And swear that it tasted like Chutney.

"The Sick Man of Tobago" in Latin: May 1869

Attempts had been made earlier to render our old friend from Tobago into Latin, but all seem to have ended up as doggerel. A pupil at Westminster School may have been the first to produce a limerick version[144]:

> Senex Insulâ in Tobaginâ
> Pulte *languet* et coctâ farina:
>   Sed nemo sic v*ixit*
>   Cum medicus dixit
> "Perna cras tibi detur ovina."
> Oratore H.G. Rawson, *Præfecte designato*

The Old Fellow of Trinity: October 1869

Arthur John Butler read classics and mathematics at Trinity College, Cambridge. When awarded a fellowship[145] in 1869, an old friend wrote "from ribald Oxford"[146]: "There was an old Fellow of Trinity Who raised × + 1 to Infinity, and, in congratulating you most heartily, I must be allowed to hope that your life will be spent on some more useful object."

Whether Butler did spend his life on more useful pursuits history can judge; among other things he became a professor of Italian, translated Dante, was an ultra-keen mountaineer, and, as the *DNB* puts it: "wrote fugitive contributions to the press, which were always trenchant, original, and humorous, and exhibited an unusual blend of inborn churchmanship with an outspoken and militant liberalism."

There are several versions of the limerick which is apparently being quoted by Stephen Fremantle. Early examples:

> There once was a fellow of Trinity
> Who raised xyz to infinity;
> And then the old brute
> Extracted the root—
> He afterwards took to Divinity.
> (Version recorded in 1878[147])

> There was an old Doctor of Trinity,
> Who discovered the root of infinity;
>   But in counting the digits
>   He was seized with the fidgets,
> So left Science and took to Divinity.
> (Known circa 1881 in Oxford and Cambridge[148])

Limerick scholarship being what it is, authorship of this limerick has been widely attributed to George Gamow,[149] seemingly because he once included it in a popular science book[150] he wrote. It's easy to prove he didn't write it; he was born in 1904.

Conclusion

Overwhelmed by the 1860s? Me too! However, this extensive examination means we have an overview of how the limerick was developing. Limericks had been written in the period 1820–1860, but they were not many. Most, but not all, were simple and probably intended for children.

It seems clear that Edward Lear's 1861 *Book of Nonsense* inspired the general public to write limericks in droves, an inspiration which spread worldwide. The reasons for this are not clear; perhaps the contents of the book just caught the zeitgeist of the time.

Three aspects of the phenomenon deserve further comment: the types of limericks being created, the type of people who were creating them, the mechanisms by which limericks were being spread.

The simple Learian form remained popular. While many were obviously aimed at children, not all were by any means. Some adherents of this style seemed to not understand more modern styles, or simply disliked them.

A second type of verse became much freer in its form, dispensing with a last line which essentially repeated the first line. This type became very creative in its content, rhyming and punning. Some were also making political statements, or referring to world events. Such clever limericks were written mainly for adults. Many limericks in this style would not be out of place in modern collections.

A third type was the dirty limerick. Because of the morals of the time, these were mainly circulated privately. I am sure that many more dirty limericks were created in the 1860s than have been recorded in diaries and letters.

A fourth type was the personal limerick; that is, a limerick which describes the personal foibles of someone known to the limerick creator, such as a friend or a public figure. Such verses have slipped under the radar of commentators on matters limerickal; I think they played an important role in the spread of the verse form.

Turning to the people who wrote limericks, there are two broad comments. The first is that almost everyone seemed to be writing them, from prime ministers to British soldiers, from American farmers to Boston matrons, from London clubmen to irate Welshmen, from Oxford dons to

Irish emigrants.[151] And they seemed to be enjoyed by everyone too, from American presidents to British schoolboys.

The second is that the era was blessed with some very good "professional" limerick writers, such as Shirley Brooks, Charles Lamb Kenney, and other writers for the "funnies."

One thing I must add—to my eyes there was also a lot of dross produced. But that seems not to have mattered, since presumably enough readers liked them or they would not have been printed.

We have also acquired some idea of how limericks were being spread. The main public routes were obviously newspapers, magazines and books. However, there are mentions of recitations in private homes; limericks were included in letters written to family members and to friends; gentlemen in private clubs exchanged limericks in conversation.

It's difficult to know how many limericks (if any) have survived to the present day solely by oral transmission; that is, by being passed orally from person to person and remembered but not written down.

When ascribing limericks to specific dates, almost by definition we can only know those limericks which were written down or printed or in some way dated. Many handwritten limericks must have perished by being thrown out or burned. Dirty limericks especially could only be passed around in oral transmission or in secret; how many of those, alas, have been lost? Hope springs eternal, and maybe some verses of either persuasion included in dated letters and diaries are still moldering away somewhere in an attic, waiting to be discovered.

One important area of limerick transmission was via singing or recitation at convivial events. I have not mentioned this in this chapter because few known limericks, if any, were recorded from this activity in the 1860s.

Chapter 9

The 1870s
The Limerick Develops

Prior to the 1860s every limerick was important—there were so few around that potentially each one contributed to the survival of the verse form. Each was also a possible indicator as to how the limerick would develop. That is why I mentioned all the ones I found. But after the 1860s the situation changes dramatically. The limerick is now so well established that we are almost overwhelmed by them. From now on we can ignore the dross and consider only those limericks which really amuse, interest, shock, amaze and/or show how the verse is developing. Of course, the choice now becomes personal but, put quite simply, a book which contained every limerick ever written would be both colossal and unreadable.

So: what memorable limerick events did the 1870s contain?

Rossetti: Two Limericks

The poet Rossetti and his friends wrote many limericks. This was often a communal activity and some verses were obviously joint productions. Most were probably written 1869–71. They can easily be found by those interested. To my mind they are not worth recording, because, as has perceptively been noted: "Howell became the subject of one of Rossetti's limericks; limericks, by the way, that sounded very gay and sharp as Rossetti recited them to his friends, but lacked felicity when recited by others or set down in print. It took a supper of bread and cheese and considerable wine to make Rossetti's limericks as witty as they were supposed to be."[1]

However, there are two which stand above the rest. The first because it is a dirty limerick, and the second because it breaks away from his usual habit of slagging off friends.

In a letter[2] of April 28, 1870, to his publisher, Rossetti included the following:

> There is a poor devil named Dallas
> Who tends, as I'm told, to the gallows
> Yet if not so well hung,
> He might never have swung,
> For it's mostly along of his phallus.

I assume the gentleman in question is Eneas Sweetland Dallas (1828–1879), a Scottish journalist and author of *Gay Science*; a treatise which tried to discover "the source in the constitution of the human mind of the pleasure afforded by poetry." Why Dallas's appendage roused such consternation I leave for others to discover.

The second limerick is so much better than Rossetti's personal squibs that I wonder if it really was written by him. The attribution to Rossetti is "oral tradition"—one Gordon Bottomley heard it from a friend of Rossetti's and happened to remember it.[3] It is also quite a late one in terms of its first printing (1956[4] is the earliest I know). Put me down as a skeptic on this one. I include it mainly as a good example of the problems of attribution. I do love the rhyme and the image the story creates, though, whoever wrote it:

> There was a young Fir-tree of Bosnia
> Which daily got ros'nier and ros'nier;
>   It at last caught on fire
>   And flamed higher and higher,
> And the Angels said: "My! But that was near!"

Cythera's Hymnal: The First Known Collection of Dirty Limericks: 1870

Of the 150 copies said to have been printed of this book, only one original is known to exist, along with two copies that have been made from it. This unique book is lodged in the Bodleian, where it slumbers under catalogue number Φ.f.123. (This is an Oxford joke. *Phi* has the same pronunciation as the word *fie* in English; it is a sort of comment of approbation on the contents of the "forbidden books" section at Oxford.)

The Bodleian book stamp is "3 Feb 1925." I would love to know where it was before then. I would also love to know if there are any more original copies extant; they would fetch a fortune if sold.

The book has been described thus: "*Cythera's Hymnal, or Flakes from the Foreskin*. A collection of songs, poems, nursery rhymes, quiddities, etc. etc.. Never before published. 'Oxford: Printed at the University Press, for the Society for Promoting Useful Knowledge' [London] 1870. (Cum Privilego.) 85 pp. 8vo."

Herbert Spencer Ashbee, in his privately printed *Bibliography of Forbidden Books* (1877), tells us most of what we know about the work, including: "In *Cythera's Hymnal* we have a gathering of cleverly written parodies and imitations of popular songs, well-known hymns, &c.; they are by different hands, and generally, as may be seen by the associations and allusions, by Oxford men ... with the exception of one or two pieces they are original, all are excessively blasphemous and obscene."

At the end of the book, between pages 70 and 82, there are limericks under the heading "Nursery Rhymes." Ashbee specifically mentions this section in his description, saying: "Lear's *Book of Nonsense* inspired the 'Nursery Rhymes.'"

Most references say there are 51 limericks. There are actually 50; one verse is in a limerick-like layout, but it's not a limerick. Where the limericks came from is unclear. At least two were known to *Punch*'s Editorial Table in 1868—the Gloucester verse and the Dagmar verse (see 1860s chapter).

The quality of the limericks can be judged by some examples:

> There was a young lady of Rhyll
> In an omnibus was taken ill,
>   So she called the conductor,
>   Who got in and fucked her,
> Which did her more good than a pill.

The popular seaside resort of Rhyl is usually spelled thus—but what the L.

> A young woman got married at Chester,
> Her mother she kissed and she blessed her,
>   Says she, "You're in luck,
>   He's a stunning good fuck,
> For I've had him myself down in Leicester."

> There was a young man of Nepaul,
> Who confessed that he'd only one ball,
>   But some meddlesome bitches
>   Once pulled down his breeches,
> When lo! He'd no bollocks at all.

> There were three ladies of Huxham,
> And whenever we meets 'em we fucks 'em,
>   And when that game grows stale
>   We sits on a rail,
> And pulls out our pricks and they sucks 'em.

> There was a young man of St. Just,
> Who ate of new bread till he bust,
>   It was not the crumb,
>   For that passed through his bum,
> But what buggered him up was the crust.

I sometimes wonder if limericks are inspired by fact. An 1865 letter[5] recorded: "A terrible catastrophe happened on Good Friday last. An old man named Dunning, aged seventy-five, ate fourteen Hot Cross Buns for his breakfast!—and, I need hardly add, he fell victim to his efforts. The medical evidence at the inquest showed that the mass of new bread in his stomach became so swollen that it pressed upon certain vital organs and suffocated him."

More Nonsense Pictures, Rhymes, Botany &c.—Edward Lear: Christmas, 1871

Lear started writing another volume of limericks in 1862 and it was ready by July 1863. However, Routledge was not interested when he approached them. I'm not sure why this was; perhaps they did not want competition for the book of his that they already owned and which was selling well. One possibility is that they thought the style of limerick which was popular had moved on from Lear's simple verses[6]; ironically a state of affairs caused by Lear's limericks themselves becoming immensely popular.

Eventually, for Christmas 1871, Lear published a book called *More Nonsense Pictures, Rhymes, Botany &c.*. This contained one hundred new limericks along with other poems. The illustrations and the style of limerick were similar to his earlier limerick books. (The title contains the word "More" because he had published a book for Christmas 1870, which contained no limericks, and which was called *Nonsense Songs, Stories, Botany, and Alphabets*.)

Arthur Clement Hilton: Mainly 1872

A.C. Hilton has been described as "a short-lived genius."[7] After Marlborough College he went to St. John's College, Cambridge. Due to his *not* being a genius at math he could only take the easier pass degree rather than the classical tripos. Fortunately for us this left him time for other activities, one of which was writing.

On an Easter break from Cambridge in 1870 he helped with a fundraising bazaar for the restoration of the parish church of Uxbridge. He started a post office department in the bazaar, and wrote a number of letters for young ladies in the style of Edward Lear's nonsense verses, which were delivered to applicants upon making a small payment. An excellent example of the style:

Are you the young lady of Uxbridge,
Who foolishly built up a duck's *bridge*?
　　Said mamma to her daughter
　　They can *swim* thro' the water,
Which vexed the young lady of Uxbridge.⁸

Hilton's biographer, who was his friend at Cambridge, has recorded some of the jokes with which he amused his fellow students. The following example may seem incongruous to the modern ear because nowadays neither smallpox nor an in-depth knowledge of Greek are commonplace: "Smallpox was rather bad about this time, and vaccination was all the fashion. There were several men in my rooms one evening, and an ingenuous freshman asked, 'Where does vaccine lymph come from?' 'Don't you know,' said Arthur Hilton, who was present, 'πανταχου.'"

This is pronounced pantacow, and means "everywhere." At the time the vaccine lymph came from calves, and of course the word "vaccination" pays homage to Jenner's discovery, since "vacca" is Latin for cow.

During his final term at Cambridge, Hilton put together the first part of the work which has brought him lasting fame. Shortly before this, a monthly magazine had enjoyed a brief existence. Called *The Dark Blue*, it affected to be the product of Oxford undergraduates.⁹ It was such a weak and feeble publication that it caused much amusement in Cambridge. Its puerility led Hilton to parody some of its scarcely intelligible nonsense, and the idea occurred to him of writing *The Light Green*, to be made up of parodies alone. It was published in May 1872, just as Hilton was going in for his final

Photograph of A.C. Hilton from *The Works of Arthur Hilton, together with His Life and Letters*, Sir Robert P. Edgcumbe, Macmillan and Bowes, Cambridge, 1904.

examination. It bore the imprint of no number since there was no intention to produce any more issues.

However, unlike nearly all Oxbridge undergraduate magazines produced before or since, it was a complete and utter success. This induced Hilton to produce a second number, which was published in November 1872, after he had taken his degree and gone down. Praise was lavished on the parodies contained therein from a variety of quarters.

Also in this second issue were nonsense verses under the byline of Edward Leary. Seven there were in total, and they are as follows:

> There was an old Fellow of Peterhouse,
> Who said, "You could not find a neater house
>   Than our new Combination-room
>   For a mild dissipation room."
> That abandoned old Fellow of Peterhouse.

> There was a boat captain of Downing,
> Whose crew were in danger of drowning,
>   But he cried, "Swim to shore,
>   For I'm sure that eight more
> Could not be collected in Downing."

> There was a young genius of Queens',
> Who was fond of explosive machines,
>   He once blew up a door,
>   But he'll do it no more,
> For it chanced that the door was the Dean's.

> There was a young student of Caius,
> Who collected black beetles and fleas,
>   He'd walk out in the wet
>   With his butterfly net,
> And smile, and seem quite at his ease.

> There was a young man of Sid. Sussex,
> Who insisted that $w + x$
>   Was the same as xw;
>   So they said, "Sir, we'll trouble you
> To confine your ideas to Sid. Sussex."

> There was a young *gourmand* of John's,
> Who'd a notion of dining on swans,
>   To the Backs he took big nets
>   To capture the cygnets,
> But was told they were kept for the dons.

> There was an old Fellow of Trinity,
> A Doctor well versed in Divinity,
>   But he took to free thinking
>   And then to deep drinking,
> And so had to leave the vicinity.

And that's it—there are no more.
But where are the others? I hear you cry. Surely he also wrote:

> There was a young critic of King's
> Who had views on the limits of things;
>   With the size of his chapel
>   He would frequently grapple,
> And exclaim, "It's biggish for King's."

—with which he is credited in several books?[10]

Alas no. This misattribution seems to have started life in a magazine article in 1918 by C.L. Graves.[11] The story is an all too familiar one in limerick lore and legend. The King's College limerick probably made its first appearance in a Cambridge undergraduate magazine of 1875 called *Light Greens*. This appeared three years after Hilton had gone down. No connection between Hilton and this magazine is mentioned by his biographer (who reproduces both issues of *Light Green* in his book), nor does Marillier make any connection in his book on Oxbridge magazines.

It is clear that Graves took the King's College limerick from *Light Greens* because in his article he refers to several of the other limericks in this magazine. Apropos of these, he comments that they seldom rise to a high level and their humor is ephemeral, adding that "Hilton was an unequal performer." He also criticizes Hilton for experimenting with the length of the verse—"his experiments in varying the meter of the 'Limerick' by lengthening the third and fourth lines cannot be pronounced worthy of imitation." That's a bit rich to say the least; criticizing one man for the deficiencies of another!

Perhaps the link was made because of the similarity of the titles of the magazines and the fact that they were both published by Metcalfe and Sons. Interestingly, both issues of *The Light Green* and the single issue of *Light Greens* are bound together in a single volume in Trinity College library, Cambridge, between—of all things—*dark* green covers.

Early in the new year of 1872 Hilton went on an odd sort of afternoon's amusement; he visited a county prison with his friends. The prisoners sat in pews, each waiting their 20-minute turn on the treadmill. Around the walls, in front of each prisoner on the mill were many scriptural texts of a personal nature. "The way of transgressors is hard"; "Thy sin shall find thee out"; "Let him that stole, steal no more"; and so on. Hilton went up on the treadmill alongside one of the prisoners to see how it felt. He observed that he wouldn't mind it very much were it not for the scriptural admonitions.

This experience notwithstanding, Hilton entered the church after graduating and became an Anglican priest in 1875. However, he had little time to walk on the treadmill of life. He died suddenly and unexpectedly on April 3, 1877. God certainly moves in mysterious ways.

Mr. Punch's Almanac: December 1872

After a break of some ten years Mr. Punch published a collection of limericks in the *Almanac* for 1873, published on December 17, 1872. Some conjure up odd visions:

> There was a young lady of Ifield,
> With whom a gay Flirter had trifled,
> Till she snatched up a pen,
> Crying, "Write the day When.
> Or I'll strangle you till you are stifled."

> There was a young person in Poland
> Who bought some Macassar of Rowland:
> Her hair grew so thick.
> It was propped by a stick—
> A thing which had happened in no land.

As usual, several subsequently appeared in newspapers.

Mr. Punch's Opinion of Limericks: 1873

January 1873 saw a pseudo-letter published in *Punch*[12] which showed how well known the verse had become (my emboldening):

THRICE GRACIOUS MR. PUNCH,

IT seems to me that **the now favorite form of poetry** might be used for the instruction of the rising generation. I have, therefore, put the list of the Roman Kings into verse, and, if this meets your approval, I will do all the Consuls of Rome, and then all the Lord Mayors of London.

Yours deferentially, ORBILIUS FLAGELLATOR

Seven "undoubted gems" in limerick form then follow.[13] Alas, the Consuls of Rome and the Lord Mayors never seem to have made the grade.

Quite what an "Orbilius Flagellator" is I'm not sure; but I do know it was one of several noms de plume used by our old friend Shirley Brooks.[14]

Elliott Roosevelt: April 1873

In 1873 15-year-old future U.S. president Theodore Roosevelt was literally floating around Egypt, shooting wildlife with gay abandon. Back at base he would dismember his catch, then apply arsenic soap with a toothbrush as a preservative prior to stuffing them. The dishevelment and mess occasioned by this operation, plus his naturally unkempt appearance, caused his 13-year-old brother Elliott to pen the following limerick:

> There was an old fellow named Teedie,
> Whose clothes at best looked so seedy
> That his friends in dismay
> Hollered out, "Oh! I say!"
> At the dirty old fellow named Teedie.[15]

Sir George Grove and Poor Old Spedding Again: July 1873

Before he died in 1863, Thackeray wrote at least two limericks about his friend James Spedding. One we have considered in the 1840s chapter. There is a reference to the second limerick being recited in the 1870s. I don't know why it was being recited at this late date, but those reciting it and listening to it show that intelligent people liked limericks.

Sir George Grove (1820–1900) was a writer on music and the founding editor of *Grove's Dictionary of Music and Musicians*. A 1903 biography[16] revealed that Groves jotted down things of interest in notebooks, and that the biographer had consulted "between seventy and eighty of the little pocket books that he invariably carried about with him."

Grove liked limericks:

> He had certain pet aversions—theological novels and gratuitous tragedies amongst others—and distrusted writers who set too great store by style, but with few reserves all subjects interested him, from puns to the Pentateuch. Nonsense verses, "limericks" and riddles are constantly entered in his pocket-books and he never tired of telling of the lover of nature who called attention to the beauty of the "autimnal tunts" or of the Frenchman who with unconscious wit replied to the salutation "Au reservoir" with "Tanks!"

His biographer quotes two limericks that Grove added "to his store of 'Limericks'" during a transatlantic voyage in 1878. If those pocket books are still in existence today, what limerick gems they must contain! And quite probably with dates attached.

The biography also records the meeting between Groves and W.H. Thompson, Master of Trinity College, Cambridge, in July 1873:

> Thompson also gave Grove Thackeray's impromptu on Spedding:
>
> > There was a young party named Spedding,
> > Who tore cigars up for his bedding.
> > His head was so bare
> > That you really might swear
> > He had danced at his grandmother's wedding.

Quite what the insult in the last line is about I'm not sure. Possibly that he was the latest in a line of inbred bastards? That notwithstanding, the limerick seems to have been memorable enough for Thompson to have remembered it. I have only come across one other reference to this limerick; this too shows how memorable it was to the listener. A letter in *The Spectator* of 1915 records:

> SIR, Your reviewer of *The Great Age* in *The Spectator* of March 20th refers to "a famous Limerick" as follows: "They are enough to have made the late Mr. Spedding 'tear up his bedding' and commit other atrocities attributed to him." I cannot refrain from quoting the whole of impromptu by Thackeray as I remember hearing it, more than fifty years ago:
>
>> There was an old fellow called Spedding
>> Who chopped up cigars for his bedding.
>>   His head was so bare
>>   It made folks declare
>> That he danced at his grandmother's wedding.
>
> —I am, Sir, &c., AILEEN ARTHUR
> The Well House, Banstead, Surrey.[17]

The Lays of Modern Oxford: 1873

Limericks were being created at the universities in the 1870s. Mostly they were published in college magazines, university magazines, and short-lived magazines created as part of the festivities during the twice-yearly student rowing weeks. Being the great seats of learning they were, some were entirely in Latin and some entirely in Greek. Most were about colleges or local characters.

A 1911 autobiography[18] by George William Erskine Russell recorded:

> For my next reminiscence of hospitality to Freshmen I must rely on the assistance of a pseudonym. At the time of which I am writing, Oxford numbered among her professors one who had graduated, at a rather advanced age, from Magdalen Hall. Borrowing a name from Dickens, we will call him "Professor Dingo, of European reputation." To the kindness of Professor and Mrs. Dingo I was commended by a friend who lived near my home in Bedfordshire, and, soon after my arrival in Oxford, they asked me to Sunday luncheon at their villa in The Parks. The conversation turned on a new book of Limericks (or "Nonsense Rhymes," as we called them then) about the various Colleges. The Professor had not seen it and wanted to know if it was amusing. In my virginal innocence I replied that one rhyme had amused me. "Let's have it," quoth the Professor, so off I went at score—
>
>> There once was at Magdalen Hall
>> A Man who knew nothing at all;

> When he took his degree
> He was past fifty-three—
> Which is youngish for Magdalen Hall.

The Professor snarled like an angry dog, and said witheringly, that, if *that* was a specimen, the book must be sorry stuff indeed. After luncheon I walked away with another undergraduate, who said rejoicingly, "You've made a good start. That rhyme is meant to describe old Dingo."

Russell was at Oxford from October 11, 1872. He left the university in 1876. The freshmen's hospitality he speaks of presumably took place in 1872/3. This means that the book he refers to would have been published around this time.

The only book I know from this period which contains the limerick is *The Lays of Modern Oxford*,[19] which was published for Christmas 1873. Perhaps Russell had heard the limerick before that. Alternatively his memory might have been a little faulty and the incident took place later, or perhaps not at all.

Lays of Modern Oxford contained several long poems and 26 limericks. It was a pseudonymous work by Adon (i.e., A Don). Possibly the author, William Frederick Traill, wanted to avoid such scenes as that described above. And presumably the author of the book was the man who actually wrote the limericks; they seem to have first been published in it. The book was well known at the time and praised in the press, with one review[20] saying: "*The Lays* are such as would deservedly be termed 'deuced good' by very young undergraduates, or 'not at all bad' by the Don, to whom Oxford is all the world."

This is an early example of a book containing university limericks, and presumably it had a wider circulation than university magazines.

Who the real "Professor Dingo" was I don't know. He probably did exist; Russell tells another story about him in his autobiography. What happened to the limerick when it appeared in later works is a good example of inflation. I've seen his age given as 73—and 93!

Rhymes of Nonsense Truth & Fiction: New York, 1874

This illustrated book of limericks[21] contains verses ranging from quite poor to quite good. A handful have stood the test of time, appearing in limerick collections over a long time span. For instance, on page 30 we find:

> A great congregational preacher
> Told a hen, "You're a beautiful creature";

> The hen upon that
> Laid two eggs in his hat;
> And thus did a hen reward BEECHER.

This was probably taken from a newspaper. For readers not familiar with the preacher in question, it is Henry Ward Beecher—whose name is punned in the last three words. The following has been a favorite in several variations:

> A chap, who don't know when he's slighted,
> And for cheek surely must be indicted,
>   Once went to a party,
>   And ate just as hearty
> As though he was really invited.

This is a good example of how false attributions arise in limerick-land. Keen readers of limerick books will be familiar with *Out on a Limerick*, a 1960 work by Bennet Cerf. Page 64 of this contains the following:

> There was a young man so benighted,
> He didn't know when he was slighted.
>   He went to a party,
>   And ate just as hearty
> As if he'd been really invited.

This is attributed to one Frances Parkinson Keyes. Cerf doesn't tell us this, but she had contributed the above limerick to his newspaper column in 1958.[22] He just assumed she had written it. Being too lazy to check the origin of this (and of most other limericks submitted to him), it appeared in his book over her name. Ms. Keyes of New Orleans was born in 1885 and by no stretch of anyone's imagination could have written this limerick.

Songs of Singularity: January, 1875

Songs of Singularity, by the London Hermit, received fair reviews in January 1875.[23] Presumably it sold well enough, as a second edition was printed the same year. Among a whole raft of long and short poems, a section headed "NURSERY NONSENSE. (AFTER THE APPROVED FASHION)" appeared over nine limericks.

The London Hermit must have led quite a secluded life; I have found out little about him, except that his name was Walter Parke, and the fact that some of his limericks have been popular for over a century, still appearing, as they do, in modern anthologies. For example:

> There was an old waiter at Wapping
> Drew corks for a week with-out stopping;
> Cried he, "It's too bad!
> The practice I've had!
> Yet cannot prevent them from popping!"
>
> There was a young man who was bitten
> By twenty-two cats and a kitten;
> Sighed he, "It is clear
> My finish is near,
> No matter; I'll die like a Briton!"

One—

> There was an old priest of Peru,
> Who dreamt he converted a Jew;
> He woke in the night
> In a deuce of a fright,
> And found it was perfectly true.

—was presumably the inspiration for a very well-known variant:

> There was an old man of Peru,
> Who dreamt he was eating his shoe.
> He woke in the night
> In a terrible fright,
> And found it was perfectly true.

Students of conspiracy theory can ponder as to why the variant appeared in the first edition of Langford Reed's book, the original replaced it in the second edition, and both were omitted from the final editions. Also, why does Walter Parke seem to get no credit for this variant limerick?

Those who like the style can read more limericks by the Hermit, published in 1890, in a section headed[24] "NURSERY NONSENSE. (ON AN OLD AND APPROVED MODEL.)"

Singing of Limericks—An Early Printed Example: 1875

The singing of limericks has played a critical part in their development, and in my opinion also explains when and why they acquired the name "Limericks." The subject is extremely important, quite complex, and warrants a whole book to itself; which I am currently writing. I will therefore confine myself here to recording the earliest *contemporary printed* evidence I know of that limericks were sung.

Mr. Mostyn Pryce of the Inner Temple was on a yacht becalmed in the Solent in the summer of 1875. What better way for the group to pass the time than by singing the limericks of Mr. Edward Lear? Not only was this done, but Mr. Pryce then published in May of the following year sheet music which contained 12 different tunes to which 12 of Mr. Lear's limericks were fitted.

Mr. Pryce included a translation into French of one of the verses. *The Graphic* of July 1876 was so impressed by this that it included it in a brief review. Mind you, it was not that impressed by some of his tunes:

> We can easily imagine the amount of fun *The Musical Nonsense Rhymes* afforded to the merry party of grown-up children "on board a yacht becalmed in the Solent last summer." The most unique of comic poets, Edward Lear, supplied the irresistibly funny words, and Mostyn Pryce composed the music, some of which is good, the rest a trifle dull. The gem of the collection is No. 1, "There was an Old Person of Ware." The French translation by a lady is so clever that we give it below—
>
> > Il-y-avait un homme de la Bourse,
> > Qui s'asseyait autrefois sur une Ourse:
> > "Trotte' t'ell?" lui dit-on,
> > Il répondit "Mais non!
> > C'est une wopsinkonne, flopsikonne Ourse."
>
> Of the remaining eleven, Nos. 7 and 9 are the most original in point of melodies. All who are capable of enjoying a hearty laugh may in this case do so at a very moderate cost.

Ah, the halcyon days when well-educated people becalmed on yachts could amuse themselves by singing limericks. Alas, gone forever. All jokes aside, it shows that people were familiar with Lear's limericks and could sing them, and translate them. One limerick came from Lear's 1871/2 book; the others from his earlier book(s). Presumably the party had at least two Lear books on board, or a good memory.

Nonsense for Girls: New York, 1875

The earliest limerick books were available in color, the colors typically being hand-painted by small children (both paid for industrially, and in their own copies at home). Later limerick books contained black and white drawings, and sometimes black, white and red illustrations.

Chromolithography was a printing process that was initially used to reproduce famous paintings and then became available to book publishers. In 1875 a New York publisher issued a series called "Aunt Louisa's big picture series. 42 kinds—25 cents each." One of these books was *Nonsense for Girls*, which contained 24 beautiful colored illustrations. Each has a limerick underneath which describes a young lady enduring some sort of misadventure. None of the limericks has a Learian last line; that is, a repetition of the first with a strange adjective.

A copy currently for sale describes it as being "Illustrated with fine and fabulous chromolithographs by C.J.H." The price is no longer 25 cents; it's $400.

Reproducing the pictures here probably wouldn't do justice to the colors in the original book, but the University of Florida has kindly put a copy online.

The limericks are good—but some do cry out to be parodied. For example:

> There was a young lady named Sue
> Who never knew what she should do;
> So she whipped all her sisters,
> Until she raised blisters –
> And then tried to mend them with glue.

> There was a young lady named Sue
> Who never knew what she should do;
> So she whipped her nude sisters,
> Until she raised blisters –
> You can see it all on pay-per-view.
> —*Bob Turvey*

I'm beginning to see how Lear's work could have inspired dirty limericks!

Christmas Chimes and New Year Rhymes: December 1875

Christmas 1875[25] was probably enlightened in some households by the reading of a book[26] which contained a significant number of limericks. In a few households mince pies probably had crusted port spewed all over them from the mouths of irate bishops as they recognized themselves being parodied by the anonymous author—a man, incidentally, who was obviously close to the ecclesiastical action, but who has not, as far as I can see, been identified publicly.

The book consists of 82 pages. The first 48 are concerned with various non-limerick verses. Page 49 bears the title:

> A GALLERY OF NOT-ABLES
> DRAWN AND QUARTERED IN
> VARIOUS VERSES, SENSE
> AND NONSENSE

Chapter 9. The 1870s

About 64 limericks and a few other verses then follow, mainly highlighting the peculiarities and shortcomings of high-ranking clergy. Typical tirades:

> There was a quaint party in Brighton,
> Who wore a tall hat, and a tight 'un,
> It so pinch'd his marrow,
> It made his wits narrow.
> Though his face was a wide and a white 'un.
>
> There bray'd a young Neddy from Dover,
> Who was cocker'd on cockle and clover,
> Now clover is grass
> And the food of an ass.
> So he soon became Donkey all over.

One verse—

> There lived an enquirer at Chichester,
> Who made all his saints in their niches stir,
> By seventy-five questions
> He probed their digestions,
> And gave the South Saxon-men—sich a stir!

—might have been the progenitor of a slightly different verse—

> There was a young lady of Chichester,
> Who made all the saints in their niches stir.
> One morning at matins
> Her breasts in white satins
> Made the Bishop of Chichester's britches stir.

—but probably not, since this verse has been credited to Oliver St. John Gogarty (1878–1957), a man who created many classic limericks[27] (although he did "improve" a few old ones as well).

A contemporary review[28] opined:

What shall be said about *Christmas Chimes and New Year Rhymes* (B.M. Pickering)? Well, it is exceedingly amusing, though sometimes it trenches on rather dangerous ground; still, the verses have an avowedly good intent, even when most bitter. The author, in a witty and subtle preface, disavows any intention of disparaging "dignities," it is only "dignitaries, if they deserve it," against whom he wages war. The lines showing up the modern craze of competitive examination are excellent, and so is

> There was an inspector of schools,
> Who reckoned all other men fools,
> But to me, do you know, sir,
> He seems an imp-oser
> (I don't say imposter) of rules.

This book is an early example of what we might call "personal limericks." Of course, many limericks are written about people. But most are generic people, like "a young lady of Here," and "an old man from There." What we have in this book are real people who are named or, at the very least, are quite identifiable. As I shall discuss in another work, I think personal limericks played a large and almost undetected part in the popularization and spread of the limerick verse form.

Limericks in Lesser Languages— George du Maurier in *Punch*: 1877

Delighting in the name of George Louis Palmella Busson du Maurier, our hero was brought up mainly in France and was bilingual. He came to England to study chemistry and his father started him off as an analytical chemist, but annoyed him by refusing to let him have a piano in the laboratory. He then became a cartoonist and author. He wrote *Trilby*, was the father of the actor Sir Gerald (who stars in one of the great limericks of all time) and the grandfather of the novelist Daphne. By one of those bizarre accidents of history, he is regarded as the man whose *Punch* cartoon gave the English language the expression "Curate's Egg," with the added explanation of it "being good in parts." But he did *not* draw the cartoon that *first* used the expression—in spite of hundreds of reference books which say he did.

Il était un gendarme, à Nanteuil,
Qui n'avait qu'une dent et qu'un œil ;
  Mais cet œil solitaire
  Etait plein de mystère ;
Cette dent, d'importance et d'orgueil.

Limerick and drawing by George du Maurier, *Punch* magazine, March 10, 1877, page 98.

Between March and May 1877, *Punch* magazine

published 32 cartoons, four to a page, each of which had a limerick beneath it in fractured French.²⁹ George du Maurier had composed each limerick and drawn each illustration. It says a lot for *Punch* readers that they were obviously thought capable of understanding—nay, enjoying—such offerings as the one describing the handsome and somewhat overdressed constable.

We may translate this: "There was a policeman in Nanteuil, who had only one tooth and one eye, but this one eye was full of mystery, and the tooth was full of importance and pride." Being an old romantic I've always hoped this ugly bug found a life partner. Perhaps he did:

> In a Greek myth, three old sisters grey,
> Shared a tooth and an eye every day.
> When they said, "Attaboy!"
> To a cop in Nanteuil—
> He proposed to them all right away.
> —*Bob Turvey*

These limericks were popular enough to be republished in a book along with other du Maurier verses in 1898.³⁰ Rudyard Kipling certainly knew du Maurier's limericks; he quoted one in one of his later Stalky tales.³¹

Limericks in other languages are usually translations of English limericks into the language in question. George du Maurier's may be regarded as some of those rare examples which were actually created in French. Even so, in the interests of fair play, I must add a 1916 critique (to use a fine English word) of these verses:

> The metrical feat here performed by the bilingual humorist was no mean one. It consisted in making the French phrasal accents fall approximately where the English word-accents would occur in an English Limerick. It must be admitted that, to obtain this metrical effect, Du Maurier's Limericks must be read so as to produce a caesura or pause after each third syllable, which is easier, perhaps, for a master of the French of Stratford-atte-Bowe than for a Frenchman accustomed to orthodox meters. I have known Frenchmen to deny that Du Maurier's Limericks could be made to scan by any one but an Englishman, and that then the result was singularly cacophonous to a French ear.³²

The Young Lady of Aberystwyth— Plus Friend: Circa 1877

It has been claimed that the verse describing the antics of the Young Lady of Aberystwyth and her erstwhile companion must be "Limerick No. 1 in any [bawdy] collection."³³ A typical version reads:

> There was a young girl from Aberystwyth
> Who took grain to the mill to get grist with.
> > But the miller's son Jack,
> > Laid her flat on her back
> And united the organs they pissed with.

The earliest reference I can find is in a letter of July 1877, from John Payne Collier to J.W. Ebsworth. Discussing poetry and rhyme, and Ebsworth's own attempts at verse, Collier asks[34]: "Do you know any song or ballad in which Aberistwith is used as a rhyme and rhymes most accurately? but the song is not one for a parson, 'tho <u>you</u> may know it."

On the verso of the page he gives the limerick thus:

> A pretty girl near Aberistwith
> Took some corn to the mill to make grist with
> > But that wicked rogue Jack
> > When he brought her corn back,
> He join'd the four things that they kiss'd with.

Collier adds: "In the original 'four' is changed to *two*, and another rhyme substituted for '<u>kiss'd</u> with.' What can it be? Do you know any such, and if you do, which version? possibly both. I am not squeamish, as you are aware."

Whether any reply was received or what it contained, I know not. Presumably Collier is quoting a limerick he has heard, and is ribbing his ecclesiastical friend, who would obviously be able to work out what the "original" was.

Who actually wrote the "original," when, where and why are questions I can't answer. I can however, trace a little of what happened to the limerick over the next few years. In 1878 a version was being sung on stage[35]:

> There was a young girl of Aberystwyth
> Took corn to the mill to make grist with
> > But she went such a pace
> > That she fell on her face
> And cut the sweet lips that she kiss'd with.

The Sporting Times was a racing newspaper which quite often gave tips in limerick form. In 1887[36] it tipped one horse as follows:

> There was once a young maid of Aberystwith,
> Who took corn to the mill to make grist with
> > But the miller's son, Jack
> > Gave her ooftish to back
> A gee-gee named Oliver Twistwyth.

Chapter 9. The 1870s

"Ooftish": there's a word you don't see often these days. It means spondulicks, moolah, simoleons, clams, lucre, smackers or scratch. It comes, of course, "from the East End Yiddish synonym for money, being derived the German 'auftische' [properly aufdem tischel], 'on the table,' because people refused to play cards for money unless the cash was on the table."[37]

Whether Oliver Twist won or not I don't know.

By 1916[38] we have another rhyme word:

> A MAIDEN of gay Aberystwyth
> Left her mark on a man she kept trystwyth;
>   Vermilion streaks
>   On his neck and his cheeks,
> With the paint on the lips that she kystwyth.

A version circa 1944[39] switched the lead proponent, but the young lady came to her usual sticky end:

> There was a young man of Aberystwith
> Who took his best girl to play whist with.
>   When she trumped his first trick,
>   He took out his prick,
> And they connected the things that they pissed with.

Bertrand Russell used to recite the dirty version with such glee that one listener wondered if he had written it.[40] Russell was five years and 54 days old when Collier committed the first currently known version to paper. Russell subsequently won the Nobel Prize for Literature, became one of the founders of analytic philosophy, a leading mathematician, and reputedly the possessor of a large penis,[41] but I don't think he was *that* precocious.

(Swinburne has, of course, been fingered by many "historians" as the progenitor of this limerick. However, a learned paper[42] on the matter concludes there is no known evidence for the claim.)

Could I do any better on the rhyme front? Probably not:

> A musical maid from Aberystwyth,
> Took a chap to her room to play Liszt with.
>   He puffed and she panted;
>   He raged and she ranted—
> Silent orgasm? Now a dismissed myth.
> —Bob Turvey

Australian Limericks: Early 1878

Inspired by Lear's book, a few limericks using Australian place names had appeared in Australian newspapers at the turn of the decade (see 1860s chapter). The *Sydney Once a Week Magazine* took things a stage further by printing many more about local places. Most were along Learian lines, with the last line echoing the first, but sometimes a freer spirit seemed to take over the writer[43]:

> There was an old man of Kilkee,
> Whose age was two hundred and three;
> When they said "Won't you die?"
> He answered "Not I!
> I'm much better off as I *be*."

> There was an old lady of Rookwood,
> Who didn't fry fish as her cook would;
> She cut off their tails,
> But left on the scales,
> And somehow the dish didn't look good.

"It is a neat, well-printed little pamphlet, containing twenty-four pages of reading matter." This is from "Opinions of the Press," which the magazine printed to let readers know how it was viewed in the wider world.

Singing Limericks on Stage: Circa 1878

The extremely popular music hall star, Arthur Lloyd (1839–1904), was apparently singing limericks on stage in the 1870s. A 1907 newspaper article[44] commented: "[Limericks] were popularized to the last generation by a comic-singer on the music hall stage named Arthur Lloyd. His plan was to sing a string of them, and he did so to shrieks of laughter and a deal of applause."

In 1878 Lloyd published a sheet-music work which contained 11 limericks. Several of these limericks appear to be cleaned up versions of verses found in *Cythera's Hymnal* (1870; see earlier). Does this mean that dirty limericks were being freely passed around at this time, and that perhaps the music hall audience was familiar enough with them to know what he was really singing about? For example, the rude version of the following has been given earlier (Silver diary, 1868):

> There was a young maiden of Gloucester
> Her friends all imagin'd they'd lost her
> But they found in the grass
> A note from this lass
> To say that she'd gone off to Worcester.

The title sheet says: "Written, composed and sung by Arthur Lloyd."

However, before I write: "Maybe we'll accept 'Rewritten, composed and sung by Arthur Lloyd'"—let me point out that one limerick in Lloyd's sheet music later appeared in a rude version in *The Pearl* of 1879. It is of course possible that the young lady of Cheadle/Treadle had been passed around by word of mouth before Lloyd cleaned her up. Equally, it is possible that his clean version was parodied by *The Pearl*. Indeed, Lloyd's verses could have been known prior to him publishing them, and could have been parodied by others.

Which came first, the chicken or the egg? That's too big a question to try to answer here, and little would be added to the subject of this chapter.

Cyprus—A Sort of Limerick Competition: 1878

The 1878 Congress of Berlin was an attempt to sort out the Balkans in the wake of the Russo-Turkish war. Everyone seemed happy at first, but problems soon set in which eventually exploded, causing the start of World War I.

A secret deal between the British and the sultan of the ailing Ottoman Empire gave control of Cyprus to the British in return for their support for Turkey at the Congress. Newspapers excitedly described the landing of British troops on the island in August 1878 in such heat that several died, thus necessitating the creation of a Protestant cemetery.[45] One overheated Englishman seemed obsessed with the fact that the name of the new possession was unrhymable, and offered a cask of Cyprus wine to anyone who could rhyme it. As one newspaper[46] put it:

> It has been said over and over again that the island of Cyprus must prove unmanageable because its name will not rhyme with any other English word. But this is scarcely true, for Mr. P. Hamerton sends the following lines to the *Daily News*:—
>
> > There was an old woman in Cyprus,
> > A vixenish one, and a vip'rous;
> > > But she caught the fever,
> > > Which silenced for ever
> > That vixenish woman of Cyprus.
>
> As Mr. Guildford Onslow has been rash enough to offer a reward for a rhyme to "Cyprus," it is to be hoped that he will now fork out his money more especially since he is connected with so respectable and fair-dealing a print as *The Englishman*.

This limerick was reported as far afield as New York[47] and Buffalo.[48] Whether Philip Gilbert Hamerton, the well-known art writer, actually won the wine I don't know. Surely he shouldn't have done—"fever" has never rhymed with "ever," has it?

I suppose technically it's correct to say that Cyprus will not rhyme with any other single English word, but it can be made to rhyme:

> Said two smelly babies in Cyprus,
> "Mum hates it when she comes to diaper us.
> She takes Russell first,
> 'cos he smells the worst;
> She heaves then says, 'Jesus: that's ripe Russ!'"
> —*Bob Turvey*

That's probably not something that's going to be snapped up by the Cyprus Tourist Board, but you never know.

The reason I quote the original verse is that it is a limerick which was entered for a competition. As such it may have been the first limerick to have won a prize. Which is funny in one sense; the rhyme could have been given as a rhyme word, in prose, or in any other poetical format. Genuine limerick competitions became common in the 1880s, and in 1907–8 there was a craze for limerick competitions which had unbelievable prizes and which probably created tens of millions of limericks. Few of which, incidentally, had any worth as limericks.

Mr. Guildford James Hillier Mainwaring-Ellerker-Onslow had been a Liberal MP and was at this time editor of *The Englishman*. There probably wasn't much that rhymed with his name either. He was involved in the trial of the Tichborne claimant. He believed that Arthur Orton was actually the missing Sir Roger and was his "staunchest advocate." (For those interested in such minutiae, there was an illustrated limerick in a pamphlet published about the claimant in 1871 to cash in on the law case[49]; it's not very good so I won't give it here.)

Allusions to Dirty Limericks in the Mainstream Press: October 1878

Victorian England is generally reckoned to have been a puritanical place—on the surface. However, all sorts of unsavory vice went on underneath.

Dirty limericks were obviously never printed in newspapers and other publications for general sale. Sometimes, though, I have come across limericks which seem pure and aboveboard, but which were probably cleaned up versions of well-known dirty verses. The following is one such example; the line following the verse suggests that the author knows that the reader knows that the original is not quite as saintly as it might be. And that the reader knows what the original actually is. It's from *The Sporting Times*:

There was a young lady of Harrow,
Whose mouth was remarkably narrow,
Oft and times without number
She'd eat a cucumber,
But never could tackle a marrow.

----------------------------------<>---------------------------------

The above can be varied to suit the customer.[50]

If by now you can't work out what words to change you probably shouldn't be reading this book. If you really want to know, the following was printed in *The Pearl* of September 1879:

There was a young lady of Harrow
Who complained that her cunt was too narrow,
For times without number
She would use a cucumber,
But could not accomplish a marrow.

This is a good example of the problems of deciding which came first—the clean or dirty version. In this case I suggest the dirty version was known orally before it was printed in *The Pearl*. But what do I know?

Making the Last Line Deliberately Too Long: 1879

Many readers will be familiar with the verse:

There was a young man of Japan
Who wrote limericks that never would scan;
When his friends asked him why
He would always reply—
"It's because I like to try to get as many words into the last line as I possibly can!"

Quite when and where this came from I leave for others to determine (variants go back to at least 1924). However, it was probably not the first of its type. In 1879 the following appeared in several American college magazines:

SPARTACUS

There was a tall soph. from Toledo.
Always spoke the same piece with great speed, O,
At his nineteenth oration,
He received an ovation
Of chalk, pieces of brick, buck-shot, black-board erasers, a boot-jack, two hairbrushes, about a barrel and a half of gravel, and a loud detonating torpedo.[51]

Snappy, eh?

The Earliest Known Non-Rhyming Limerick—W.S. Gilbert: 1879

I recognize the potential flaw in describing a non-rhyming verse as a limerick. However, I once wrote a list of ten attributes a limerick should possess; rules, if you like. The last one read: "All rules may be broken if the result is a limerick of genius, which of course can't be defined, but can be recognized when seen."

I submit that the following is such a verse:

> There was an old man of St. Bees
> Who was stung on the arm by a wasp
> When they said, "Does it hurt?"
> He replied, "No, it doesn't.
> But I'm so glad it wasn't a hornet."

For reasons too lengthy to go into here, I believe this was written by W.S. Gilbert in 1879. But he didn't write it like this. What he wrote was the following pedestrian verse:

> There was an old man of Tralee,
> Who was stung in the arm by a wasp.
> When they asked, "Does it hurt?"
> He replied, "No, it doesn't;
> It may do it again if it likes."

This was then improved dramatically by our old friend *Anon.* who substituted a much better town to be stung in, as well as adding a much better insect to be stung by.

Nonsense Scribbles at Cambridge: 1879

This work is almost completely unknown to limerick scholars, let alone the general public. I include it show the range of people who were writing—and publishing—limericks at this time. The author was one "Naughty Boy," a person or persons as yet unidentified.

Apparently going through four "editions" (which just means four reprints), it was still on sale into the 1920s,[52] and still at the original price of three shillings and sixpence. Despite this, there are but half a dozen copies extant that I know of.

Advertised as containing "Thirty droll sketches, illustrating certain matters of interest to Undergraduate and other members of the University," it does indeed contain 30, and each (save the cover sketch) is accompanied by a limerick. Some of the amateurish drawings owe a lot to Lear and are possibly by diverse hands. The 29 limericks describe colleges, clubs, work, boating and bedders. The printed dedication suggests that the whole exercise might have been a collective attempt to cheer up an ill fellow student—

> There was an old "Sweetie" called "Will"
> Who worked 'till he made himself ill –
> So they made him this book,
> And with laughter he shook,
> To think it was made for "old Will."

—an attempt which perhaps got a bit out of hand. *Alumni Cantabrigienses* unfortunately does not readily offer any clue as to who our "old Will" might have been.

The Pearl Magazine: July 1879–December 1880

The Pearl was a monthly magazine which contained upward of 60 limericks—depending on how you want to define our dear old friend. Some have a known provenance; for example Godfrey Morgan's young fellow at Bicester, which had been declaimed at the *Punch* editorial table in January 1863. The young woman of Chester had appeared in *Cythera's Hymnal* in 1870. Most, however, seem new to the work.

What are they like? Well, one recent review described *The Pearl* as being composed of "prose [that] is reasonably imaginative and erotic, but the limericks, of which there are a fair number, are almost uniformly tedious, having no virtues but the inadequate one of form alone."[53] This is by one of the best writers of modern limericks, Dr. Robert Conquest.

I must say that, despite Dr. Conquest's reservations, I like them. For instance, I think the following is both clever and funny:

> There was a young man of Bombay,
> Who fashioned a cunt out of clay;
>   But the heat of his prick
>   Turned it into a brick,
> And chafed all his foreskin away.

They seem to have been fairly well known at the time; for instance, a parody of this limerick some 20 years later in a major newspaper manages to capture the flavor of the original and get in a good play on words by using "forehead" to replace "foreskin":

> There was a young man of Bombay,
> Who fashioned a hat out of clay;

> But the sun did the trick—
> Turned that clay into brick,
> And wore all his forehead away.⁵⁴

Those who would like more along the lines of—

> There was a gay Countess of Bray,
> And you may think it odd when I say,
> That in spite of high station,
> Rank and education,
> She always spelt Cunt with a K.

—can read all of the limericks in reprints of the magazine in book form, or online.⁵⁵

Conclusion

The 1870s seem to have been about expansion of subject matter, about all and sundry having a go at writing limericks, about people in every station of life creating, swapping and collecting limericks. Limericks were certainly being sung, in private and on stage.

Despite censorship, dirty limericks made their mark in the published field and in private notes and correspondence—and God knows how many of them have gone unrecorded. Many would not be recognized as being nigh on 150 years old if they were printed unattributed in a modern book.

A couple of experiments in extending the last line or in doing away with all rhyme schemes were a lurch away from the conventional limerick. Such variants are amusing, and they do show how the old verse can withstand rough handling. (Over many years of study I have seen a few others of that ilk, such as a modern series of limericks which successively lose a line until nothing is left. But, surprisingly, there are only a handful of such variants. The standard model seems to be by far the fittest.)

Chapter 10

The 1880s
The Limerick Expands

The 1880s started off with a bang when Krakatoa went up, Coca-Cola fizzed into existence and several women were murdered by Jack the Ripper. The decade ended with the birth of Adolf Hitler and the construction of the Eiffel Tower. And, sadly, the death of Edward Lear.

As regards limericks, a couple of interesting things happened. Competitions were run which specifically asked for limericks to be submitted, and limericks began to be used as advertisements. Mainly, though, it was more of the same: good limericks were being written and these were being printed and distributed worldwide.

Truth Magazine—Limerick Competitions: 1880 Onward

Truth was a weekly magazine published in London between 1877 and 1957. It regularly ran all manner of literary competitions. The magazine's readership was described as: "Labouchere's *Truth*, a weekly journal largely read by discontented English butlers and valets, and rivaling *Argos* in the number of its 'I's."[1]

Discontented they may have been, but my goodness they could write some good limericks.

The earliest competition I know of in which the public was invited to create limericks in order to win prizes was announced in *Truth* magazine in 1880, as follows:

This week the Prize will be given for the best
ORIGINAL NONSENSE VERSE,
written in the well-known meter popularized by Mr. Edward Lear. Every one knows what I mean, I presume; but it will be safer, perhaps, to give a sample verse—

> There was an old man with a beard,
> Who said, "It is just as I feared;
> Two larks and a wren—
> Three cocks and a hen,
> Have all built their nests in my beard!"

I need scarcely repeat, I hope, that the verses must be entirely original. I lay down no limit as to their subject, but an effort should be made to embody in them, if possible, some quaint or incongruous notion, and temper their wild absurdity with humor.[2]

The stricture about originality seems to have fallen on deaf ears, because the competition editor complained: "On the whole, I cannot think the 'Nonsense Verses' were well done, and, in spite of my warning, several very old friends were sent in as original."[3]

The attempted "passing-off" of other people's limericks in competitions is one that has persisted through the ages. Often this is missed by the judges; can they really be supposed to have an encyclopedic recall of every verse written? Occasionally the miscreant is found out, publicly shamed and made to repay the cash. One famous example (Tenby/Denbigh) has been described in the 1860s chapter.

It's still a common problem—I've even seen children do it, or at least it was done by those who submit entries in the child's name.

An 1881 issue contained a very similar invitation to write limericks, with a double prize of four guineas. Entries for this competition seemed to irk the competition editor in the much the same way they had done a year earlier: "This proved a most popular competition, judging by the exceptionally large number of verses received. It was curious to notice, though, how many competitors failed altogether to keep to the prescribed meter. Others, in spite of the conditions laid down, sent in verses copied verbatim from Mr. Lear's *Book of Nonsense*; and a few such, I find on re-perusal, have been included in the published 'specimens.'"[4]

It was also noticeable, although the editor didn't point it out, that several entrants submitted more than one verse, despite that being forbidden as well.

Some of the limericks were clever; the following was one of the four winners:

> There was once an elderly sow,
> Who exclaim'd "Goodness gracious! pray how
>   Shall I learn what the dose is
>   Which cures trichinosis?
> For I feel that it's coming on now."—GHOUL.

Another seems to be a very early example of a multiple-rhyming style which became particularly associated with the American limerick writer Miss Carolyn Wells; she was 19 at the time of the competition:

> A high art young fellow of Crewe,
> Was running to catch the two two;
>   He cried, "I'll be late.
>   The train will not wait,
> It's a minute or two to two two."—A.L.E.[5]

Truth is a difficult journal to run to earth, because the word "truth" exists in many book and magazine titles and a typical online search throws up thousands of results. It was edited by Henry Labouchere and published by the Truth Publishing Company. The subtitle of this work is "Cultores Veritatis Fraudis Inimici," which makes it easier to find. The magazine was a leading exposer of fraud in all its forms. Those exposed did not take the exposé lying down; Labouchere was prosecuted about 42 times for libel in his first 25 years. He won virtually every case.

Limericks Being Used in Advertisements: 1880 Onward

It's often quite difficult to find the first example of something being used in a particular way. Langford Reed claimed that an ad in Limerick form was used in the 1850s for Allcock's Corn Plasters.[6] Reed, unfortunately, is quite an unreliable source. Mr. Allcock was certainly an early—and prolific—user of limericks for advertising, but the oldest I have been able to find date from December 1880.[7] There were so many of them in newspapers in the 1880s that I will just select a couple of examples:

> A lady said, "Bother these boots,
> When I wear them my corn always shoots."
> So she tried "Allcock's Shields,"
> And exclaimed "Now it yields,"
> As she pulled out the corn by the roots.
>
> Said a wicked corn, "Fiddle-de-dee,
> Allcock's Corn Shields'll never cure me."
> So he got one and tried,
> And the next day he died,
> So the verdict was "Felo-de-se."

A corn committing suicide? Only in a limerick! The use of "felo-de-se" in a limerick is rare, by the way. I only know of six other examples, one of them by Rudyard Kipling.

Early photography seems to have been a thrilling activity. Among other exciting chemical recipes, *Anthony's Photographic Bulletin* for 1884 reprised a method for "Stripping Gelatin Negatives or Positives by the Aid of Hydrofluoric Acid." It also included a four-limerick advert for Mr. Anthony's camera, Mr. Dallmeyer's lens and Mr. Eastman's dry plates.[8]

While not as thrilling a chemical as hydrofluoric acid, baking powder is probably more useful to the average person:

> There was a young maid in Jamaica
> Who quarreled one day with the baker
> So her mother allowed her
> To buy BORWICK'S POWDER,
> And excellent bread it doth make her! (1885[9])

I have seen ads in limerick form in 1887 for Sapolio soap[10] and, if you'll pardon a slight excursion from the 1880s, in 1895 for Carter's Little Liver Pills:

> There was a young man of Carlisle
> Who suffered extremely from Bisle
> He took CARTER'S PILLS
> Was relieved of his ills,
> And received all his friends with a smisle.[11]

There are hundreds more in later years, advertising everything from tea to beer to Harris Tweed to breakfast cereals to Maidenform bras.

For those seeking a brief overview of the early days in America, a 1938 magazine article commented:

> The limerick contest is absolutely standard in advertising technique and there is practically no reputable type of product—oranges to silk stockings, cigarettes to dandruff removers—which has not at one time or other been promoted by means of a limerick contest.
>
> Partly for reasons of sentiment, and partly because the Readers' Service Department of PRINTERS' INK receives every so often a request for such information, it seems timely to set forth a brief and fairly definitive history of the limerick as a handmaiden of American advertising.[12]

After all that, I think I'll give the last word on the subject to the *Columbia Encyclopedia*: "Of unknown origin, the limerick is popular rather than literary and has even been used in advertising."[13]

You learn something every day, don't you?

A Fine Spell of Limericks in America: 1881

Dr. C. Grant Loomis was an American with an interest in limericks.[14] Just after he died, an article by him was published titled "American

Chapter 10. The 1880s

Limerick Traditions."[15] In this he remarked: "The following two years [1878 and 1879], however, saw the introduction of spelling rhymes, a habit which became a mania in the limerick boom of 1881."

A number of limericks were then quoted, mainly from magazines like *Puck* and *The Argonaut*. An example from the latter:

> There was a young woman of Worcester,
> She petted an old Shanghai rorcester;
> When asked what indorcester
> To fondle the rorcester,
> She blushed, for the question conforcester. (1879[16])

(Perhaps such verses should have been included in the 1870s chapter, but since this type seems to have exploded in the 1880s I have put this topic here.)

The word "Sioux" seems to have been popular in 1881, with different examples being published in August,[17] September[18] and October. The October effort consisted of five stanzas. The first verse went:

> A wandering tribe called the Siouxs
> Wear moccasins, having no shiouxs;
> They are made of buckskin,
> With the fleshy side in,
> Embroidered with beads of light hiouxs.
> —*Charles Follen Adams*[19]

This sequence enjoyed a considerable circulation at the time and still appears in collections today (often only printed in part, and often ascribed to *Anon.* even though the author is well known[20]). It's a good example of how limericks spread, and how many different types of people were interested in them. For instance, it appeared in an English public school magazine in 1882,[21] where it was introduced by the immortal sentence: "I should like to quote one poem from a late number of Scribner's Magazine: which is, I suppose, inaccessible to most fellows and so this will not be stale—." In 1903 it appeared in a pamphlet on German phonetics.[22]

In early 1882 a puzzled reader of the *Boston Journal* wrote a letter to the editor:

> Mr. Editor: Tell me why Colonel
> Is spelled in a way so infolonel?
> Shed one ray of light
> On a sorrowful wight
> Who for years has subscribed for the Jolonel.[23]

This limerick subsequently appeared in many newspapers around the world. It's not the first outing of "colonel" as a rhyme word but it is a nice one, tying in as it does with the name of the newspaper.

Quite a few limericks exist using rhyme words based on "colonel." Indeed, several scurrilous stories have been woven around an upstanding officer of his rank. A well-known example has a padre upset by an oath-emitting choleric colonel, while still managing to write the oaths down in his notebook.[24]

Spellings such as Greenwich, Harwich, St. John, Caius, yacht, corps, Grand Prix, Vaughan, daughter and many others were rhymed with similarly spelled words. Gloucester was also used; we have come across limericks using this word earlier, but then the rhyme words were conventionally spelled.

Whether *Puck* was the "originator" of this type of limerick I don't know, but it was certainly known for such verse. An American student magazine[25] published an article in 1881 in which the editor was driven mad by inferior limerick submissions and wound up stuffing them into an envelope and posting them to *Puck*.

Examples of similar verses which use differences between spelling and pronunciation can be found widely in newspapers, magazines and books of the time in several countries, especially the UK and the U.S. They have appeared on and off over many years and are still written today. Readers keen on this type of limerick can easily find them. For example, in Langford Reed's *Mr. Punch's Limericks* there is a whole chapter called "Nomenclatory Limericks," which contains various versions of Cholmondeley (1896), Marjoribanks (1896), Beauchamp (1896), Geoghegan (1904) and Menzies (1928). An example from the 1929 *Encyclopædia Britannica* reads:

> The lifeboat that's kept at Torquay
> Is intended to float in the suay:
> The crew and the coxswain
> Are sturdy as oxwain,
> And as smart and as brave as can buay.[26]

Gershon Legman has given his considered opinion about such verses. He seemed to think they dated from *Punch* in the 1900s, were based on stupid mispronunciations of English place names and surnames, and were among the worst limerick innovations ever attempted.[27] Perhaps he just did not understand that the English really do pronounce such words in such ways.

Abbreviations of such words as Mister, Company, Maine, and Maryland also made appearances in limericks in the 1880s, along with rhyme words similarly abbreviated. I wonder if Legman might have been more inclined to accept such limericks, since several were written by his fellow American William Sydney Porter, better known as O. Henry. The following appeared in a 1919 magazine[28]:

Who has written the most ingenious example of those limericks that end in abbreviated words whose pronunciation (or mispronunciation) is to be filled out by the reader? Many would vote for O. Henry, one of whose effusions of this kind is as follows:

> An old woman who lived in Fla.
> Had some neighbors who all the time ba.
> Tea, sugar, and soap,
> Till she said: "I do hope
> I'll never see folks that are ha."[29]

The Sporting Times: 1887

The *Pink 'Un* contained its fair share of "Unorthodox Orthography" limericks in the 1880s. On January 1, 1881, it opened with a double verse using rhyme words of colonel / infolonel / etolonel / patolonel / volonel / matolonel.

The issues of 1887 in particular were positively jammed with them. However, from that year I would like to draw attention to a rare form of the old verse, in which the obvious ending is substituted by an apposite long sentence, which ends in a non-rhyme:

> There was a young girl of Nantucket
> Seen rubbing her knee 'gainst a bucket;
> She'd been stung by a bee,
> But a rustic Johnnee
> Most gallantly offered to—do all he could to allay any local
> inflammation that might possibly ensue.[30]

At least I think I know what the last two words should be.... Or maybe I don't. Whatever they should be, this variant never really seemed to take off. One or two good ones were written, though. The following made an appearance in 1924.[31] Langford Reed said this was his choice of "the best limerick"[32]:

> We thought him an absolute lamb,
> But when he sat down in the jam
> On taking his seat
> At our Sunday school treat,
> We all heard the vicar say—"Stand up please while I say grace."

Interestingly, there exists a later variant of this which may be judged by some as an improvement.[33]

You can of course have fun writing your own:

A war-time brickworks in old Hatham
Fulfilled a rush order from Chatham.
   When a bomb in the Blitz
   Blew the bricks all to bits
The foreman sat down and he—shhh; it's an Official Secret
how this important order for the Naval Dockyard was in fact completed.
                                               —Bob Turvey

Newspapers and Magazines Worldwide

In the 1880s newspapers and magazines all over the world sometimes seemed awash with limericks; singly, in twos and threes, and often whole columns of them. One or two conjured up a rather exciting mental picture. What a pity the following New Zealand offering was not illustrated:

There was a young lady of Brighton,
Who buttoned her jerseys so tight on,
   That whenever she stirred,
   Off the buttons all "whirred,"
And much did the people it frighten. (1881[34])

THAT tough old citizen, Beggs,
  Lived on whiskey, tobacco, and eggs,
     Nor was he put out,
     When, because of the gout,
  A doctor chopped off his hind legs.

Illustration from *Life* magazine, May 24, 1883, page 250.

The American *Life Magazine* on the other hand did illustrate some of its limericks.[35]

Whether such illustrations—or indeed such limericks—were suitable for general public consumption I leave to your judgment.

Sometimes illustrations did manage to capture the innocence of the verse. Examples can be found in the American magazine for children, *St. Nicholas*. One of my favorite verses is the legendary "Ichthyosaurus" from 1887, written by Isabel Frances Bellows.[36]

Chapter 10. The 1880s

Limerick by Isabel Frances Bellows, illustration by R.B. Birch. *St. Nicholas: An Illustrated Magazine for Young Folks*, Century, New York, March 1887, page 333.

(Perhaps because his name is so difficult to spell—or he really was ashamed of it—this verse sometimes appears in later books using the word "plesiosaurus." But a plesiosaur is a horse of a quite different color.)

The Baby's Own Æsop: 1886

William Linton wrote a series of limericks based on Aesop's fables. These were illustrated by Walter Crane and published as a book by Routledge in time for Christmas 1886. Though expensive, this was apparently a children's book.[37]

However, an online sale listing described it thus: "Series of 66 limericks of critical or socialist content. The misleading title tries to cover the political brisance of the publication."

In 1991 this book was analyzed in a 22-page article titled "Depiction vs. picturing: subversive illustrations in a Victorian picture-book."[38] Whether this semiotic analysis explains what this book is really about I leave you to work out. What Victorian children thought of the book I don't know.

Leviora: Being the Rhymes of a Successful Competitor: 1888

Thomas Frank Bignold, BA, died in Melbourne as the latter half of his book, bearing the above unusual title, was still in the press in Calcutta. The author was an Anglo-Indian Caian. What this work is actually about I leave for others to discern. However, it contains several limericks. One or two almost seem to inject a degree of thoughtful logic into the humor:

> There was a young lady in Shihuri
> Who cut her aunt's throat in a fury;
> She was duly committed
> But promptly acquitted
> On blowing a kiss to the Jury.[39]

On reading this verse, Fox News viewers and *Daily Mail* readers will probably howl in rage that a woman has got off again and that if a man had committed this crime he would have been sent to prison or worse. I agree with them, but I have to point out that despite the author being a judge in India, it is only a limerick and the event probably never happened.

Journal of Education: 1888

Doubtless keen to educate its readers on local geopolitics, the *Journal of Education* printed a selection of "Nursery Rimes" on European capitals. A couple will give the flavor:

> There was a young lady of Stockholm
> Who was vex'd they'd not sent her new frock home;
>   So she went to the ball
>   Dressed in nothing at all,
> Which astonished the good folk of Stockholm.
>
> There was an old man at Belgrade
> Who bought all his clothes ready made:
>   When they asked, "Do they fit?"
>   He replied, "Not a bit
> But just think how little I paid."—BRAND[40]

The first one was a bit racy for public consumption in 1888, don't you think?

Anti-Chinese Sentiment in America: 1888

Despite the rhetoric on the Statue of Liberty reading "Give me your tired, your poor, your huddled masses yearning to breathe free," some immigrants were more welcomed than others. The American attitude toward its Chinese citizens has not always been positive.[41] A limerick published in several American newspapers[42] even made it into an English paper[43]:

> **An Example to be Followed.**
> The bodies of sixteen Chinese
> Are homeward bound over the seas;
> If the live ones would skip
> On a similar trip,
> New York would be more at its ease.

A Trifle to End On: 1889

Just as the Eiffel Tower was about to open, *The Sporting Times* published a verse commemorating the event. Its comment about Monsieur Eiffel rifling the tourists' pockets was true—he had a 20-year concession on trips up the tower and that was how most of the construction cost was paid off:

> There was a constructor named Eiffel,
> Who proposed tourists' pockets to reiffel;
> They might climb by the hour
> To the top of his Tour
> At a charge of five francs—quite a treiffel.
> —*George Piesse*[44]

So there we have it; bizarre spelling, insulting Johnny Foreigner and a comment on current events, all in one limerick. And it really was five francs to get to the top as well.

Conclusion

Limerick competitions became firmly established, limericks started earning their keep by advertising, the peculiarities of English spelling were harnessed to the service of Calliope, the range of topics included politics and current events, and children were catered to in several books and magazines.

Chapter 11

The 1890s
Who Wrote What?

Industrial chemists and connoisseurs of ladies' clothing will remember the 1890s as the Mauve Decade. The mass production of the dyes mauveine and alazarine, which had been discovered many years earlier, made the world much brighter. So thanks for that, William Henry Perkins.

As regards limericks, it was mostly steady as she goes. No fantastic outbursts of color as far as I can see, apart from the odd blue one of course, written by folk such as Aubrey Beardsley in letters to a friend.

Another Fine Spell of Limericks

Whatever Legman thought about limericks which use odd spellings—indeed, whatever you or I or anyone else thinks of them—the 1890s had lots. University magazines seemed to love them. For example, the *Isis* printed the following in 1893:

> **LUSUS ORTHOGRAPHIÆ.**
> There was a young man named Colquhoun,
> Who went out to shoot a balquboun,
> With a comrade called Cholmondeley;
> But they came back quite glolmondeley,
> For they met nothing but a ralqucoun![1]

Some, however, would probably have puzzled even native English speakers, were it not for the explanations occasionally given. For example an 1898 verse:

> In Kent there's a village called Trotterscliffe*
> In style most distinctly "one-hotterscliffe."
> If you said so in joke
> To one of its foke,
> He'd eye you uncommonly crotterscliffe.[2]

The asterisk reads: "Pronounced 'Trossley.'" (Nowadays the name seems to be spelled Trottiscliffe; it is a real village and it is pronounced Trosley.)

Even with the explanation offered, as to what the limerick actually means…. I can only assume the second rhyme is "one-hossley" and the insult is therefore that it is a one-horse town; i.e., a place with few and poor facilities.

A Problem for Limerick Historians: Too Many Wheres

A verse from the 1890s provides me with an opportunity to comment on a problem often faced by those who study the history of the limerick verse form: namely, how to find information about a particular limerick, such as its author and date of creation. Imagine our student has come across the following in a 2013 book about Somerset:

> There was a young woman of Durston,
> Who thought her third husband the worst 'un
> For he justly was reckoned,
> Far worse than the second,
> And the second was worse than the first 'un.[3]

Durston is a village in Somerset and our researcher wonders if he should contact the book's author. However, before he does this, he finds the following in a 1918 Welsh newspaper:

> The following Limerick was found among the M.S.S. papers of a late local classical scholar:
>
> > There was an old lady of Thurston,
> > Who thought her third husband the worst 'un
> > For he, as she reckoned,
> > Was worse than the second,
> > And the second was worse than the first 'un.[4]

The learned scholar looks up Thurston, finds it is a village in Suffolk, and wonders if he should deploy his efforts in contacting the local library. Fortuitously, just before he does this, the Library Angel intervenes and he finds the following in a 1912 book:

> **DEVONSHIRE IDYLLS.**
> THERE was an old woman of Churston
> Who thought her Third husband the worst 'un;
> For he justly was reckoned
> Far worse than the Second,
> And the Second was worse than the First 'un.[5] 1894

This book describes the writings of Dr. Herbert Kynaston. At the date given for the creation of the limerick, he was at Durham University.

So, after thankfully missing out on a wild goose chase around the UK, our scholar appears to have identified not only the author and the date and place of creation, but also the Devonshire village it was actually written about.

I think this shows that those who recall and reprint memorable limericks often concentrate on the important parts of the verse, and forget the least important parts—in this case the place. Of course, the problem this causes for limerick historians is obvious; if you don't know the original verse you can waste time and effort. A good tip is to put each of the lines into search engines and try variations of rhyme words. Also—adopt a cynical view toward those who claim to have found the handwritten literary remains of local scholars.

Having a Ball

Another example of multiple and confusing names is the following verse. An early sighting is in *The Sporting Times*:

> There was a young man of Bengal,
> Who went to a fancy dress ball;
>   And just for some fun,
>   He went dressed as a bun,
> And got munched by the dog in the hall.[6] 1892

The following will give an idea of the range of the places our protagonist came from and what activities he got up to. The limericks also raise the question: are they variations of the original limerick—or new verses?

Our first variant is an example of another perennial problem, plagiarism. The following was an entry to an 1898 competition. Did the lady who submitted it write the original?

> There was a young man of Nepaul,
> Who went to a fancy dress ball.
>   He went just for fun
>   Dressed up as a bun,
> But a dog eat him up in the hall.[7]
>   —Blanche

A 1904 example seems to record an entirely different problem for our intrepid balleteer—if such a word exists:

> There was a young man of St. Paul
> Who went to a fancy dress ball;
>   By some sad mischance
>   He fractured his pants
> And had to go home in a shawl.[8]

Chapter 11. The 1890s

Our next example illustrates a problem we often encounter with dates. In 1905 a book of verse was published. However, it is quite clear that the verses were written much earlier in the author's life. The following stands over the word *Anon.*:

> There was a young man of Nepal
> Who went to a fancy-dress ball.
>   He thought t'would be fun
>   To go as a bun,
> But the dog ate him up in the hall.

The reason for including this limerick in the book was so the author could show the original of his French translation to those who might not know it:

> À Nepal, un jeune homme enjoué
> Se rendait à un bal costumé.
>   Il le trouvait fort beau
>   D'y aller en gâteau,
> Mais le chien le mangea à l'entrée.[9]

Our next three examples add only minor variations to our protagonist's activities; in these he is called Paul,[10] McCall,[11] and Small.[12] These are followed by a man from Pall Mall[13]—who is obviously tone deaf since Pall Mall doesn't rhyme with ball.

A nice variant of disguise appears in a 1910 version:

> There once was a man named McCall,
> Who attended a fancy dress ball.
>   He thought he would risk it,
>   And go dressed as a biscuit,
> But was "et" by a dog in the hall.[14]

It would probably also have been a mistake to go dressed as a cake, to paraphrase the French version.

Two variants with a different type of disguise recall the well-known propensity of dogs to mark their territory, even in such a new venue as a masquerade ball:

> There was a young man of Bengal
> Who went to a masquerade ball
> Arrayed like a tree
> But he failed to foresee
> His abuse by the dogs in the hall.[15]
>
> There was a young man of Bengal
> Who went to a fancy dress ball.
> He was draped like a tree
> Having failed to foresee
> Being pissed on by dogs, cats, and all.[16]

Finally, of course, we encounter the obvious filthy variant:

> There was a young man of Bengal,
> Who went to a fancy dress ball.
> Just for a whim
> He dressed up as a quim,
> And was had by the dog in the hall.[17]

In another incarnation: "just for a stunt he dressed up as a cunt."[18]

After all the abuse the poor chap suffered, the following verse probably summarizes what we've all been thinking. Of course, it uses another rhyme word:

> There was a young man of Southall,
> Who went to a fancy dress ball;
> Information we lack
> As to how he got back—
> Or whether he got back at all.[19]

With Repetition Confusion Begins: Another Problem

Magazines and newspapers in the 1890s often had whole columns filled with limericks. Where all these limericks came from is not entirely clear. Probably staff writers created them; perhaps the public sent in some. Others, however, were clearly "stolen" from previous publications—an action often not acknowledged. This, of course, adds another problem for the limerick historian; it is now becoming increasingly difficult to find the first printing of any particular verse, unless one is possessed of either a prodigious memory or a vast and searchable database. Even equipped with both, if the original publication was in an obscure journal—or in a publication which has no copies left in existence—there can still be a nagging doubt: has the earliest printing really been found?

Let me give a few examples, none of which bear any acknowledgment as to their origin. An issue of *The Sporting Times* in 1891 printed:

> There was a young man of the Cape,
> Who always wore trousers of crape.
> When they said, "Do they tear?"
> He replied, "Here and there;
> But they keep such an excellent shape."[20]

This had appeared in several newspapers in 1887.[21] The serious student of limericks can ascribe this verse to a known author; and it's *not* Robert Louis Stevenson, as so many have claimed.

Chapter 11. The 1890s

Keeping with *The Sporting Times*, in 1896[22] it reprinted the "Ichthyosaurus" limerick, which we have already encountered in 1887, when it was still attached to its authoress's name.

An 1894 issue of *Judy* magazine contained a page containing 12 limericks. Somewhat disingenuously titled "Rhymes of the Times," they included the following, which had had its first outing in *Punch's Almanac for 1863*[23]:

> There was a young lady of Harrow,
> Who would go to church in a barrow,
> It stuck in the aisle
> And she said, with a smile,
> "They build these here churches too narrow."[24]

Mind you, to be fair—many newspapers "borrowed" all sorts of limericks from the likes of *Punch*, *Judy* and *Fun*, printing them shortly after their initial outing. Credit where credit's due, they usually attributed them to the magazine from which they were taken.

As a final example, the legendary Rio limerick from 1868 was reprinted in 1893 in *The K.P.*, a Cambridge undergraduate magazine, complete with a little drawing.[25] Three weeks later the verse appeared in *The Isis*, an Oxford undergraduate magazine,[26] whereupon *The K.P.* commented, presumably about this "theft":

> A smart little paper the *Isis*,
> When hard up for a verse at a crisis,
> Takes the *K.P.'s* best rhyme—
> But we'll pardon it's [*sic*] crime,
> If t'will only give up such devices.[27]

A bit rich, eh? And to spell the possessive "its" incorrectly—unforgivable at Cambridge. No wonder *The K.P.* folded shortly afterward.

Obviously, reprinting old limericks with no attribution was not started in the 1890s—earlier examples exist—but it perhaps became more noticeable. This may have been because there were simply more old limericks to reprint. Some of those reprinted certainly seem to be of the memorable and well-known type.

Timely Tongue-Twisters

There is a small group of limericks which both illustrate the multiple place-names problem and also give us a little insight into the problem of attribution.

A motley Crewe

Let's start off with an 1892 UK magazine. The following was used as an exemplar of the type of nonsense stanza contestants were supposed to emulate, which suggests it was well known at the time:

> There was a young lady of Crewe,
> Who wanted to catch the 2.2;
> When she seemed in a flurry,
> They said, "Do not hurry!
> It's a minute or two to 2.2."[28]

Crewe is a well-known railway town in central England. Readers would understand that a train leaving at two minutes past two is being referred to.

A UK newspaper recorded in 1894:

> There was a young lady of Crewe,
> Who wanted to catch the two-two;
> But the guard said, "Don't hurry,
> There's no need for flurry,
> It's a minute or two to two-two."[29]

In a February issue of *Judy* in 1896 we find an illustration showing a lady talking to a porter, with a clock in the background. The verse underneath reads:

> There was a young lady of Crewe
> Who wanted to catch the 2.2;
> Said the porter, "Don't hurry,
> Or scurry or flurry,
> It's a minute or 2 2 2 2!"[30]

In addition to some UK newspapers subsequently printing this verse, several U.S. newspapers also printed it, an early version being in March 1896.[31] Most cite *Judy* as the source.

An 1897 competition in *Truth* omitted to stipulate that only original nonsense verses should be submitted.[32] One entry therefore read:

> There was a young lady of Crew,
> Who wanted to catch the two-two;
> When the guard saw her flurry,
> He said, "Oh don't hurry!
> There's a minute or two to two-two."—ZEN[33]

Pausing only to remark how similar these are to a previously discussed limerick from 1881, there are versions which have first line endings such as Typhoo[34] (1895), Kew[35] (1898), Bellew[36] (1899), "in blue"[37] (1899), "old man of Chifu"[38] (1901), Peru[39] (1905), "named Sue"[40] (1908), Boo Loo[41] (1909) and "named Lou"[42] (1921).

The Tait gallery

Let's consider another verse, reportedly a favorite of President Woodrow Wilson.[43] The following is from *Truth*.[44] Pear John is given as the name of the person who claimed to be the author:

> There was a young fellow called Tait,
> Who dined with a girl at 8.8,
>   But I cannot relate
>   What that fellow named Tait
> And his tête-à-tête ate at 8.8. (Sept. 1898)

Several U.S. newspapers reprinted the above limerick in late 1898 and early 1899, attributing it to *London Truth*.

A variant spelling of the hero's name is found in some papers:

> There was a young fellow called Tate
> Who went out to dine at 8.08,
>   But I cannot relate
>   What that fellow called Tate
> And his tete-a-tete ate at 8.08. (Dec. 1898)[45]

Minor variants appeared in the *person* of our hero, and in the fact that the reciter *will not* tell what they ate, rather than merely being unable to say.

> There was a young person named Tate
> Who went out to dine at 8:8,
>   But I will not relate
>   What that person named Tate
> And his tête-à-tête ate at 8:8. (May, 1899)[46]

The Crewe and Tait limericks exhibit a problem the historian often runs into: attribution. In order to examine this a little more carefully, let me introduce you to someone who was both a writer of limericks and a student of limerick history.

Carolyn Wells: 1862–1942

I won't describe the American author Carolyn Wells in great depth. The internet and her autobiography will oblige. Suffice it to say she wrote many detective stories and children's books. She also wrote limericks and wrote about limericks. She knew Oliver Herford; he illustrated some of her limericks.

In her autobiography she recalls how in the 1890s she would write humorous jingles, post them off with a stamped return envelope to *Puck, Life, Judge* or *Texas Siftings* and hope for the best. Many a dollar came back as payment. Presumably there was an odd limerick or two among them. When she visited the World's Fair in Chicago, most of the staff of *Puck* were on holiday and she was sending so much verse to the magazine that "the editor was forced to sign my stuff with other names than my own, with initials, with no signature at all,—or his would have become a one name paper."

So lesson one is: never believe all attributions you read in a newspaper!

Miss Wells has been credited with authorship of both the tongue-twisting limericks cited above. Let's examine each claim separately.

Crewe at 2:2

An early claim for the 2:2 limerick is in a 1908 book, where "a lady named Sue" nearly misses her train. This and some other limericks are attributed to Miss Wells in the List of Sources.[47]

In the first edition of Langford Reed's 1924 book, many limericks had no attribution to an author. However, in subsequent editions he included the authorship of many limericks; presumably authors or those associated with them wrote in to claim parentage. The Crewe limerick was assigned to Bishop H.T. Foss (Anglican Bishop of Osaka, Japan). So far, so badly. Especially as Bishop H.J. Foss was probably meant.

Let's look at Wells's own works. In an article in 1903 she included the Typhoo variant as if it were not her own, because the next section starts: "I venture to quote one or two of my own," and we find in this such limericks as "There's a train at 4:4."

In her 1925 *Book of American Limericks*, she has a section titled "Anonymous Limericks." This includes "a young woman named Sue Who wanted to catch the 2:02."

In contrast to the above books, in her 1906 *Whimsey Anthology* there is a section headed "By Carolyn Wells," and the section concludes with her name. A version of the Typhoo limerick is included among the limericks in this section.

Miss Wells seems to me to be guilty of some very sloppy proofreading of her own books; there are several other instances in the above books where verses are both claimed to be by her and claimed to be anonymous.

If forced to come to a conclusion, I say she didn't write this one. However, she kept a huge pile of clippings of her verses of hers which were printed in U.S. and UK magazines and newspapers; if they still exist, someone might like to plow through them.

Tait at 8:8

Let's now turn to Tait and what he and his tête-à-tête ate at 8:8. An early claim for Wells is in the 1908 book mentioned in connection with the Crewe limerick. In the second and subsequent editions of Langford Reed's book, this limerick stands over the name Carolyn Wells. Reed also changed the rhyme name from Tate to Tait, which suggests that someone sent him some definitive information. An American book[48] published in 1945 also claimed authorship for her, and a 1946 review of this book in *Life* magazine[49] repeated the claim.

In her own books, we find exactly the same confusion as for Crewe: two which don't claim authorship, and one which does. The position of the verse in her 1903 magazine article suggests that she didn't write it.

What are we to make of this? Well, I've included these sections to show how confusing it can be to try to find the authorship and date of publication of any particular limerick. And by God I think I've succeeded.

I'm not saying these problems arose in the 1890s or are confined to them—I've just used this decade to draw attention to a problem which becomes increasingly frustrating for the historian as we get further and further away in time from the first outing of any particular limerick.

Current Affairs: 1898

Occasionally limericks are written about current events. Earlier we saw one about the opening of the Eiffel Tower in 1889. The following caught my attention:

> A lady once said to Herr Rontgen,
> When sitting beside him at luncheon,
> "The rest you'll amaze,
> If you turn on X-rays,
> And discover just what I've been munchin."[50]

(The dirty-minded can doubtless ascribe a secondary meaning to the verse, depending on what they think the lady might have been munching.)

A History of the Limerick: 1898

The Idler was an illustrated monthly magazine published from 1892 to 1911. In 1898 it published an eight-page overview of some aspects of the history of the limerick verse form, perhaps because it felt that the verse had by now a history. Titled "Nonsense Verses, New and Old," its accuracy left a lot to be desired.[51]

Truth: New Competitions, Same Old Problem

Truth continued to run limerick competitions in the 1890s. One problem I find with *Truth* is that it's not opaque enough, by which I mean that the show-through of print from the other side of the page is sometimes so great that it can substantially interfere with your ability to read the text you want to. This probably also upsets the OCR systems that scanning software uses.

I would like to examine a competition announced in *Truth* on August 11, 1898. After carefully explaining (yet again) exactly what a nonsense verse was, the puzzle editor concluded by saying that entries had to be in by August 22.

After the competition ended a variety of submissions were printed in the magazine, under the usual heading: "Assorted Specimens—Good and Otherwise."

However, for quite a while the winning entries were not printed. The editor mentioned that "In several cases I have had reason to doubt the originality of the verses sent to me in connection with this competition. This has involved correspondence which is not yet completed, and I must therefore postpone for one more week the announcement of the prize winner's name."

Finally, on October 6, the editor wrote:

> I am sorry to have to repeat what I stated last week and to say that several competitors sent in for this competition stanzas which they must have known were not original. The explanations I have been furnished with, I am bound to add, fail to fully satisfy me that the breach of the conditions laid down was made innocently. I am very loath to pillory the offenders by publishing their names in the page; but in calling attention to conduct which I consider indefensible I would again urge on all who take part in these competitions the necessity of doing so in a strictly fair and honorable way.[52]

The editor then awarded prizes to two of the decent souls who had contributed original entries.

The editor was quite right to upbraid those dishonest enough to submit ringers. I can see at least four myself. I presume there were more in the entries he did not print.

Although the editor did not actually shame the miscreants by unmasking their noms de competition, he did print the following comments during his search to uncover the truth:

OLD DUTCH.—Your "Nonsense Verse" is familiar to me. (September 1.)
VIRESCO.—The originality of your "Nonsense Verse" has been challenged. Are you ready to vouch for it? (September 15.)
PEAR JOHN.—Many thanks for your classical versions of two well-known Nonsense Verses. (September 22. Possibly refers to Tait limerick and an unknown other.)
VIRESCO.—This verse, I am assured, had already been seen in print. (September 29.)
VIRESCO.—The lines appeared in the Gentlewoman for January 14, 1893, over the signature of "Old China," and gained the Prize offered in that journal. (October 6; refers to Young Lady of Wilts/stilts/kilts.)

That VIRESCO, eh? The bastard wouldn't give in even when caught with his trousers down. OCR is very poor when searching *Truth*. The old-fashioned technique of actually reading the paper shows that Viresco entered earlier competitions, but I haven't yet been able to find his real name. I want to; the guilty should be shamed, even after all these years.

Profane Limericks: 1899

You may think it's a bit late to have a section on profanity in this work, but here I am using the word in its older, more literal sense of irreligious or irreverent behavior, originating as it does from the classical Latin "profanes," meaning "outside the temple."

In 1899 one G.L. MacKenzie got so fed up with Christianity that he penned and published a work titled *Brimstone Ballads and Other Verse*. It was subtitled *Bible Bosh; or Jingles of Christian Nonsense*, and for some strange reason it was seemingly passed over for review by the mainstream press. A handful of copies of this work still exist and the keen student of public profanity in limerick form will find 11 limericks inside, among other types of verse. The last stanza of the group reads:

> There once was the son of a ghost,
> Whom godly men pinned to a post;
> I don't say it's true.
> But priests say that you
> Have all to believe it—or roast![53]

That has the ring of truth about it, don't you think?

Conclusion

I shall conclude this decade by briefly commenting on how limericks seemed to spreading at this time, based on my observations.

1. A clean limerick is created by a private person, a professional writer or an employee of a newspaper. Both men and women were writing such verses.

2. The limerick is submitted to a newspaper competition, posted on spec to a humorous magazine, or just printed because it has been written in-house.

3. Other newspapers pick it up and reprint it. Typically the origin is one of the "funnies." There can be quite a number of reprintings, often many within a short time. Further "reprinting clumps" can occur subsequently in foreign countries, following arrival of a printed source in that country.

4. The limerick then typically disappears. Sometimes it reappears at random intervals separated by many years.

5. If printed in a book or an anthology, the limerick can go on to have a long life, often being stolen by successive anthologists or the editors of newspapers and magazines. It has usually lost any attribution of authorship, if it ever had one.

Dirty limericks had a quite different path in life. Printing in mainstream literature was not allowed. There seem to have been only a few privately printed books or magazines which contained them. I assume they were created exclusively by men, who then regaled other men with them at private clubs, at their places of work such as the Stock Exchange or newspaper offices, in university Common Rooms or at sports clubs. As the London magazine *Pick-Me-Up* put it on June 13, 1896: "Some of the current Limericks being only suitable for recitation when the gas is turned down and the girls looking the other way."

I also assume that these limericks had a considerable degree of memorability. I say this because they were probably passed from one man to another by word of mouth and would have to be remembered over long periods of time. An alternative method of transmission might have been via notebooks, or handwritten or typed selections bound together in some way. Oh, to be able to find such material—if it ever existed. On occasion private letters between good friends contained dirty limericks.

Over the years I have collected many examples of "the same limerick" in both clean and dirty versions. It is impossible to be sure in every case which came first, but I think it is certain some clean limericks were degraded and that some dirty limericks were cleaned up. So there was transfer between the two types, probably by men who knew both sorts and could tailor any particular limerick for the audience they happened to be speaking to at that moment.

CHAPTER 12

The 1900s
The Limerick Explodes—Again

Between 1900 and 1910, Queen Victoria died, the new King Edward had a potato named after him, Japan emerged as a world power, Albert Einstein told the world that $e = mc^2$, the first powered flight took off, and the *Wizard of Oz* was published.

One of the most amazing events in the history of the limerick occurred in the 1900s. I propose to devote an entire chapter to it.

The Great Limerick Competition Boom of 1907–8

The 1900s saw what is arguably the most unexpected and unbelievable event in the history of the limerick: competitions in which contestants had to create a last line to follow four lines given by the organizers. The incredible popularity of these competitions was on a scale which had never been seen before and almost certainly will never be seen again. For a year and a half it seemed that almost an entire nation was involved in creating the last lines of limericks and submitting them in the hope of winning prizes.

It was limerick production on an industrial scale. It started in the UK and spread round the English-speaking world.

What was even more astonishing was the colossal value of many of the prizes on offer—with a very small submission charge to enter the competition. This was in an age where lotteries were prohibited by law in the UK, football pools were some years away in the future, and television and radio competitions didn't exist.

The phenomenon was well described in newspapers worldwide at the time; some later books on limericks, such as Langford Reed's 1924 work, gave an overview of the outbreak and spread of limerick competition fever. In 2007 several articles marked the 100th anniversary of the outbreak of limerickitis. Some were accurate; some contained egregious mistakes.

Many of the ancillary events associated with this phenomenon are so interesting that I would like to describe them at great length; for example, how the events provoked suicides, resulted in at least one marriage, caused bankruptcies, caused a government enquiry into their legality and morality, allowed one winner to emigrate and become an authority on Canadian weeds, riled the Church, brought lawsuits from failed entrants, and engendered attempted bribery of competition judges via both cash and sexual favors.

But this book is about the development of the limerick verse form—not about the excitement, social upheaval, frustration and occasional calamity occasioned by the Great Limerick Competition Boom of 1907–8. I shall therefore concentrate on the task at hand. I do need to describe some aspects of the background of what was driving the event, so please bear with me.

Limerick Competitions Prior to 1907

A competition in a January 1907 issue of *London Opinion* was the spark which ignited the Great Limerick Competition Boom of 1907–8. This competition gave the first four lines of a limerick and the general public was invited to supply a fifth. Before we get to that, let's briefly look at limerick competitions which preceded it.

Competitions to create whole limericks

Competitions involving the creation of limericks prior to 1907 were not uncommon by any means. For example, competitions can be found in *Truth*, a London weekly newspaper, in 1880, 1881, 1887, 1897 and 1899. In all of these, some of which I have described earlier, contestants were invited to write a full limerick on any topic of their choice. The large number of entries printed in the sponsoring magazines showed that such competitions were popular.

In the early 1900s, competitions which required contestants to write whole limericks were quite common. A trawl through newspapers of the period will throw up many. Some asked for limericks on famous footballers, others on local places. Some papers ran regular competitions. Prizes were usually modest sums of money, rarely more than a guinea.

Not all competitions were open to the wider general public. Some were more restricted. For example, in 1903 in the small town of Winslow, "The 'Limerick' form of verse, which has caught on so much in magazines and comic papers lately, was made the means of amusement at a public competition held by the Mutual Improvement Society on Monday night. We quote a few of these 'Limericks.'"[1]

Seven undoubted gems using the rhyme word "Winslow" then followed. A few months later another meeting of the same society was reported:

> WINSLOW SOCIAL EVENING—On Monday the members of the Mutual Improvement Society gave a public "social" which was well attended. Among the items of amusement was a book title competition in which each person competing had to wear a design emblematic of the title of a book, which the audience had to guess. Miss J. Cripps and Miss Yeulett were the winners in this, and Master Illing for the design ("Robinson Crusoe"). Another competition was Limerick verses on "Japan." This was a keen contest, and with one exception all were sympathetic with Japan in her struggle against "The Bear." Miss E. Emerson took first prize.[2]

(The Russo-Japanese War began on February 8, 1904. Britain had entered an alliance with Japan in 1902 and there was much suspicion about Russia's intentions in Afghanistan, Persia, etc., which explains why the Mutual Improvement Society sympathized with Japan, even before the Dogger Bank Incident in October 1904, when Russian warships fired on British fishing boats.[3])

Competitions where only the first line was given

A competition in *Today* on the last day of 1898[4] gave the first line only. Announcing the winner three weeks later, the competition editor mentioned in passing how popular such contests were compared to other literary puzzles:

> For some reason or other the number of people who entered for Competition No. 52, a five-lined nonsense verse beginning "There was an old lady of Kew," was more than double the average. Consequently the classes are large. I regret to say the number of unclassed is still larger. It is somewhat difficult to award the prize when so many are good, but I think on the whole it should go to Miss Minnie G. Hopwood, 180, Church Street, Stoke Newington, N., and I shall forward to her a postal order for 10s. for the following
>
>> There was an old lady of Kew,
>> Who wanted to catch the 2.2;
>>   Said the porter, "Don't hurry,
>>   Or scurry, or flurry,
>> It's a minute or two to 2.2."[5]

Observant readers will remember a discussion in the last chapter about the provenance of this limerick. Looks like young Minnie was another chancer who played fast and loose with copyright laws and the concept of honesty.

This demonstrates one of the problems with competitions which ask for whole limericks, or those which give just a first line: plagiarism. I have come across many other such examples. Occasionally the miscreant is spotted, but usually he—or she—is not. Can judges be expected to have an encyclopedic knowledge of all limericks ever written?

In 1899, Boots Cash Chemists of Nottingham invited the public to enter four different competitions. The second offered a prize of £2 for "a nonsense rhyme of five lines on Spring Cleaning, beginning—'There was a young lady in Crewe.'" Competitors had to include a receipt for any cleaning product bought at any branch of Boots.[6]

Looking at contemporary newspapers shows that this type of limerick contest was both common and popular.

Competitions where the first four lines were given

Although this sort of competition became wildly popular via the *London Opinion*, it seems that virtually no one had ever thought of it before. I know of only one example of this type prior to 1907; that was in ads for B.D.V. cigarettes. These were produced by Godfrey Philips and Sons from the early 1900s until 1948. The brand name came from Boyd and Dibrell Virginia, who supplied the tobacco. I'm not sure how many of these last-line B.D.V. contests there were; I only know of two different first-four-lines.

The *London Opinion* Limerick Competition: 1907–8

London Opinion was a magazine which had started in 1903. It ran regular weekly literary competitions; one of these was to complete a story, the first part of which was given. Contestants had to paste the printed commencement of the story onto their postcard or paper entry. In other words, they had to buy the journal to enter; there was no entry fee. Prizes were typically a guinea.

London Opinion also ran limerick competitions before 1907. Full limericks were required, with readers being asked to describe famous people of the day in limerick form.[7] In one it asked readers to describe David Lloyd George. The winner of the one guinea prize wrote[8]:

> His brow is as broad as his smile;
> His eye is as bright as his style
>   His tongue is as smart
>   As his wit; and his heart
> Is as free as his face is from guile.

If only we had politicians of such moral probity around today!

In the January 5 issue of 1907, in addition to the weekly conclude-a-story competition, the journal included a drawing of a man in a dinner jacket seemingly warming his hands over a small fire of cigarettes, paper and spilled wine bottles. Either that, or he is throwing things onto a heap to get rid of temptation. Over this drawing stood the following text:

LIMERICK COMPETITION
A GUINEA FOR A LINE

We offer a prize of One Guinea for the best conclusion to the following Limerick. These *printed* lines must be sent:

> There was a young man of Portslade
> Who many New Year resolves made,
> He would lie less and drink less,
> Of evil things think less,

The winner was announced two weeks later, the last line being: "I've heard that before," Satan said.

Not a ripper in my opinion, but there we go.

Each subsequent week the *London Opinion* had a similar competition, illustrated by a drawing, and variously headed "Last Line of a Limerick Wanted," "Who will Complete This Limerick?" and so forth.

By January 26 it appeared that lots of entries had been sent in, since the prize was one guinea for the winner, and 10 crown consolation prizes.

February 2 saw more largesse being distributed; the usual guinea and 65 other prizes.

Public interest can be judged by this remark on February 9: "Our last-line-of-a-limerick has proved so vast a success, and the number of entries each week have grown so amazingly, that we have decided to increase the number of prizes to a proportionate ratio."

In the issue of February 16, the heading was "Five Pounds in Prizes for a Line," and there were "New Conditions for Completing our Unfinished Limericks." These included asking for sixpence to accompany each entry, as a postal order or stamps. It was also announced that Mr. G.L. Jessop would judge the competition.

In the issue of March 2, the rules were really laid down:

£12 10s. IN CASH PRIZES FOR A LINE
Ten Limerick Competitors Get Twenty-five shillings Each.

The Limerick Competition in which we set our readers the task of completing the fifth line of an unfinished "Limerick" week by week provides genuine opportunities for the exercise of skill and wit, both in neat rhyming and in conception of bright and fitting ideas, and in making money thereby.

The adjudication of the awards is entirely in the hands of Mr. Gilbert L

Jessop, the famous University cricketer and sporting writer, who has kindly consented to act as judge, and whose decisions must be regarded as final without appeal.

RULES.—(Which must be strictly complied with.)

    1. Competitors must send the four lines of the unfinished Limerick *with each attempt* in print, cut from this page and affixed to a sheet of paper, the completing line being written beneath the print in each case. Any number, up to ten, may be sent in on one sheet.

    2. Each attempt must also have sent with it a Postal Order for 6d. (*not* stamps), made payable to LONDON OPINION and crossed "&Co."

    3. No one competitor may send in more than ten attempts for any one week's competition.

    4. Envelopes must be marked "Limerick" in the top left-hand corner, and addressed "Competition Editor, LONDON OPINION, 36 Southampton St., Strand, W.C."

    5. Entries must reach the offices not later than the first post, Tuesday, March 5th. The award will appear in the issue dated March 16th (published on March 14th).

Competitors are advised that the merely obvious idea, or the line which does not rhyme and scan thoroughly, stands no chance, as among the many replies there is always a good proportion of lines of undoubted skill and cleverness. But the vast numbers who possess wit and literary ability, which at present they are not turning into money, we say—"Here is your chance!"

The advice to competitors as to how to write "winners" changed a little soon after that, the suggestion being: "Competitors are reminded that the better their lines rhyme and scan, the better chance they have of being selected to participate in the prize, though few will be required to be told that humor and originality count also. If too obvious, an idea may lose its chance by being seized on by many people."

Initially the whole of the money received from competitors, "without any deduction whatsoever for expenses or anything else," formed the prize money. At first it was divided among the ten best lines. As the prize money grew, more and more winners were rewarded. The prize money for the June 29 competition was £844 and 12 shillings. This equates to 33,784 sixpences, so you might think that that is how many entries there were. Actually, since the paper had started deducting 5 percent of the entry fees for overheads by this time, there were probably 35,562 entries.

In the same issue, the magazine justly crowed: "THE NATION'S NEW PASTIME ... London Opinion has set a new fashion throughout the United Kingdom—'Limerick-last-lining!' In the Literary Competition we had the pleasure of inventing, and respecting which our contemporaries are exhibiting the sincerest form of flattery."

In 1907 a loaf of bread cost 2d. and the average UK wage was perhaps

£70 per year.⁹ This latter figure might be a little low; in his 1924 book Langford Reed commented that "The author knows of a young Civil Service clerk who ran a business of this kind [supplying 'sure-to-win' last lines for the 1907–8 limerick contests] during his ample leisure hours and who, in less than six months, cleared a profit of more than £200—or nearly three times his salary during that period!"

Most of the four-line starter limericks were what you might call "general"; that is, they were not about anyone in particular, though sometimes they were about people in the news. These often led to what we might call "better quality limericks." However, in such cases, unless you know the back story, the last lines are incomprehensible. A good example is the following from the *London Opinion* of May 4, 1907:

> A Nigger, unknown in "Who's Who,"
> Masqueraded as "Prince Makaroo."
> But the law very soon
> Caught this picturesque coon,

Winning last lines included:

> Taking "cod" into Grimsby won't do.
> And cut short his bluff—and hair too.
> And he's nae hair apparent the noo.
> Like me, he's a sentence to do.

The back story is that a con man tried to mulct the mayor of Grimsby for 40 or 50 shillings. The mayor promptly had him arrested. During his trial he was described as: "Thomas Makaroo, a comedian." He said he was an Abyssinian prince, a claim which caused laughter in the court. Known locally as Khaki Jim, he had "previous" for wandering around Grimsby in military uniform while wearing a self-awarded VC. As might be imagined, the newspapers had a field day reporting the event; even the *Times* mentioned it. The story is also told in several books; it's amusing and easy to find.

The origin of the London Opinion *limerick competition— and the effect it had on the magazine*

In no book describing the history of the limerick have I seen an account of how and why the great limerick competition boom came into being, or what effect the competitions had on the *London Opinion*. However, the information exists, in great detail, in the autobiography of the man who started the ball rolling: the editor of the magazine, Lincoln Springfield.¹⁰ It was an advertising gimmick, designed simply to increase circulation, and it worked: "The competition lifted the circulation of *London Opinion* from 30,000 to 160,000, and the contents of the paper having been vastly improved, nine-tenths of this new circulation was retained when the limerick craze, in the course of a year or two, died down."

Competitions in other newspapers and journals

As the *London Opinion* so clearly remarked, imitation is the sincerest form of flattery. Solicitor Mr. Scott Duckers, in a pamphlet published by the National Anti-Gambling League around November 1907, said that over 200 papers were running "Limerick" competitions.[11]

Some of the prizes were organized by the papers themselves. Most paid out the entry money submitted, after typically skimming off 5 or 10 percent for administration costs. The *London Opinion* also did this after a few months of paying out all the money submitted, commenting: "So great has become the cost of this competition, necessitating as it has the engaging of additional offices and extra sorters, checkers, etc., that henceforth 5 per cent must be deducted from the prizes to cover expenses."

Other competitions were essentially advertisements in which the competitor had to buy samples of the product and submit a proof of purchase.

The scale of the contests

The number of limerick last lines sent in to competitions in 1907 and 1908 can be worked out approximately. I estimate that over 15 million last lines were submitted in the UK. The greatest number in a month was probably in October 1907, when just over two million entries accompanied by sixpenny postal orders were submitted, along with an unknown number using vouchers and other forms of entry payment.

The Prizes

Cash was probably the king of the prizes. Talking of which, I am sure that my mathematically minded readers can spot the flaw in the following: "One of the most interesting modern Limerick competitors is said to live at Gotham, in the shape of an old gentleman, who sends in an immense quantity of last lines (with postal orders) to the paper of his choice each week, so that, if he wins, the prize may be a big one."[12]

(It is a joke, by the way; it appeared in *Punch*. At least, I think it's a joke.)

My favorite comment about cash prizes is one which demonstrates the high moral tone taken by those who opposed limerick last-lining. After describing a competition in *Answers*, which had attracted 85,000 entries at sixpence a go, Mr. John Hawke of the National Anti-Gambling League remarked: "The fortunate winners, of whom there were twenty, received £80 a-piece, I think, four times as much as Milton received for 'Paradise Lost.'"[13]

Mr. Samuda

The pinnacle of prizes was probably those offered by one Mr. J. Samuda in a series of contests. This is certainly the opinion of the promoter; the full-page ad proclaiming his first competition in the *London Opinion* was headed in large letters:

THE GREATEST OF ALL LIMERICKS

The word "limericks" was used colloquially at the time to mean limerick last-line competitions. For a while it also meant a sixpenny postal order; people would ask for a "Limerick" at the post office counter and the assistant would know exactly what was required.

The prize was eye-watering: "Mr. Samuda will pay £3 a week for life to the actual winner.... Try and realize what £3 a week would mean to you.... If you go on working it would double your income at a stroke."

Mr. Samuda went on to explain the reason for his largesse:

> Mr. Samuda is the well-known manufacturer of the celebrated "Avoca" Cigars, Cigarettes, etc., and he has recently placed on the market a new Virginia Cigarette, the "Traylee" Cigarette, which is sold in boxes of 100 at 2s. 6d. As all readers will understand, it is most costly to successfully place new Cigarettes on the market. Most firms spend tens of thousands of pounds before they secure regular sales. After careful consideration Mr. Samuda decided to establish this Limerick Competition for the express purpose of bringing the "Traylee" Cigarettes prominently before the notice of the British public.

The competition was not quite the same as the normal one of sending in a sixpenny postal order with each entry. What happened here was that the entrant had to submit a postal order for two shillings and eight pence. Most of this went toward buying 100 Traylee cigarettes, and twopence went toward the postage of these cigarettes to the entrant.

The limerick to be completed:

> That the Traylee's the best cigarette
> Is a tip that you cannot regret;
> And in buying I'll mention
> There's three pounds a week pension—

And the winning last line:

> "Two good 'lines'—one you give, one you get."[14]

Doubtless buoyed by increased sales of his cigarettes, Mr. Samuda announced a second competition:

> A FREEHOLD FURNISHED COUNTRY HOUSE, A HORSE AND TRAP, AND £2 A WEEK GUARANTEED FOR LIFE.

Mr. Samuda's largesse was widely reported in newspapers, presumably gaining him much-appreciated free advertising. The house, incidentally, was to be built where the winner wanted it. I have no idea if it was built, or if it still exists today, but the second ad in many newspapers began with the words: "Residents in this district should note that Samuda's Limerick First Prize House will be built in this locality if the winner is resident and desires it."[15] A neat trick to convey a sense that the winner might well be local and that you should therefore get your entry in ASAP.

The same conditions applied as before. The limerick to be completed:

> There's a Cigarette commencing with "T,"
> Its full name is Irish, "Traylee";
>   It's Samuda's, the best,
>   Of fine leaf from the West

The winning line this time:

> It's not "tipped" but "runs first" believe me.

Keen to extract maximum publicity from the winner, Mr. Samuda immediately launched a third limerick competition—and included in its newspaper ads a fulsome description of the lucky gentleman receiving the previous prize, along with a letter of thanks from the man himself.

Mr. Samuda's third competition offered a thousand pounds for completing the following:

> Unique is the prize so say we,
> And not less unique is 'Traylee';
>   You've no loss to repine
>   If you send a last line

The winning line, announced on March 10, 1908:

> "You've one end in view—so have we!"

I don't know what you think of this last line—but I do know what a contemporary writer thought; it "moved his respectful astonishment." After describing the competition, he gave the last line, and then continued:

I confess that I am entirely unable to conjecture what merit the judges discerned in this feeble production to render it worthy of the first—or, for that matter, of the second, or third, or even a consolation prize. It has neither point, humor, nor wit. The very scansion of the line halts somewhat, unless you lay artificial stress on certain syllables; and, moreover, the repetition of the "we" constitutes a vicious rhyme. It may, perhaps, be retorted that the goodness or otherwise of a last line is purely a matter of opinion, and that if the judges were of opinion that this particular line was the best sent in, that is a complete and sufficient answer. Possibly. But are these judges—(three gentlemen of considerable literary standing)—really prepared to stake their critical reputation on such an award? Is Mr. Mostyn Pigott, for instance—who is an acknowledged expert on smart verse—prepared to declare that he honestly considers this line a good one, or that there were not hundreds of better lines sent in for the competition? Are he and his two colleagues prepared to say that they took any serious pains to examine and adjudicate upon the bulk of the entries? Like Brutus, I pause for a reply; and I imagine I am just about as likely to get one.[16]

Undaunted by such remarks, Mr. Samuda plowed on. His fourth and apparently final competition had a first prize consisting of a "Freehold Furnished Country House" and £2 a week for life to keep it going. Ads contained a picture of the house, with a lady playing croquet, and a Pekingese dog in attendance. The limerick to be completed:

> There was a young man of Soho,
> To Brighton he wanted to go,
>   So he sent a last line
>   For the "Traylee" so fine

Like Mr. Samuda's previous competition, the result ruffled a few feathers; the following is from *The Sphere*:

The winning line ran:—
> The best draw through a paper I know.

Which is not even a pun as the prize was not offered by a newspaper but by a commercial company.

I find it very difficult to believe that certain of my distinguished literary friends were adjudicators—Mr. Greenhough Smith of *The Strand Magazine*, Mr. Mostyn Pigott of *The World*, and Mr. G.B. Burgin, the well-known novelist—should really think this to have been the finest imaginable line or that it should or that it should even have been the best that was received in response to the competition. My correspondent tells me that his line to complete the verse ran:

> And won a week two quid pro quo.

He does not deny that there may have been hundreds of equally good or even better solutions I at least am inspired by his—but he does protest, and I think justly, against the possibility of such a line as—

> The best draw through a paper I know

having been the best in actual merit of all the contributions. The probable explanation is that the three literary gentlemen that I have named did not see one-quarter of the replies, and that these replies were sifted through less competent hands. It is this that makes the thing an utter gamble of a most deplorable kind. It is, of course, equally deplorable that the capacity for versification among the "masses" is at so low an ebb.[17]

This resulted in the reviewer metaphorically getting a good kicking since he hadn't actually bothered to find out the facts before putting pen to paper. Some weeks later he wrote a more reasoned column, but notice how he still managed to end on a nasty self-justifying note:

Mr. G.B. Burgin asks me to state that he was not one of the three adjudicators in the recent Samuda limerick competition. It would seem that it was another of the many limerick competitions in which he adjudicated. In connection with this limerick question I have received several letters pointing out that I had missed the real point of the winning line in that Samuda limerick competition, the reference being to smoke drawing through paper. One of the adjudicators assures me moreover that the line sent to me by a friend as his suggested answer was repeated by a hundred competitors, whereas the line that won the prize stood quite alone. I am still, however, left regretting that cultivated and capable men should have allowed themselves to intervene in these competitions. I am glad to know in any case that such competitions are now practically dead, and I hope that before substitutes are found the law will intervene to put down all forms of newspaper gambling.[18]

The Antipodes

Newspapers in Australia and New Zealand reported on the limerick craze occurring in England. For example, a Tasmanian paper wrote in June 1907:

The latest craze is the construction of that amusing form of rhyming called the Limerick. Wherever one goes now—society at homes, clubs, hotels, seaside boarding houses—one finds little groups and syndicates busy working out Limericks, or, rather, adding the last lines to "uncompleted Limericks." Even sweethearts are heard in conservatories saying to each other, not the customary sugary inanities, but 'There was a young lady of Lynn—what are some of the words that rhyme—din, shin, win, or what about sin?' We are all poets now![19]

In September 1907, a Sydney newspaper said it had inaugurated a limerick competition along the usual last-line lines, titled "Money for Brains." Interestingly, in Australia, for some years at least, these contests were not judged to be lotteries. Doubtless those interested in such legal matters can find out more.

Probably the most remarkable prizes given Down Under came from

Chapter 12. The 1900s

the Laxo-Tonic Company. The product they peddled, a gelatin capsule containing several herbs or natural products, came in little wooden boxes. It was a "unique combination of laxative and tonic principles," hence the name. One testimonial claimed that "Laxo-Tonic removed an unsightly batch of pimples from my face, which for two months had resisted every possible remedy." Apparently it would also "chastise a lazy liver," cure complicated stomach troubles, relieve pains between the shoulders, and alleviate the symptoms of acute rheumatism.

You wouldn't think such a wonderful product would need any advertising, but seemingly it did. In early November 1907, ads appeared inviting the public to submit whole limericks which not only praised the product, but also included its name. No entry fee was required, but each entry had to be accompanied by a wrapper from a tenpence ha'penny packet, or two entries for a wrapper from the 1/6 packet. The adverts stated: "This competition is for the purpose of getting Limericks for advertising purposes, and Limericks are judged according to their value for this purpose. Competitors will do well to bear this in mind, and to make their Limericks rational, and not to submit verses recommending the Pills for Bubonic on account of the fact that the word rhymes with Laxo-Tonic."

In other words, this was not a last-line competition but a "write a whole limerick on a given topic" competition.

The first prize was £3, with several runner-up prizes, totaling 10 pounds. This obviously attracted enough entries for a second competition to be run, in which the first prize remained at a staggeringly modest £3. Over 2,500 entries poured in. Ads for the product appeared regularly in newspapers along with entries already submitted.

The third competition, however, went stratospheric, with a first prize of "a 7000-MILE TOUR From Sydney to the South Sea Islands, New Zealand, Tasmania and Victoria Return. Six Weeks' Trip, embracing 16 Ports of Call." First class, too!

The fourth competition outdid even that, with a first prize of "an 18,000 MILE TRIP to Brisbane, New Britain, Philippine Islands, China, Japan, Strait Settlements, Penang, Ceylon, return via West Australia, South Australia and Victoria." Naturally it was First Class, and estimated to take 11 weeks without any break of journey. Doubtless readers will be agog to know the gem that won this prize. Well, here it is:

> No need any more to be ill,
> Because there's a wonderful Pill,
> Ever-growing in fame,
> Laxo-Tonic its name
> The summit of medical skill.
> —J. Wallace, Sandford, Stock Exchange Club, Adelaide, S.A.

Presumably feeling that nothing could top that, the fifth competition reverted to a first prize which was the same as the third. A sixth competition could only manage a first prize of a boat trip to New Zealand, in a competition which finished in October 1909. Then, presumably guessing correctly that the fad had run its course, there were no more limerick competitions.

What eventually happened to the company and its wonder product I have no idea.

America

American newspaper readers were well aware of the limerick mania sweeping the UK. It was often commented on, and the number of entries and the prize monies were faithfully reported.[20] However, similar contests were slow to materialize in the States, and prizes seemed modest.

One suggestion I have read to explain this is that limerick last-lining "embodied lottery features which made it illegal under US law."[21] I'm not an expert on U.S. lottery law of a century ago, but I think this referred to the payment needed to enter, and the illegality of this action under postal laws.[22] Free entry seemed de rigueur in U.S. contests, and I assume that lack of submission fees from competitors would have curtailed the value of prizes which could be offered. Another suggested reason was the Knickerbocker Crisis in Wall Street in mid-October 1907, brought about by bankers attempting to corner the market in shares of the United Copper Company.[23] This attempt failed, causing panic, bankruptcies and a loss of confidence throughout the country. The result was a lengthy economic contraction, at a time when there was already a recession.[24]

Last-lining was certainly carried out by several newspapers. For example, *The Washington Times*, in September 1907, had last-line competitions. The initial verse to be completed was about the local baseball team's eternal but misplaced optimism about the following season. "Several thousand suggestions by Washington poets and near-poets" poured in. Ten bucks went to a lucky winner.

The New York Evening World ran a series of last-liners starting in October 1907. Each day three winners received $5, $3 and $2.

Magazines such as *McClure's* and *Pearson's* in May, June and July 1908 carried limerick contests advertising "Old English Curve Cut."[25] This article was not, as I initially assumed, a delectable marmalade. After reading that it could be smoked, it became clear that it was actually a product of the American Tobacco Company. Each month a different starting four lines were given. Local newspapers often commented whenever a local person won anything. For example, a Miss Howard, of West Randolph, Vermont, received $2 for a winning last line. The prizes for the three months aggregated $3,000 in cash and $750 in presents.[26]

Pantasote

All of which brings us to Pantasote. From Greek roots, the name meant "to serve all purposes." It was an imitation leather produced in New York. Cheaper than real leather, it came in several colors and was widely used in tents, awnings, automobile seats, railway carriage seats, upholstery and so on. The manufacturers claimed it was "waterproof, greaseproof, stain-proof and germproof. Does not rot, peel or crack. Is not affected by heat or cold, and is not inflammable." It could also resist exposure to gasoline and oils.

Despite all these wonderful properties, the material apparently needed advertising. The chosen vehicle was a limerick competition, starting on October 1, 1907, and running until January 10, 1908.

At first each competitor had to submit a whole limerick, and some entries were used in subsequent ads:

> A lady who lives down in Me.
> Left some Pantasote out in the re.
> Said she, "Tis all wet,
> And ruined I'll bet!"
> But she looked for the damage in ve.[27]

However, this did not generate the response required, so the rules were changed. It became a last-line contest. Nine "four-liners" were created and printed in a booklet, which contained cuts of the Pantasote-covered furniture that contestants could win, along with a sample of Pantasote itself. The first print run consisted of 150,000 booklets; they were sent free to anyone who asked for one. I have been unable to find a copy of this booklet, although images of the cover and opening pages can be found online.[28]

A 10th incomplete four-liner appeared in newspapers and magazines:

> Said the pretty and thrifty young bride,
> "To housekeep will now be my pride—
> With a couch and some chairs
> All of Pantasote wares—"

Competitors could thus submit last lines for any of these 10 partial limericks, and enter for free as many times as they liked. The only stipulation was that each entry had to be submitted separately.

The response was such that the advertising company received nearly one million entries. This necessitated opening a new, temporary department, in which a large staff labored for four and a half months reading, sorting, eliminating and classifying prior to the meeting of the judges. The four judges were Carolyn Wells, Marie Nehlig, Gelett Burgess, and Oliver Hertford. All were well known at the time, and at least three wrote limericks.

Several people sent in as many as 250 postcards, and one determined (or deranged) individual sent in 473. I am a little surprised at this; the prizes were ... well, not that incredible. The ads read: "$2,500 for a line to complete a limerick." So far so good, but the largesse was to be distributed in 600 prizes. One ad read: "[prizes] consisting of fine furniture, hand made illuminated tooled leather table mats, handsome books, 100 annual subscriptions to *Harper's Bazar*, etc..". So obviously there were not 600 prizes at $4.17 each ... but still.

Contemporary newspaper articles stated that the 10 winning last lines had been published in the May 1908 issue of *Harper's Bazar*. I have examined several online copies of this issue and as yet have found nothing. Advertising pages and inserts are often removed from magazines when they are stored or bound, so perhaps that explains my lack of success.

Miscellany

Some folk seemingly did not have the wherewithal to actually enter these competitions, but were clearly influenced by them. For example, a 1907 newspaper reported:

THE BLIND MAN AND HIS LIMERICK

Limericking seems to have invaded the world of mendicancy. On Monday morning in South London a sightless ancient mariner was being led about by a small boy. The story of his misfortune was told in a limerick inscribed on a card hung round his neck, thus:

> "Through a boiler that bursted at sea,
> When I had just turned twenty-three,
>   I am blind as a bat,
>   And poor as a rat,
> Please help me good folks who can see."[29]

Others were clearly outraged by limerick last-lining. Groups such as the National Vigilance Society and the National Anti-Gambling League, plus quite a few rabid vicars, wrote pamphlets, gave lectures, or sent letters to the newspapers to express their condemnation and explain why they felt the way they did. For example, in September 1907, a Reverend

Doctor Horton made "a scathing denunciation of the prevalent Limerick madness." He concluded that "the drift into insipidity and silliness were provoked by love of money, and that this would be a proper limerick to describe the situation:

> There was a great country of old,
> Which was ruined, dishonored and sold.
>   You ask how she fell.
>   The legions of hell
> Bought the Press, to seduce her, with gold."[30]

I wonder if the good doctor understood the irony of using a limerick to condemn—er—limericks. The legions of hell ... where they are today?

The rhythm of limericks passed into daily speech. In an article titled "The Limerick Lilt," *The Daily Express* reported (a little tongue-in-cheek but probably with more than an element of truth) that people were using short sing-song sentences in everyday exchanges. Those who had the disease worst used whole limericks to say, for example, to a waitress:

> I regret very much to complain,
> But the tea is much weaker than rain,
>   And the cook hasn't learnt
>   To make toast—this is burnt.
> You must ask her to try it again.[31]

Another newspaper commented:

THE CRAZE SPREADS TO THE BUILDING TRADE

The "Limerick" craze is responsible for sundry notice-board effusions in London. One of these runs as follows:

> This building estate, you must know,
> Has been let by J——and Co.
>   They've let this choice piece
>   On a long building lease,
> And smart villas will soon be on show.[32]

How good were the "limericks" produced by these competitions?

The answer to this question has to be "not very," inasmuch as few if any have made it into the public stock of limericks, either verbally or in printed form. It has certainly been claimed that some were good; for example, the following was written by the Australian poet John Shaw Neilson for a 1907 limerick contest:

> They were hanging a man up at Bright
> He had been a temperance light.
> When they showed him the rope,
> He said "I do hope
> That it isn't inclined to get tight."

It has appeared in several books, mainly those about Neilson. But it is *not* a last line limerick; the contest was to write a limerick using the name of a country town in Australia. (If anyone could have done with winning a monetary prize it was Mr. Neilson; he was a hard-up manual laborer for much of his life.)

Perhaps the following comment is a suitable one with which to finish this section: "The prize-competition nuisance, however, was responsible for one extraordinary incident. A very famous Victorian man of letters was a constant competitor under an assumed name in these tournaments, but never succeeded in gaining a prize. He consoled himself, however, by the reflection that, in view of the quality of the prize contributions, his consistent failure proved that his brain had not given way."[33]

A suggestion as to why "last-line limericks" are not very good

There are perhaps two main reasons for the "poorness" of even winning last lines. The first is that many last lines seem to me to have been "overworked" and are too polished. They often contain labored puns. By definition they were aimed at winning a prize—and most of those we find in contemporary newspapers had done just that. This made them "prize-limericks" or "show-limericks." Indeed, an analogy could be made with prizewinning fruit and vegetables; they are fruit and they are vegetables, but the 28-foot-long carrot and the half-pound sprout are probably inedible, which is really the main purpose of food. I think the best limericks, like the best fruit and veg, are probably the misshapen ones which have real flavor and character.

I think a second reason is that many good limericks start life with the last line being created first, which is the opposite of how these verses were created. And the initial four lines of competition verses never really seem to contain anything that grips the reader; these lines are just there to provide the subject matter.

The End

As *The Pall Mall Magazine* put it: "The limerick craze died a natural death because the majority of 'last liners' grew weary of getting nothing for their sixpence."[34]

Conclusion

The phenomenon of last-lining probably caused the limerick verse form to become better known worldwide than it had ever been before or has ever been since. In a way this is somewhat perverse, since the limericks created were not very good.

Chapter 13

The 1910s
The Limerick Does Its Bit

The 1910s opened with the death of the British King and ended with the deposing of the German Kaiser. In between was the First World War, which put a bit of a crimp into the general jollity of the time.

Because the War dominated the decade, a military theme is as suitable as any for this chapter. The first reference is interesting in that it shows one mechanism by which limericks were spreading: soldiers were singing them in India.

The next two references show how the limerick did its bit during the conflict, cheering up the Allied troops. The fact that one of the books was being sold to raise money for soldiers shows that the editors of the book (both newspapermen) believed that the public liked limericks enough to buy the book in large numbers. They did; it ran to a second edition.

German Erotic Folklore

Let's start off with a colossal German study of erotic folklore. The seventh annual volume was published in 1910 and it had the wonderfully catchy title of:

> ANTHROPOPHYTEIA
> Jahrbücher
> für
> Folkloristische Erhebungen und Forschungen
> zur
> Entwicklunggeschichte der geschlechtlichen Moral

Underneath this were an impressive number of editors' names and qualifications (including, I notice, one Prof. Dr. Sigmund Freud of the K.K. Universität in Vienna).

This volume contained a section titled "Englische Volkleider aus

Indien." This included three limericks, among other verse, probably collected from British soldiers in India. Scholarly explanations were given in German. The three limericks:

> There was once an old king of Siam,
> Who said: For women I don't care a damn.
> You may think it odd o' me,
> But I prefer sodomy.
> They call me a bugger: I am.

> There was a young man of Natal,
> Who slept with a Hottentot gal,
> Said she: You're a sluggard;
> Said he: You be buggered,
> I want to fuck slow and I shall.

> There was a good curate at Eltham,
> Who never fucked women, but felt 'em.
> In the lanes he would linger
> Playing stink finger;
> And when he got home he smelt 'em.[1]

The following year saw the publication of the eighth annual volume, and again we find three limericks:

> Englische Soldatenlieder aus Zentralindien.
> Mitgeteilt von Dr. Susruta II.

> There was an old man named Skinner,
> Who asked a girl out for dinner;
> At a quarter to nine they sat down to dine;
> At half past nine it was in her—
> The dinner, not Skinner!

> Anhang zum "Limerick," den König von Siam betreffend:

> Then up spake the Dey of Algiers,
> Who was fat and well stricken in years;
> There may be some joy in the arse of a boy;
> But I prefer women.—Loud cheers.

> A well-bred young man of Salamanca
> Caught crabs, clap, pox and soft chancre.
> The whole of the four he caught from one whore,
> So he sent her a post-card to thank her.[2]

All of these limericks have appeared in anthologies over the years. The Natal and Eltham verses first made a printed appearance in *The Pearl*, August 1879, so these two limericks were being "sung" 30 years after their first printing. It is difficult to say whether officers or privates were the source; the collector does not say.

The Book of William: November 1914

Shortly after the start of World War I, the work of that fine Englishman Edward Lear was pressed into the service of his country. A propaganda book appeared which was heavily based on his drawings and limericks, 22 of them being revised to degrade Kaiser Wilhelm.[3] Only a handful of copies exist today. Looking at my own copy, it's easy to see why; poor quality paper and board and poor construction.

Comparing a page from this book to its progenitor will give a flavor of the work. Anyone wishing to read the whole book can do so online courtesy of the State Library of Victoria.

The Book of Limericks: August 1916

There is a subset of limerick books which are produced for a charitable cause or to promote a local event. Such books are typically typewritten and stapled together. The verses contained therein are usually written specially for the book; they are often poor, although some do achieve an unexpected height.

Quite different from most such books was one published in 1916[4]:

THE BOOK OF
LIMERICKS
A COLLECTION OF THE MOST FAMOUS RHYMES
OF THIS TYPE IN THE WORLD
FROM THE EARLIEST AGES TO THE PRESENT TIME,
TOGETHER WITH MANY
NEW ONES, BEING THE RESULT OF A COMPETITION INAUGURATED
IN THE *DAILY EXPRESS* ON BEHALF OF ITS CHEERY FUND
FOR SAILORS AND SOLDIERS
By TAURUS and ORION
FIRST FOLIO EDITION (*warranted to become rare*)
1916
WITH ILLUSTRATIONS *by* FAMOUS ARTISTS

Among other things, the preface stated:

"The book itself is the result of a competition in the *Daily Express*. 14,361 Limericks were received, fully three-quarters of which were duplicates of popular favorites. With the exception of those from Edward Lear's book, all the old favorites were included.... Only a few Limericks on current topics will be found, as most of these, being of little permanent interest, would soon require explanatory footnotes—a practice we abhor.... Excluded, of course, are those

Chapter 13. The 1910s

There once was a Man, Kaiser Will, who seldom, if ever, stood still;
He ran up and down with a horrible frown,
And his ideas of culture were *nil.*

Picture from *The Book of William*, Anon., Frederick Warne, London, November 1914.

There was an Old Man on a hill,
Who seldom, if ever, stood still;
He ran up and down, in his Grandmother's gown,
Which adorned that Old Man on a hill.

Picture from *The Book of Nonsense*, Edward Lear, Routledge & Warne, London, November 1861.

which offend good manners by reason of their Rabelaisian tendency.... This book contains many amusing and audacious rhymes which appear for the first time in this book; and it is not too much to hope that in the midst of the Empire's mighty struggle it will serve to lighten these dark days a little."

For one shilling and sixpence the purchaser got a total of 765 limericks, with quite a few of them illustrated. As the preface indicated, many indeed were *very* old favorites, and despite the injunction against Lear, two of his verses somehow slipped in along with an improved version of a third.[5] The following give a flavor of the work; one or two have a rather philosophical feel, don't you think?

> THERE was an old man of Dumbarton
> Whom nothing on earth could dishearten.
>   When his daughter went blind
>   He said, "Never mind;
> There ain't much to see in Dumbarton."

> A MAN to a maiden so Fair
> Said, "Pray give me a lock of your hair."
>   She said, with a stare,
>   "Sir, are you aware
> That these curls cost five shillings a pair?"

> THERE was a young man who would Growl
> When the visiting team made a foul;
>   But if during the game
>   The home team did the same
> He would utter a jubilant howl.

> I GATHER that beer is a Juice
> Which a soothing effect can produce.
>   Great contentment it brings,
>   But, like most other things,
> We should strongly condemn its abuse.

> SAID a lady reporter in Kent—
> While searching for notes—to a gent,
>   "Do people round here
>   Often die?"—with a leer.
> He replied, "Only once"; and she went.

> JONES had a night out in Sept.,
> The rest he could never rem.
>   It turned to Oct.
>   Before he was s.,
> But he felt quite himself in Nov.

> THERE was an old bore of Torbay
> Who would telephone, "What did you say?"
>   When assured, "I said nought,"
>   He would cry, "So I thought;
> But all doubt is now taken away!"

Despite the comment that "only a few Limericks on current topics will be found, as most of these, being of little permanent interest, would soon require explanatory footnotes," the ones that were included are today of historical interest, although some probably do need an explanatory footnote:

Chapter 13. The 1910s

> IN a story the officers tell
> The Chaplain one night had a sell.
>   To the sentry outside
>   "I'm the Chaplain," he cried;
> "Pass, Charlie," said Tommy, "all's well."

(Try Charlie Chaplin. A "sell" means being sold a joke or being made the butt of a joke; a contrivance or fiction by which a person is deceived or disappointed.)

> SOME ladies were making Munitions
> Under fearfully rigid conditions.
>   In order to cough
>   They must ask for time off
> And to sneeze they must get up petitions.

> AN Anzac there was from down Under
> Who filled his companions with wonder.
>   In the worst cannonade
>   He was quite undismayed,
> And said he preferred it to thunder.

The book ran to a second edition. Those of us who bought it in the hope of finding some "acknowledgement of any invasion of copyright in our next editions"—in other words the identification of authors—were doomed to disappointment. The second edition was exactly the same as the first.

Most reviews of this charitable book predictably took a charitable view of it. Not quite so *The Spectator*. The text started off with a long description of the history of the limerick. The contents of the book were then described. Quite a few verses were cited and commented on, mainly unfavorably. The review then ended somewhat snippily: "But these gems [Khartoum; Syndicate], few and far between, only serve to emphasize the literary deterioration and vulgarization of the Limerick brought about by journalistic competitions."[6]

(Come on, *Spectator*. I'm as critical as the next man, but 42 and a half limericks for one penny, many illustrated—with all proceeds going to the lads risking life and limb for King and Country in the bloodiest war ever fought—has got to be a bargain. What more do you want?)

The review resulted in several letters being sent to the paper on matters limerickal. One was commented on as follows:

> A propos of our article on "Limericks" which appeared last week, a correspondent sends us a delightful piece of nonsense metaphysics in the form of a Limerick:—
>
> > There was an old man of Cadiz
> > Who affirmed that life is what it is,
> > For he early had learnt

> If it were what it weren't
> It could not be that which it is.⁷

It has been said that in this verse: "The versatile author Anon has defined the elusive term 'life'—whose definition great biologists have discreetly sidestepped."⁸

A tongue-in-cheek remark or the truth? Readers who are biologists or philosophers might care to comment. All I know of the author is that he was a friend of John St. Loe Strachey.⁹

A Final Conclusion

The First Century: 1820–1920

I believe that limericks started life in the 1820s as illustrated verses for children. Like the little lads and lasses they entertained, they had a simple outlook on life. Like children themselves they slowly grew in complexity, bit by bit becoming noticed by the adult world. In the early 1860s they were like teenagers entering puberty. A sudden mental growth spurt increased their vocabulary and the form and structure of the language they used. Their imagery became expansive, poetic and memorable. Some reveled in puns. Some experimented with sex. It can be argued that the creation of the dirty limerick was a pivotal moment in its success, because people liked them.

Suddenly limericks had friends everywhere: in print, in parties, in songs. And not just in England; they became world citizens. They became so well known about town that these poetic tearaways acquired a nickname, goodness knows exactly how, where or when: Limericks. Then, like young adults, from the 1870s onward they developed their own individual and idiosyncratic lives. Some flirted with philosophy, some with religion. Others took the road into politics. Some went into advertising. A goodly number become fine upstanding examples of humor, of twisting wordplay and wondrous mental images. Many, of course, preferred the dark side of life, reveling in the foulest of thoughts. All of them entertained people in so many ways: in competitions, in raising money for military charities, and by simply making people laugh out loud. A singular achievement for such a small verse.

The Second Century: 1920–2020

The limerick swept into the second century of its existence with a competition which saved a New York newspaper from bankruptcy. A mid-century competition to publicize a film had a Pacific island as a prize. It swept out of its second century with a competition which awarded the future prime minister of the United Kingdom a thousand pounds for writing an obscene limerick about the president of Turkey.

Following the relaxation of censorship laws in the UK and the U.S., dirty limericks were published openly for the first time. Books containing thousands of limericks were published, some becoming standard works on the subject. The Devizes limerick was involved in the construction of the atomic bomb. Mentally creating limericks helped an American missionary resist brainwashing in communist China. A limerick was reputedly written by a ghost. Great limericks were written by real people such as Philip Heseltine, Edward Gorey and Robert Conquest. The limerick's second century definitely has tales to tell.

What Will Become of the Limerick?

The old verse form is now into its third century of existence. There are new dynamics at play regarding a critical aspect of the limerick which is rarely thought about: how they are transmitted, how are they spread. In the old days it was word of mouth between friends, handwritten letters, verses were printed in books, magazines and newspapers. Newspapers in particular had wide circulations, and limerick competitions have always been popular.

A critical aspect of this method of transmission was the winnowing out of poor verses by editors, and by those who recited, sang or relayed the verses. It can also be argued that there was a mechanism for unwitting improvements of limericks as people misremembered them, thereby sometimes creating a better version.

Today, though, the internet spreads things almost instantaneously. Self-publishing is readily accessed, and cheap. Neither of these routes seems to offer any critique of the form. I have seen hundreds of recently self-published "Limerick Books" for sale. The ones I have read contain—to be polite—mainly quite poor examples of limericks. There is no editing, no evaluation, no mechanism for improvement. So how will good limericks be created and how will they spread? That's a good question.

As regards limericks spreading via books, modern publishers seem reluctant to publish books which contain only limericks.[10] Perhaps they think readers already know the classic examples from previously published books, which are widely available, and are sometimes even free online.

Competitions which require a limerick to be written are still widespread and popular. I have entered many. Such activity shows that people still enjoy creating limericks. This suggests to me that there is a market for limerick books. However, since it is very difficult to create a whole book's worth of top-notch new limericks, another approach is needed. One way would be to tell something interesting about the old verse form, for example the backstories about individual limericks and their creators. Another approach would be to write an accurate in-depth analysis of the history and development of the verse form.

Will the limerick live long enough to celebrate its 300th birthday? I think so; it has been part of the literary landscape for over 200 years and it shows few signs of dying. The rude variety survived censorship by going underground from the 1860s until the 1960s—and I am sure it will survive the next bout of prissy public moral outrage. Why? Because intelligent people love limericks, their bawdy humor, their clever wordplay and the outrageous mental images they create—and such people do not take kindly to those who tell them how they should think, what words they can and can't use, and how their lives should be run. Liking a non–PC limerick is one way of sticking it to the system; creating one is even better.

I hope it will survive, because a world without limericks will be missing something very special indeed.

Appendix
Pre-1820 Verses in English Which Have Been Claimed to Be Limericks or Proto-Limericks

This is an attempt to list in chronological order all pre-1820 verses in English which have been claimed to be limericks or proto-limericks, with as much information as I can find about each one.

Sources cited are in the bibliography. Gershon Legman references are to the 1974 Panther paperback edition.

Verses which I believe have not been considered by previous researchers are not included here as they have been chronologically discussed in the appropriate chapter.

POEM: Sumer is icumen in

The version below is in "modern" English, from an 1829 magazine. (I have chosen this date so the reader can see what people would have been familiar with around the date of the publication of the first known children's limerick books.)

> **Summer is i-coming in!**
> Loud sing cuckoo!
> Groweth seed and bloweth mead,
> And springeth the woods now.
> Sing, cuckoo!
> Ewe bleateth after lamb,
> Loweth after calf cow.
> Bull starteth,
> Buck verteth,
> Merry sing, cuckoo!
> Cuckoo! Cuckoo!
> Well sing'st thou, cuckoo.
> Nor stop thou never now.

Author of poem and original source: Possibly the oldest English song extant. Some say it was written in the middle of the thirteenth century.

Date poem first published: 1250 (circa).

Citation in limerick literature: Legman, pp. 12–13, Bibby, p. 57.

Comments: Legman says: "To avoid controversy, I do not insist that 'Sumer is i-cumen in' (about 1300), the oldest popular song in the English language, is in the limerick form, but a rather good case can be made for its stanzaic portion at least, and the possibility ought not to be overlooked."

To avoid controversy, I say that the only connection with limericks is that the author is anonymous.

POEM: The Lion

> þe lion is wondirliche strong
> & ful of wiles of wo.
> & weþer he pleye
> oþer take his preʒe
> he can not do bot slo.

The above is as given in the Harleian ms, as transcribed by Furnivall. The symbol þ can be pronounced as th. Both þ and ʒ are as close as I can get to the original medieval letters.

Author of poem and original source: Harleian reference 7322 (see below for description).

Swann and Sidgwick p. 102 say: "The meter is just audible in a snatch of the fifteenth century:

> The lion is wonderly strong,
> And ful of wilès of wo;
> And whether he playe
> Or take his preye,
> He can not do but slo (slay).
> —(from *MS. Harl. 7322*)"

Date poem first published: Late 1300s (date from Furnivall).

Citation in limerick literature: Morse p. 7 refers to Swann and Sidgwick.

Legman, p. 13, says of Swann and Sidgwick: "and that it is a limerick they clearly state." What they actually say is given above.

Parrott p. 10 for some reason thinks this verse is eleventh century.

It is still being touted as a limerick, for example in an article in *The Oxford Times* by Tony Augarde, December 3, 2007.

Potter, 2013, p. 25, describes it as a limerick form.

Comments: 8-6-5-4-6. Also rhyme scheme is abccb. Again, an obvious story, which is just a simple statement.

This verse shows how poorly some "researchers" understand references. Marsh p. x says that the Harleian manuscript is dated 1322 instead of having the acquisition number 7322! Possibly the editor was influenced by Harrowven, as she stated the verse came from the fourteenth century rather than the fifteenth as Swann and Sidgwick state.

Harleian reference 7322 is a large collection of poems in manuscript form, of which The Lion is just one. It was seemingly first available to the general public in the following: *Political, religious, and love poems. From the Archbishop of Canterbury's Lambeth ms. no. 306, and other sources*, edited by Frederick James Furnivall, London, 1866.

The "short religious poems" from Harleian 7322 are on pp. 220–243. The chapter heading says: "First treatise, of the end of the fourteenth century, which has English verses mixed in the Latin prose." The Lion poem is on p. 237. The work can be read online at several sites.

POEM: A Religious Use of Taking Tobacco

> The Indian weed witherëd quite,
> Green at morn, cut down at night,
> Shows thy decay;
> All flesh is hay:
> Thus think, then drink tobacco.
>
> And when the smoke ascends on high,
> Think thou behold'st the vanity
> Of worldly stuff,
> Gone with a puff:
> Thus think, then drink tobacco.
>
> But when the pipe grows foul within,
> Think of thy soul defiled with sin.
> And that the fire
> Doth it require:
> Thus think, then drink tobacco.
>
> The ashes that are left behind,
> May serve to put thee still in mind
> That into dust
> Return thou must:
> Thus think, then drink tobacco.

Author of poem and original source: Robert Wisdome, d. 1568. Two stanzas added later by George Wither (1588–1667).
Date poem first published: 1568 or earlier.
Citation in limerick literature: Legman, p. 15; Bibby, p. 58. These references only give the first verse.

Comments: 8-7-4-4-7. Said to occur in 1690 *Pills to Purge Melancholy*, and in 1710 edition.

POEM: The daughter of debate
　　　　 Who discord aye doth sow
　　　　　　Hath reaped no gain
　　　　　　Where former reign
　　　　 Hath taught still peace to know.

See comments below for a full explanation of where this "stanza" comes from.

Author of poem and original source: Written by Queen Elizabeth I. Recorded in contemporary books.

Date poem first published: 1568 (around this date; perhaps a year or so later).

Citation in limerick literature: The claim that this is *almost* a limerick seems to have been made by the poet Leonard Bacon. This was seemingly first picked up by Baring-Gould—see his comments on p. 25. It was then apparently just copied in such books as:

Wordsworth Book of Limericks p. x.
Mammoth Book of Limericks p. 25.

Bibby, p. 58, and Potter, 2013, p. 31, cite the verse, but carefully comment that there is doubt about the internal rhyme.

Comments: This is a ridiculous claim. The stanza quoted comprises two lines of the original poem. The layout has been changed, along with several of the words, and an internal rhyme has been introduced where there was none originally. The original two lines are usually given as:

> "The daughter of debate that discord aye doth sow
> Shall reap no gain where former rule still peace hath taught to know."

The "daughter of debate" is Mary, Queen of Scots.

The entire 16-line original poem can be read in total at several sites online under the title of *The Doubt of Future Foes*.

Legman, pp. 18–19, in a crushing comment, puts the literary boot into this so-called limerick. Not all subsequent writers on matters limerickal seem to have bothered to read his remarks.

An excellent example of the truth of the adage "always verify your references."

POEM: By Gis and by Saint Charity,
Alack, and fie for shame!
Young men will do't,
if they come to't;
By cock, they are to blame.

Quoth she, before you tumbled me,
You promised me to wed.
He answers:
So would I ha' done,
by yonder sun,
An thou hadst not come to my bed.

Author of poem and original source: Shakespeare, *Hamlet*, one of Ophelia's mad songs, in Act 4, scene 5.
Date poem first published: Written between 1599 and 1602 (?), published 1603.
Citation in limerick literature: I have seen this referred to online as being in limerick form. Also in Potter, 2013, pp. 31–2.
Comments: Rhyme scheme abccb. Most lines too short of beats. Simple story.
Gis is Jesus.
The intrusion of "He answers" in the second stanza throws everything to pot.

POEM: And will he not come again?
And will he not come again?
No, no, he is dead;
Go to thy death-bed;
He never will come again.

His beard as white as snow,
All flaxen was his poll.
He is gone, he is gone,
And we cast away moan.
God ha' mercy on his soul!

Author of poem and original source: Shakespeare, *Hamlet*, one of Ophelia's mad songs, in Act 4, scene 5.
Date poem first published: Written between 1599 and 1602 (?), published 1603.
Citation in limerick literature: Legman, p. 20, cites first line, using a variant which reads "And will he not come home again?"
Legman says the second stanza especially shows "the limerick form" in Shakespeare's work.
Comments: First stanza has repeated first line. 7-7-5-5-7.

Second stanza has rhyme scheme abccb. 6-6-6-6-7. Just a statement.

POEM: And let me the canakin clink, clink;
And let me the canakin clink;
A soldier's a man
A life's but a span;
Why, then, let a soldier drink.

Author of poem and original source: Shakespeare, *Othello*, Act II, Scene III. Iago's drinking song.

Date poem first published: Written around 1603. Printed 1622.

Citation in limerick literature: Morse, p. 8. Legman p. 20 cites first line.

Comments: 9-8-5-5-7. First line essentially same as second.

POEM: Swithold footed thrice the old;
He met the night-mare, and her nine-fold;
Bid her alight,
And her troth plight,
And, aroint thee, witch, aroint thee!

Author of poem and original source: *King Lear*, William Shakespeare. Part of Edgar's mad speech in Act 3, scene 4.

Date poem first published: Written around 1605. Published 1608.

Citation in limerick literature: Legman quotes on p. 20, saying there is "no mistake about the couplet."

Comments: 7-9-4-4-8. Just a simple statement.

POEM: O metaphysical Tobacco
Fetched as far as from Morocco,
Thy searching fume
Exhales the rheum,
O metaphysical Tobacco.

Author of poem and original source: *A Book of Madrigales for Viols and Voices*.

Date poem first published: 1606.

Citation in limerick literature: Edsall, 1924, p. 135, quotes this verse of 1606, suggesting that he is the first person to recognize it as the first dated limerick.

Comments: This just states something obvious; tobacco comes from a long way away, and the smoke clears your nose. The first and last lines are identical. So I don't think it is a limerick.

For some reason John Leonard wrote in 1993 that this verse was: "an almost perfect limerick, a fact which I believe has not been noted before" (*N&Q*, June 1993, pp. 207–8).

POEM: *Love love*

> Love is a peculiar pedlar
> Whose pack is fraught with sorrows,
>   With doubts and fears
>   With sighs and tears.
> Some joys—but those he borrows.

Above verse is stanza five in a six-stanza poem. This is the stanza Legman quotes.

Author of poem and original source: Robert Jones' *The Muses Gardin for Delights; or, The Fift Book of Ayres.*

Date poem first published: 1610.

Citation in limerick literature: Legman, p. 17.

Comments: Rhyme scheme abccb. Beats are 8-7-4-4-7.

A copy of Robert Jones' book can be read online (archive.org). The first poem is called *Love love*. It consists of six verses, the fifth verse being the one quoted. All are similar in layout and rhyme scheme.

POEM: The master, the swabber, the boatswain and I,
> The gunner and his mate
> Loved Mall, Meg and Marian and Margery,
> But none of us cared for Kate;
> **For she had a tongue with a tang,**
> **Would cry to a sailor, Go hang!**
> She loved not the savour of tar nor of pitch,
> Yet a tailor might scratch her where'er she did itch:
> **Then to sea, boys, and let her go hang!**
> This is a scurvy tune too: but here's my comfort.

Author of poem and original source: Stephano's song in *The Tempest* by Shakespeare, scene 2.

Date poem first published: Written around 1610 to 1611. Published 1623.

Citation in limerick literature: Legman, p. 20, and Bibby, p. 60, quote the part I have emboldened.

Legman claims it is the first sighting of the "modern rising anapaestic meter of the limerick, replacing the older iambics." Legman then goes on to comment that "the innovation of the double-length couplet was never followed up, and is seldom used in modern limericks."

Well, he got that right.

Comments: I find this claim simply unbelievable. At least Bibby had the grace to say: "This might almost be described as a sort of 'anti-limerick,' with the third and fourth lines longer instead of shorter than the other three."

It might also be described as the most stupid claim ever made about a possible early limerick sighting.

POEM: Shear sheep that have them, cry we still,
  But see that nó man 'scape
   To drink of the sherry
   That makes us so merry
  And plump as the lusty grape.

Author of poem and original source: William Browne (*fl* 1614).
Date poem first published: around 1614.
Citation in limerick literature: Legman, p. 17. Says song is chorus in drinking song called *Now that the Spring hath filled our veins*, which antedates by almost a century the presumed use in Limerick, Ireland.
Comments: Legman says, "Note that the first line still does not rhyme." No shit, Sherlock!

Beats are 8-6-6-6-7.

POEM: Tom o'Bedlam

  From the hagg & hungry Goblin
  That into raggs would rend yee,
   & the spirits that stand's
   by the naked man,
  in the book of moones defend ye …

  Of thirty bare years have I
  twice twenty bin enragèd,
   & of forty bin
   three times fifteene
  in durance soundlie caged.

  On the lordlie loftes of Bedlam,
  with stubble softe and dainty,
   brave braceletts strong,
   sweet whips ding-dong,
  with wholesome hunger plenty …

The three stanzas given above come from Legman—the full poem is usually not given in the above layout. See comment below.
Author of poem and original source: Author unknown. One source says discovered in a commonplace book of about 1620.

Appendix 211

Date poem first published: 1615?
Citation in limerick literature: Legman, p. 14, says first recorded in Giles Earle's manuscript music book about 1615, though probably decades older. Claimed to be in "limerick meter throughout."
Comments: Quoted three segments are abccb. Beats are 8-7-6-5-8 and 7-8-5-4-7 and 8-7-4-4-7.
Whole poem can be read online; typically, the poem has eight verses of eight lines each, each verse ending with a four-line chorus.
Variants exist of the verses, and it is not possible to know what the original was.
To my eye and ear there is little resemblance to a limerick.

POEM: Tobacco's a Musician
And in a Pipe delighteth:
 It descends in a Close
 Through the Organ of the nose
With a Relish that inviteth.

This makes me sing, So ho, hó --
 So ho hó, boyes!
Ho boyes, sound I loudly:
 Earth ne're did breed
 Such a Joviall weed
Whereof to boast so proudly.

Author of poem and original source: Barten Holyday's play *Technogamia, or The Marriage of the Arts* (1618), Act II, scene iii.
Date poem first published: 1618.
Citation in limerick literature: Legman, p. 16.
Comments: abccb rhyme scheme. So, not a limerick. Beats are 8-7-6-7-8.
Second verse; abccb, and 11-6-4-5-7.
 ho hó, boyes—if you think it's a limerick!

POEM: Come kisse, come kisse, my Corinna
And still that sport wee'l beginn-a
 That our soules may meet
 In our lippes, while they greet,
Come kisse, come kisse, my Corinna

Author of poem and original source: Barten Holyday's university comedy *Technogamia, or The Marriage of the Arts* (1618), Act III, scene v.
Date poem first published: 1618.
Citation in limerick literature: Legman, pp. 16–17; p. 17 claims that,

as in this example, the "correct" aabba rhyme scheme is in existence in the 1610s.

Comments: Last line repeats first line. All the verse says is: "give us a kiss, dear."

Beats 8-8-6-6-8. Rhyme scheme is aabba.

POEM: "To the old, long life and treasure!
To the young, all health and pleasure!
To the fair, their face
With eternal grace!
And the soul, to be loved at leisure!
"To the witty, all clear mirrors!
To the foolish, their dark errors!
To the loving sprite,
A secure delight!
To the jealous, their own false terrors!"

Author of poem and original source: Ben Jonson (1572–1637). See also next entry.

Date poem first published: 1621.

Citation in limerick literature: Wallace and Francis Rice, 1911, p. xiv.

Comments: Poem is in *The Masque of the Gypsies*, presented three times by Jonson to James I in August 1621.

Subsequent printings usually called *The Masque of the Metamorphosed Gypsies*.

This is the third song sung by Patrico, a wandering hedge-priest.

See short discussion in chapter dealing with pre–1820 verses in English.

POEM: The fairy beam upon you,
The stars to glister on you;
A moon of light
In the noon of night,
Till the fire-drake hath o'ergone you.
The wheel of fortune guide you,
The boy with the bow beside you
Run aye in the way
Till the bird of day,
And the luckier lot betide you.

To the old, long life and treasure,
To the young, all health and pleasure;
To the fair, their face
With eternal grace,
And the soul to be lov'd at leisure.
To the witty, all clear mirrors,

> To the foolish, their dark errors;
>> To the loving sprite,
>> A secure delight;
> To the jealous, his own false terrors.

Author of poem and original source: Ben Jonson (1572–1637). See also previous entry.

Date poem first published: 1621.

Citation in limerick literature: Legman, p. 21, refers to this quite elliptically, without quoting anything useful or telling us anything useful.

Bibby, pp. 60–61, also mentions the song cited by the Rices, 1911, and prefaces it with another song sung in the play.

Comments: These are the second and third songs sung by Patrico, a wandering hedge-priest.

In the play there is a gap between the songs, which is filled by the captain talking. They are not sung as one song, as could be inferred from Bibby.

These songs are just a linear statement. No fire, just boredom. Beats are 7-7-4-5-8 then 7-8-5-5-9 then 8-8-5-5-9 then 8-8-5-5-9.

POEM: *A pleasant new Northerne Song called the two York-shire Lovers* (23 stanzas, of which the following is one).

> My lambs new gowns shall beare thee,
> No daglockes shall e'er come neere thee;
>> The poultry of the town
>> Shall cackle without downe,
> Ere He want a soft bed to cheere thee.

Author of poem and original source: See comments below.

Date poem first published: circa 1635.

Citation in limerick literature: Legman, pp. 17–18.

Comments: Around 1635 a poem appeared in print entitled: *A pleasant new Northerne Song called the two York-shire Lovers*. This was to be sung: "To a pleasant new Court tune, or, the tune of Willy." Quite what these airs were I don't know. The poem itself consists of 23 stanzas, each in a limerick-like layout.

POEM: The Distracted Puritan

> Am I mad, O noble Festus,
> When zeal and godly knowledge
>> Have put me in hope
>> To deal with the Pope
> As well as the best in the college?

> Boldly I preach, I hate a cross, hate a surplice,
> Mitres, copes, and rochets!
> Come hear me pray nine times a day,
> And fill your heads with crotchets.

(First verse only given above; there are 12 in all.)

Author of poem and original source: Bishop Corbet (1582–1635).

Date poem first published: 1636 or earlier. First printed 1660 (Legman).

Citation in limerick literature: Legman, pp. 23–4. Legman (p. 24) quotes the following:

> "Of the beast's ten horns (God bless us!)
> I have knock'd off three already;
> If they let me alone
> I'll leave him none;
> But they say I am too heady.
> Boldly I preach, I hate a cross, hate a surplice,
> Mitres, copes, and rochets!
> Come hear me pray nine times a day,
> And fill your heads with crotchets."

Comments: All stanzas are too long. All stanzas have the first line not rhyming with lines 2 and 5.

POEM: *Mondayes Worke*
    or
    The two honest neighbours both birds of a feather
    Who are at the Ale-house both merry together.
    To the tune of *I owe my hostess money.*

> Good morrow, neighbour *Gamble*,
> Come let you and I goe ramble:
> Last night I was shot
> Through the braines with a Pot
>   and now my stomacke doth wamble:
> Your Possetts and your Caudles;
> Are fit for babes in Cradles;
> A piece of salt Hogge
> And a haire of the old Dogge
>   is good to cure our drunken Noddles.
> *Come hither mine Host, come hither,*
> *Here's two birds of a feather,*
> *Come hither mine Host*
> *With a Pot and a Tost*
>   *And let us be merry together.*

The above is the first verse of the poem. The rest of the poem consists of four more verses of a similar rhyme scheme and nature, i.e., a ten-line stanza, each followed by the chorus given above (*Come hither* etc.).

The poem is then followed by: "The Second Part, to the Same Tune." This consists of four verses similar to the above first part in layout.

Author of poem and original source: *Roxburghe Ballads.* The whole poem can be read online in various editions.

Date poem first published: earlier than 1640.

Citation in limerick literature: Legman, p. 28; Bibby, p. 56. These references give only two five-line verses, taken from two different ten line stanzas, and given a layout as in conventional limericks.

The layout in older books is as given here; this is from an 1874 edition.

Comments: Legman calls it "a perfect modern limerick." Bibby says: "here, it is worth noting, there is not only the rhyme and rhythm of the limerick, but each stanza relates to a separate individual, whose name terminates the first line and sets the scheme of rhyming."

Bibby's comment about each stanza relating to a separate individual is incorrect. Some do; some don't. I don't think he saw the original but merely copied the two verses Legman gave.

Despite the above rave reviews, my comment is still this: it's just a linear poem that has no mystery, just an description of what happened at a drinking session the night before with an invitation to drink some more, etc.

POEM: *Jone* is a wench that's painted,
    Jone is a Girle that's tainted;
        Yet *Jone* she goes
        Like one of those
    Whom purity had Sainted.

    Jane is a Girle that's prittie,
    Jane is a wench that's wittie;
        Yet, who would think
        Her breath do's stinke,
    And so it doth? that's pittie.

Author of poem and original source: Robert Herrick, *Upon Jone and Jane.*

Date poem first published: 1648.

Citation in limerick literature: Legman, p. 23; Bibby, p. 61.

Comments: Both 7-7-4-4-7. The sentiment is limerick-like, and rhyme scheme is aabba.

POEM: The Night piece: To Julia

    Her eyes the glow-worm lend thee,
    The shooting stars attend thee;
        And the elves also,
        Whose little eyes glow
    Like the sparks of fire, befriend thee.

    No Will-o'-th'-Wisp mis-light thee,
    Nor snake or slow-worm bite thee;
        But on, on thy way,
        Not making a stay,
    Since ghost there's none to affright thee.

    Let not the dark thee cumber;
    What though the moon does slumber?
        The stars of the night
        Will lend thee their light,
    Like tapers clear without number.

    Then Julia let me woo thee,
    Thus, thus to come unto me;
        And when I shall meet
        Thy silv'ry feet,
    My soul I'll pour into thee.

Author of poem and original source: Robert Herrick.
Date poem first published: 1648.
Citation in limerick literature: Cited by Ralph A. Lyon, 1908, in un-paginated Introduction. Also by Bishop, p. 2, and Belknap, p. 14.

Bibby, p. 61 states: "No doubt about the limerickality of these verses!"

Edsall, 1924, p. 135, claims this is the first signed poem in limerick form.

Comments: To my mind there is no way, shape or "form" this poem is a set of limericks. It is merely a poem in four stanzas which have a limerick-like layout. The clincher for me is that, with the possible exception of the first stanza, none of the four can stand alone as a limerick. As Belknap remarks: "Certainly no orthodox limerick approaches the poetic excellence of Herrick's 'The Night-piece: to Julia,' a sequence of stanzas with an easy continuity carried by the iambic tempo. But, one by one, these stanzas lack the specific though limited qualities and virtues in the strict modern form."

In a review of Lyon's book in *The New York Times* of June 13, 1908, it is stated: "Possibly, Irishmen may forgive him for applying the name to Moore's 'I Can no Longer Stifle,' and, consequently to 'The Time I've Lost in Wooing,' but a 'set of limericks' is almost blasphemous when used as a description for Herrick's 'The Night Piece, to Julia.'"

POEM: A Relation of a Quaker that to the Shame of his Profession Attempted to Bugger a Mare near Colchester.
First two verses read:

> All in the land of Essex,
> Near Colchester the zealous,
> On the side of a banck
> Was play'd such a prank,
> As would make a stone-horse jealous.
>
> Help *Woodcock, Fox* and *Nailor,*
> For Brother Green's a stalion
> Now alas what hope,
> Of converting the Pope,
> When a Quaker turns Italian ...

Author of poem and original source: Sir John Denham (1614/15–1669). For example in *J. Cleaveland Revived, Poems, Orations, Epistles, and other of his genuine Incomparable Pieces*, 4th edition, London, Nathaniel Brooks, 1668, pp. 64–65.

Date poem first published: 1659—date given by Oxford Text Archive.

Citation in limerick literature: Legman, p. 27, cites a 1662 reference. Ogden, p. 530, gives the last two verses.

Comments: Original is a seventeen-stanza poem in which stanza two is repeated as stanza seventeen. Later versions are sixteen stanzas, omitting the repeated stanza.

Editions by Dr. Johnson record "To the tune of Tom of Bedlam."

A simple story with rhyme scheme abccb. Some lines seem short of beats, too.

In his article Ogden mentions eight poems described in this Appendix. He also cites two other songs which, in my opinion, are so far from even a limerick-like layout that I have not included them here.

POEM: Joan Easie got her a Nag and a Sledge
To the Privy-house for a slide, a:
   The hole was beshit
   That she could not sit,
But did cack as she lay on her side, a:
   She was not wind
   For she sent forth a sound
Did stretch her fundament wide, a.

Author of poem and original source: *Wit and Drollery*, 1661. (This work was originally published in 1656 by John Playford.)

Date poem first published: 1661.

Citation in limerick literature: Legman, p. 25. He cites 1661 for the verse.

According to Mark McDayter at a University of Western Ontario website, this verse functions as a kind of conclusion to another poem. In the 1656 edition this verse is printed as though it were prose; the layout as a limerick-like verse appears in the 1661 edition.

Comments: Legman says under this: "So many examples of these evident predecessors of the modern limerick ..." So even he thinks it is not a limerick, but a "predecessor."

I wonder why Joan needed a horse-drawn sledge to get to the outhouse. Either she was drunk, disabled or it was a long way away.

POEM: Here comes Sir HENRY MARTYN
As good as ever pist,
This wenching beast
Had Whores at least
A thousand on his list.
This made the Devils laugh,
So good a friend to see,
At *Pluto*'s Court
There's better sport,
Come thou shalt dwell with me.

Author of poem and original source: THE BLOODY BED-ROLL *Rump: Or an Exact Collection.*

A "celebration" of Oliver Cromwell's death. Consists of 18 stanzas, each of ten lines, as in the example given here. Sir Henry is stanza four.

Date poem first published: 1662.

Citation in limerick literature: Legman, p. 27. He only gives the first half of the ten-line stanza I have quoted.

Comments: Rhyme scheme abccb. Beats are 7-6-4-4-6 and 6-6-4-4-6.

Whole poem can be read online. Sir Henry Martyn (usually spelled Marten) was one of Cromwell's men, and a regicide.

POEM: Make ready fair lady tonight,
And stand at the door before,
For I will be there
To receive you with care,
And to your true love you shall go.

And when the stars twinkle so bright,
Then down to the door I will creep.
To my love I will fly
Ere the jealous can spy,
And leave my old daddy asleep.

Author of poem and original source: John Dryden's first and most successful play, entitled *Sir Martyn Mar-all, or The Feign'd Innocence*. It had its first performance on August 15, 1667, and was based on two French plays.

Date poem first published: 1667.

Citation in limerick literature: Ogden, p. 530. He gives both verses, commenting that "Warner sings the first verse and Millicent the second."

Comments: These two verses seem to be the only songs or text in the play which are in a limerick-like layout.

The obvious comment is the rhyme scheme is wrong: abccb. Again, just simple statements of fact.

POEM: Her lips are two brimmers of claret,
    Where first I began to miscarry,
        Her breasts of delight
        Are two bottles of white,
    And her eyes are two cups of Canary.

Author of poem and original source: Sung by one of the characters in Act IV, Scene I of *Epsom Wells, a comedy*, by Thomas Shadwell, the poet laureate (licensed and printed, 1673).

Date poem first published: 1673.

Citation in limerick literature: Bunting/O'Sullivan, 1927, p. 32. Part of the text reads: "The earliest printed limerick in English appears to be the following single stanza... The air to which it was sung is not known."

Comments: Lines 1, 2 and 5 are poor rhymes—at best. Also, the so-called limerick is part of a longer poem, and is not a stand-alone verse. It's just a description of a handsome lass.

POEM: When first I laid siege to my Chloris

I have not found an original copy yet; a 1720 version is given later in this Appendix, said to be an altered copy of the original.

Author of poem and original source: Sir Charles Sedley's *Bellamira, or The Mistress*, Act III, Scene I.

Date poem first published: 1687.

Citation in limerick literature: Bunting/O'Sullivan, p. 32.

Comments: *The Weekly Amusement Etc.* of Saturday, February 8, 1734, p. 357 gives this (and the subsequent 4 verses) in a four-line layout, viz–

    "When first I laid siege to my Chloris,
        Cannon oaths I brought down
        To batter the town,
    And boom'd her with amorous stories."

POEM: SHINKEN's Song to the Harp

Of Noble Race was Shinken,
The Line of Owen Tudor,
But her Renown was fled and gone,
Since cruel Love pursu'd hur:

II.
Fair Winny's Eyes bright shining,
And Lily Breasts alluring,
Poor Shinken's heart, with fatal Dart,
Have Wounded past all Curing:

III.
Hur was the prettiest Fellows,
At Bandy once and Cricket,
At Hunting-Chace, or High-foot Race,
Gadsplut, how hur could kick it:

IV.
But now all Joys defying,
All pale and wan hur Cheeks too,
Hur heart so akes, hur quite forsakes
Hur Herrings and hur Leeks too:

V.
No more must dear Metheglins,
Be top'd at goot Mountgomery,
And if Loves sore, smart one Week more,
Adieu Creen Cheefe and Flummery.

Author of poem and original source: Thomas D'Urfey's stage comedy called *The Richmond Heiress*. Original tune is of unknown origin, sometimes claimed to be Welsh, but most likely written by John Eccles or Henry Purcell. Can be found in the Fourth Act.

The original text contains various "musical" directions to aid singing, such as *"trum tery, tery, tery; trum trum."* I have removed them for clarity.

Date poem first published: 1693.

Citation in limerick literature: Legman, p. 29, mentions first line in passing.

He also suggests that "neighbour Jinkin," a character who appears in *Mondayes Work* (Roxburghe Ballads, 1640 or earlier) is a variant of the Shinken character; no evidence given.

Comments: Several variants on the name: Shinken, Jinkin. The song appeared in several later works, for example *Pills to Purge Melancholia*.

The Weekly Amusement Etc. of Saturday, February 8, 1734, p. 358 has a song in limerick-like layout, called "Of a noble race called Shenkin"—but again the rhyme scheme is abccb.

Several early compilations contain both a tune and the verses.

The eponymous hero is a comic Welshman, Rice ap Shenkin, and the song is apparently sung in a cod Welsh accent.

Many later versions contain different words, e.g., stool-ball for bandy, and cream cheese for Creen Cheefe, but the layout and meaning are essentially the same.

POEM: To drink is a christian diversion,
    Unknown to the Greek or the Persian:
        Let Mohametan fools
        Live by heathenish rules,
    And be damned over tea cups and coffee.
        But let British lads sing
        Crown a health to the king
    And a fig for your sultan or Sophy.

Author of poem and original source: *The Way of the World*, a play by William Congreve, premiered in March 1700, in London. The verse is sung by Sir Wilfull Witwoud in Act IV.

Date poem first published: 1700.

Citation in limerick literature: *The Archive*, a monthly publication by the Senior Class of Trinity College, Duke University, Durham, NC. Article titled "A Limerick Fiend Speaks," by A.B. Gibson, March 1925, pp. 263–266. See p. 266.

Comments: Rhyme scheme aabbc, for the first part, the whole being aabbcddc.

POEM: When first I laid siege to my Chloris

When first I laid siege to my Chloris,
When first I laid siege to my Chloris;
    Cannon oaths I brought down
    To batter the town,
And boom'd her with amorous stories.

Billet deux like small Shot did so ply her,
Billet deux like small Shot did so ply her;
    And sometimes a Song
    Went whistling along,
But still I was never the nigher.

At length she sent Word by a Trumpet
At length she sent Word by a Trumpet
    That is I lik'd the Life
    She would be my Wife
But she would be no man's Strumpet.

I told her that *Mars* wou'd ne'er marry,

I told her that *Mars* wou'd ne'er marry;
   I swore by my Scars,
   Got in Combates and Wars,
That I'd rather dig Stones in a Quarry.

Author of poem and original source: D'Urfey's *Pills to Purge Melancholy*, volume VI, p. 308.
Date poem first published: 1720.
Citation in limerick literature: Bunting/O'Sullivan, p. 28.
Comments: Said by O'Sullivan to be an altered copy of Sedley's 1687 work. Can be read online.

A five-stanza simple story; in each the first line is repeated as the second. It could therefore be more correctly described as a four-line poem, abba.

This is just a simple story, with no particularly redeeming features, no great rhymes, and no obvious claim for any stanza to be a limerick.

POEM: My mither's ay glowran o'er me,
   Tho' she did the same before me:
      I canna leave
      To look at my love,
   Or else she'll be like to devour me …

Author of poem and original source: Ramsay's *Tea-table Miscellany*.
Date poem first published: 1724.
Citation in limerick literature: Legman, p. 29.
Comments: Just a simple statement of fact, telling a boring storyette. Beats are 8-7-5-5-9.

POEM: At the Tree I shall suffer with pleasure,
   At the Tree I shall suffer with pleasure.
      Let me go where I will,
      In all kinds of ill,
   I shall find no such furies as these are!

Author of poem and original source: Gay's *Beggar's Opera*, Air XXV, p. 23. Air to which it is sung is: *When first I laid Siege to my Chloris*.
Date poem first published: 1728.
Citation in limerick literature: Bunting/O'Sullivan, p. 28.
Comments: O'Sullivan comments that the singer sees a prospect, through hanging, of finally being rid of his female entourage. Also, says it is an exact copy of the version in *Pills to Purge Melancholy*. So original presumably 1690?

POEM: I'll never get drunk again,
For my head's full of pain,
And it grieves me to think
That by dint of a drink,
I should lie with my Phillis in vain.

Author of poem and original source: Star of Coventry (an inn), on a window, dated 1712.

I have recorded this as 1731, since first appearance in print seems to be in *The Merry-Thought: OR, The Glass-Window and Bog-House Miscellany. Part I* (1731), p. 26.

Date poem first published: 1731.

Citation in limerick literature: None. I found this in a modern book and traced it back.

Legman quotes from later editions of the book this first appeared in, but he seems to have missed this verse. Perhaps it is not in later editions.

Comments: Does not seem to have been commented on by limerick scholars.

Beats are 7-6-6-6-9.

An early example of Brewer's Droop.

Whole book can be seen at Horntip.com.

This verse has led an interesting life; a World War II American version had Betty Grable as the disappointed paramour.

POEM: Hickory Dickory Dock

Author of poem and original source: Unknown author. Langford Reed quotes a Scottish variant from 1821.

Date poem first published: 1744.

Citation in limerick literature: Langford Reed.

Comments: See my comments in main text. The date given is from the first known printing. Reed implies it is much older.

POEM: *On JOLLITY: an* Ode, *or* Song *or both.*

I.
There was a jovial Butcher,
He liv'd at *Northern-fall-gate*,
He kept a Stall
At *Leadenhall*,
And got drunk at the Boy at *Aldgate*.

II.
He ran down Houndsditch reeling
At *Bedlam* he was frighted,

>He in *Moorfields*
>Besh—t his heels
>And at *Hoxton* he was wiped.

Author of poem and original source: *The Midwife: or, The Old Woman's magazine*, volume 2. London, pp. 175–6. Followed by an extensive explanation until p. 180.

Christopher Smart, writing as Mary Midnight.

Date poem first published: 1751.

Citation in limerick literature: Legman, p. 30, cites *The New Boghouse Miscellany, or A companion for the Close-Stool*, 1761, p. 207.

Legman and those who just copy him use an accent in the last word thus: wipèd. Perhaps the word is accented in later books.

Comments: The original can be read online. It is followed by an in-depth pseudo-serious explanation which does add to the humor.

Despite knowing the original appeared in *The Midwife*, and *The Non-pareil* (1757, pp. 165–170), Legman (p. 31) wondered if Oliver Goldsmith wrote this addendum; but it does seem to be Christopher Smart.

The problems here are the rhyme scheme (abccb), the lack of beats in most lines, and the fact that it is just the telling of a simple linear story.

POEM: Ralph's Ramble to London.

The two references given below can be read online. The 1768 reference contains a tune to which the song can be sung.

The poem describes a journey to London, with visits to the theatre and a pleasure park.

Mr. Alan Thompson can be heard singing a five-stanza version of the song online.

Author of poem and original source: The earliest reference I know is: *The Gentleman's Magazine*, volume 38, February 1768, p. 89. The page is headed "'Ralph's Ramble to London,' Sung by Mr. Vernon, at Vaux-hall. Set to Mufic by Mr. Potter." There are six verses in this reference.

In *The Ladies Polite Songfter; or Harmony for the Fair-Sex* ... (London, no date. 1780?) pp. 123–5 give 14 verses. The additional verses are by Mr. Adam Smith, as sung by him at the Theatre-Royal on Richmond-Green.

Date poem first published: 1768 (or earlier).

Citation in limerick literature: The only reference I know was made by Ronald Knox in 1925. As seen in the comments below, he had no idea of the age or origin of the poem.

See Ronald A. Knox, "Lyra Limerica," *English Life*, London, vol. 4, no. 3, February 1925, pp. 202–203. See p. 202.

Comments: Ronald Knox wrote: "Meanwhile the actual form of the

Limerick crops up in odd sources which would really be worth tabulating. Thus, I find in a book called "Old English Melodies" a poem, (undated, of course, and unattributed) called "Ralph's Ramble to London," the first verse of which runs—

> I am a poor innocent clown,
> And lately I rambled to town;
> And I've heard the folks say
> 'Twas a place fine and gay
> And I wanted to view it, I own.

The remaining four verses are equally perfect Limericks, so far as scansion is concerned. There is a wide field of research here which still remains to be explored."

POEM: Dance a baby, diddy,
What can mammy do wid'e,
But sit in her lap
And give 'un some pap,
And dance a baby diddy?

Author of poem and original source: Italian showman called Piccini. Script only transcribed in 1828, and this rhyme called a common nursery ditty.
Date poem first published: 1780.
Citation in limerick literature: Source is the Opies, p. 60. They say it was included in the performance of an Italian showman about 1780.
Bibby, p. 51.
Comments: Note the Opie's comment about no limericks prior to 1820—they obviously did not regard this or the Feedum verse as limericks.
First and last lines same. Beats are 6-6-4-5-7.

POEM: I CAN NO LONGER STIFLE

I.
I can no longer stifle,
How much I long to rifle
    That little part
    They call the heart
Of you, you lovely trifle!
You can no longer doubt it,
So let me be about it,
    Or on my word,
    And by the Lord,
I'll try to do without it.

II.
This pretty thing's as light, Sir,
As any paper kite, Sir;
   And here and there,
   And God knows where,
She takes her wheeling flight, Sir.
Us lovers, to amuse us,
Unto her tail she nooses;
   There, hung like bobs
   Of straw, or nobs,
She whisks us where she chuses,

Author of poem and original source: Thomas Moore.
Date poem first published: 1805.
Citation in limerick literature: Cited by Ralph A. Lyon, 1908. He gave no date for the poem. He gives the layout as four separate "limericks," and prefaces the verses with the following text: "Thomas Moore, the famous Irish poet, uses the limerick form for several of his poems, both serious and humorous. A characteristically limerickian poem by Moore follows …"
Comments: Beat scheme is: 7-7-4-4-7.

A song called "I can no longer stifle," by T. Moore, with an accompaniment for the piano forte, was published in circa 1805 by C. Wheatstone. Copy in British Library. Not seen by me.

I believe it was printed with tune in *A Selection of Irish Melodies with symphonies and accompaniments by Sir John Stevenson Mus. Doc and Characteristic words by Thomas Moore, Esq.*, Volume 3, 1810—but I have not seen a copy.

I don't know what the tune was called it was sung to.

Many subsequent collections of Moore's work contain the words but not the tune. The earliest I know of this nature is: *The works of Thomas Moore, comprehending all his melodies, ballads, etc., never before published without the accompanying music*, Galignani, Paris, 1819. See volume 4, pp. 250–1.

POEM: Kate Kearney

Oh, did you not hear of Kate Kearney?
She lives on the banks of Killarney:
From the glance of her eye, shun danger, and fly,
For fatal's the glance of Kate Kearney;

For that eye is so modestly beaming,
You'd ne'er think of mischief she's dreaming;
Yet, oh! I can tell how fatal the spell,
That lurks in the eye of Kate Kearney.

> Oh, should you e'er meet this Kate Kearney
> Who lives on the banks of Killarney,
> Beware of her smile, for many a wile
> Lies hid in the smile of Kate Kearney.
>
> Tho' she looks so bewitchingly simple,
> Yet there's mischief in every dimple;
> And who dares inhale her sigh's spicy gale,
> Must die by the breath of Kate Kearney.

Author of poem and original source: Song composed by Miss Sydney Owenson. She later became Lady Morgan.

Date poem first published: 1806 (possibly 1804).

Citation in limerick literature: Russell, 1898, p. 87: "We have not seen it noticed that these nonsense-verses copy the meter of Lady Morgan's 'Kate Kearney' …"

Comments: *A select collection of songs: or, an appendage to the pianoforte,* printed by and for S. Hodgson, Newcastle upon Tyne, 1806; p. 213 records the text given here, as sung by Mr. Incledon.

Bunting/O'Sullivan, p. 28, cites Crosby's *Irish Musical Repository* (1808), p. 143.

Kearney is pronounced Kerney or Karney.

POEM: "CUPID'S LOTTERY"

> A lottery, a Lottery,
> In Cupid's court there used to be;
> Two roguish eyes
> The highest prize
> In Cupid's scheming Lottery;
> And kisses, too,
> As good as new,
> Which weren't very hard to win,
> For he who won
> The eyes of fun
> Was sure to have the kisses in
> A Lottery, a Lottery, etc.

Author of poem and original source: Thomas Moore.

Moore wrote the libretto for a comic play called "*M. P., or The Blue Stocking.*" It was first produced on the London stage on September 9, 1811. The song is sung by Susan and starts Act Three. The text of the play was published in London in 1811 and in New York in 1812. Copies can be read online, and the poem can be found on pp. 60–1. The poem has no title in the libretto.

Date poem first published: 1811.

Citation in limerick literature: Cited by Reed in second edition (1926) of *The Complete Limerick Book*.

Legman p. 9 just refers to the song by name only.

Comments: Reed states (p. 66): "In Moore's forgotten lyric, *A Lottery, a Lottery,* the choruses are in complete Limerick form. (See the 1825 edition of his collected works.) That this delightful Irish poet is, most appropriately, the real pioneer of the Limerick, the present editor has no doubt."

We can note the beats are 8-8-4-4-8 for the first five lines. The whole poem is not in separate five-line stanzas, and it could never be because the poem cannot be split into a limerick-like layout—there are not enough lines to do so.

POEM: Edward Lysaght (1811)

No examples can be given here from Edward Lysaght's 1811 *Poems* as none of the poems in English look like limericks.

Author of poem and original source: Edward Lysaght's *Poems* (1811). This book can be read online.

Date poem first published: 1811.

Citation in limerick literature: Baring-Gould, p. 35, quotes Morris Bishop as stating that in an 1811 book titled *Poems*, Edward Lysaght, a Munster barrister, published "a serious celebration of Ireland in limerick form, and also a series of limericks in Irish."

Morris Bishop did indeed state that in *The New York Times Book Review*, January 3, 1965, p. 2. But he was wrong—see comments below.

Comments: I agree with Bibby, who states on p. 55: "Unfortunately, I was unable to find in that collection more than one verse of even approximately limerick form, and none that could be unambiguously so called."

The poem version of "Garnavilla" in Irish has a first verse that looks like a limerick in shape. But the phonetic version shows lines 1, 2 & 5 end in the same word, and lines 3 & 4 don't rhyme. (See pp. 100–1 in Lysaght's book.)

POEM: Oh! Where's the slave?

Oh! where's the slave so lowly
Condemn'd to chains unholy,
Who, could he burst
His bonds at first,
Would pine beneath them slowly?
What soul, whose wrongs degrade it,
Would wait till time decay'd it,
When thus its wing
At once may spring
To the throne of Him who made it?

Chorus:
Farewell, Erin,–farewell, all,
Who live to weep our fall!

Less dear the laurel growing,
Alive, untouch'd and blowing,
Than that whose braid
Is pluckd to shade
The brows with victory glowing.
We tread the land that bore us,
Her green flag glitters o'er us,
The friends we've tried
Are by our side,
And the foe we hate before us.

Chorus:

Author of poem and original source: Thomas Moore.
Date poem first published: 1815 or earlier.
Citation in limerick literature: Bibby, p. 53.

Comments: Earliest reference I have found: *Irish Melodies, by Thomas Moore*, Philadelphia, published by M. Carey, 1815, pp. 137–8. Air: "Sios agus sios liom."

POEM: The Young May Moon

The young May moon is beaming, love.
The glow-worm's lamp is gleaming, love.
How sweet to rove,
Through Morna's grove,
When the drowsy world is dreaming, love!
Then awake!—the heavens look bright, my dear,
'Tis never too late for delight, my dear,
And the best of all ways
To lengthen our days
Is to steal a few hours from the night, my dear!

Now all the world is sleeping, love,
But the Sage, his star-watch keeping, love,
And I, whose star,
More glorious far,
Is the eye from that casement peeping, love.
Then awake!—till rise of sun, my dear,
The Sage's glass we'll shun, my dear,
Or, in watching the flight
Of bodies of light,
He might happen to take thee for one, my dear.

Author of poem and original source: Thomas Moore.

Date poem first published: 1815 or earlier.
Citation in limerick literature: First reference seems to be Edsall, 1924, p. 135.

Legman p. 9 just refers to the poem by name only, and says it was obviously inspired by Herrick's "The Night-piece; To Julia."

Comments: Earliest reference I have found: *Irish Melodies, by Thomas Moore*, Philadelphia, published by M. Carey, 1815, pp. 109–10. Air: "The Dandy, O!"

POEM: THE FOURTH SONG OF PEACE

    O Thou that art our Queen again,
    And may in the sun be seen again,
        Come, CERES, come.
        For the war's gone home,
    And the fields are quiet and green again.

    The air, dear Goddess, sighs for thee.
    The light-heart brooks arise for thee,
        And the poppies red
        On their wistful bed
    Turn up their dark blue eyes for thee.

    Laugh out in the loose green jerkin
    That's fit for a goddess to work in,
        With shoulders brown,
        And the wheaten crown
    About thy temples perking.

    And with thee come, Stout Heart in,
    And Toil, that sleeps his cart in,
        And Exercise,
        The ruddy and wise.
    His bathed fore-locks parting.

    And Dancing too, that's lither
    Than willow or birch, drop hither,
        To thread the place
        With a finishing grace,
    And carry our smooth eyes with her.

Author of poem and original source: Leigh Hunt.
Date poem first published: 1815.
Citation in limerick literature: First reference seems to be Edsall, 1924, p. 135.

Bibby, p. 52, states, "And there is really no doubt at all in the case of 'Song to Ceres' ..." He then quotes the jerkin/perking stanza.

Comments: This is an interesting reference. Commentators do not seem to know when the poem was published—for example, Bibby (p. 52) and *The Wordsworth Book of Limericks* (p. x). Seemingly the poetry collection book they took the verse from did not have a date. They also refer to the poem as Song to Ceres.

It took me some while to find the original. In 1815 Leigh Hunt published an 82 p. book entitled *The Descent of Liberty, a Mask*. A second edition was published in 1816. Both editions can be read online. The work was widely quoted from, for example, *The Eclectic Review*, May 1815, pp. 517–521, see p. 520. *The Analectic Magazine*, August 1815, pp. 113–118, see pp. 116–7. Both of these were printed in London. A January 1817, Philadelphia magazine called *The Port-Folio*, contained much the same information on pp. 237–241, see p. 239.

All these references quoted the poem called "The Fourth Song of Peace." The poem then became detached from its origin and appeared just above the author's name, with no date, in later poetry collections, often with the title "The Song of Ceres." Without the internet I doubt I would have found the original or the reviews.

POEM: *The Metamorphosis of the Royal Honours of Scotland*
A typical verse:

> And sometimes he's the honour,
> And sometimes he's the honour,
> When summer's hat
> To cool her twatt,
> And put the sheare upon her.

Author of poem and original source: *A Banquet of Dainties for Strong Stomachs* by James Maidment, 1815. Contains a poem entitled *The Metamorphosis of the Royal Honours of Scotland*. Mss written 1815, book privately printed 1828.

Date poem first published: 1815.

Citation in limerick literature: Not previously discussed in limerick literature.

Comments: Brought to my attention by Doug Harris. Can be read online at Horntip.com. The poem mainly describes how the regalia of Scotland can be used for immoral purposes, usually involving the private parts of ladies. It certainly has a limerick-like layout, and each stanza is essentially self-contained. However, most of the lines have the wrong number of feet, and I feel they lack that elusive "snap" that fires a verse into a limerick. It can have had no effect on the history and development of the limerick verse form since it was only known to a handful of friends, and it was published in a very limited printing *after* 1820.

POEM: Feedum fiddledum fee,
    The cat's got into the tree.
        Pussy, come down
        Or I'll crack your crown,
    And toss you into the sea.

Author of poem and original source: Douce MS circa 1815.
Date poem first published: 1815—but only in manuscript form.
Citation in limerick literature: Bibby, p. 51. He does not mention it was only in *ms*.
Comments: This verse is recorded as being in a manuscript dated circa 1815 (*The Oxford Dictionary of Nursery Rhymes*, edited by Iona and Peter Opie, see 1975 edition, p. 114). There is no record of it being known or printed prior to 1820.

Beats are 6-7-4-5-7. First line meaningless, so really a four-line verse.

POEM: "The Time I've Lost in Wooing"

The time I've lost in wooing,
In watching and pursuing
The light, that lies
In woman's eyes,
Has been my heart's undoing.
Though Wisdom oft has sought me,
I scorn'd the lore she brought me,
My only books
Were woman's looks,
And folly's all they've taught me.

Her smile when Beauty granted,
I hung with gaze enchanted,
Like him, the sprite,
Whom maids by night
Oft meet in glen that's haunted.
Like him, too, Beauty won me,
But while her eyes were on me,
If once their ray
Was turn'd away,
Oh! winds could not outrun me.

And are those follies going?
And is my proud heart growing
Too cold or wise
For brilliant eyes
Again to set it glowing?
No, vain, alas! th' endeavour
From bonds so sweet so sever;

> Poor Wisdom's chance
> Against a glance
> Is now as weak as ever.

Author of poem and original source: Thomas Moore.
Date poem first published: 1815 or earlier.
Citation in limerick literature: Despite the comment in *The New York Times* of June 13, 1908, this is not actually cited by Ralph A. Lyon in his 1908 book. This seems to have been a deduction by the reviewer from the text Lyon used to introduce Moore's *I Can No Longer Stifle*. This read: "Thomas Moore, the famous Irish poet, uses the limerick form for several of his poems, both serious and humorous. A characteristically limerickian poem by Moore follows …"

Seemingly cited independently by Reed in second edition (1926) of *The Complete Limerick Book*. Reed (p. 66) quotes the "Wisdom Oft" verse from "The time I've lost in wooing."

Legman p. 9 just refers to the song by name only.

Comments: In a review of Lyon's book in *The New York Times* of June 13, 1908, it is stated: "Possibly, Irishmen may forgive him for applying the name to Moore's 'I Can no Longer Stifle,' and, consequently to 'The Time I've Lost in Wooing,' but a 'set of limericks' is almost blasphemous when used as a description for Herrick's 'The Night Piece, to Julia.'"

Earliest reference I have found: *Irish Melodies, by Thomas Moore*, Philadelphia, published by M. Carey, 1815, pp. 135–6. Air: "Pease upon a Trencher."

Several authoritative sites online say it came from Moore's poem Lalla Rookh; it does not.

There is no truth in the conjecture that the original first stanza read:

> The time I've lost in wooing,
> In watching and pursuing.
> The light, that lies
> In woman's eyes,
> Has been my britches' undoing.

Mainly because I wrote this.

Chapter Notes

Chapter 1

1. Willard R. Espy, *An Almanac of Words at Play* (New York, Clarkson N. Potter, 1975), 230.
2. *New Scientist*, London, July 27, 1978, 283.
3. Carole R. Fontaine, "A Modern Look at Ancient Wisdom: The Instruction of Ptahhotep Revisited," *The Biblical Archaeologist*, vol. 44, no. 3 (Summer, 1981), 155–160. (A substantial description of this paper was given by Richard Severo, *The New York Times*, August 25, 1981, Section C, page 1.)
4. Bennett Cerf, *Out on a Limerick: a Collection of over 300 of the World's Best Printable Limericks: Assembled, Revised, Dry-Cleaned and Annotated by Mister Cerf* (New York, Harper, 1960. London, Cassell, 1961), 114.
5. *The Century Illustrated Monthly Magazine*, New York, Century, vol. 61, April 1901, 960.
6. Henry B. Hass, *Collected Poems* (privately published, January 1982), 28.
7. P. Selver, "Pastiche. Some aspects of the Limericks as a verse-form," *The New Age, A Weekly Review of Politics, Literature, and Art*, London, October 24, 1912, 620.
8. *The New Age, A Weekly Review of Politics, Literature, and Art*, London, November 14, 1912, 47. Letter to the Editor from P. Selver.
9. Paul Selver, *One, Two, Three* (Jarrolds, London, 1926), 80–81.
10. F.A. Wright, *Greek Social Life* (London, J.M. Dent & Sons; New York, E.P. Dutton, 1925), xii–xiii.
11. H.I. Brock, *The Little Book of Limericks* (New York, Duell, Sloan and Pearce, 1947), 8–9.
12. John Armstrong, *There Was a Young Lady Called Alice, and Other Limericks* (New York, Dell Publishing, Inc., 1963), 12.
13. Cyril Bibby, *The Art of the Limerick* (London, Research Publishing Company, 1978), 16. Translation by Benjamin Rogers, 1915.
14. David R. Slavitt and Palmer Bovie, eds., *Aristophanes, 2* (Philadelphia, University of Pennsylvania Press, 1999), 3. Comment by Campbell McGrath on how he translated *The Wasps*.
15. *The Athenæum; a Journal of Literature, Science, the Fine Arts, Music and the Drama*, London, January 2, 1909, page 10.
16. *Punch*, London, January 15, 1933, 94.
17. *The Classical Journal*, The Classical Association of the Middle West and South, June 1933, 709. Note seemingly by the editor, commenting on a communication to him from Robert A. MacLean of the University of Rochester.
18. *The Classical Journal*, The Classical Association of the Middle West and South, December 1933, page 218. Letter from W.A. Oldfather.
19. *American Notes & Queries*, New York, January 1948, 152. A letter from Herbert N. Crouch, headed "Limerick Hoaxes." The letter was reproduced in *Pentatette*, Moffett, CA, July 2009, 8.
20. For example, Caroline Levine, *Provoking Democracy: Why We Need the Arts* (Malden, MA, Blackwell, 2007), 40.
21. *The Commonweal, a Magazine for Catholics*, New York, January 28, 1925, 330.

22. *The Times*, London, Saturday, April 6, 1935, 8. Letter headed "Accidental Verse," by the Rev. E.J. Pizey.

23. *The Saturday Review of Literature*, New York, June 8, 1946, 32. Letter from George Dwight Kellog.

24. *John O'London's Weekly*, London, August 2, 1946, 170. In the regular column by "Jackdaw."

25. *The Listener*, London, August 2, 1951, 190. Letter by Jack Werner.

26. Jack Werner, *Small Latin and Less Greek* (London, Dennis Dobson, 1954).

27. Eric Cross, "Limerick—the Poem and the Town," *The American Mercury* (New York, August 1953), 105–8.

28. *The Spectator*, London, March 29, 1963, 388.

29. *Notes & Queries*, London, November 1968, 409. Letter from Peter Horwath.

30. NB's column, *Times Literary Supplement*, London, May 28, 2004, 16.

31. By June 2004, this quotation about Aquinas's verse had already made it onto a Catholic website, Leithart.com.

32. A.N. Wilkins, "Prelimerick," *Pentatette* (Moffett, CA, May 1985), 3. R.J. Winkler, "Some thoughts on St. Thomas Aquinas," *Pentatette* (Moffett, CA, July 1985), 2–3. William D. Loring, "Thomastic Limericks," *Pentatette* (Moffett, CA, December 1985), 2–3. (These three articles are online at the Nonsenselit.org site / Edward Lear Homepage, under the title "Thomastic Limericks.")

33. Arthur Deex, "St. Thomas Aquinas Revisited," *Pentatette* (Moffett, CA, December 2009), 6.

34. Christopher M. Brunelle, *The Church Year in Limericks*, MorningStar Music Publishers, Inc. (St. Louis, MO, 2017), 7–8. Can be read online.

35. Ronald A. Knox, "Lyra Limerica," *English Life*, London, vol. 4, no. 3, February 1925, 202–203. See page 203.

36. Elbridge Colby, "The Priest in Medieval Literature," *The Ecclesiastical Review*, Washington, DC, Catholic University Press of America, vol. 57, July 1917, pages 30–43. See page 30.

37. *The Nation*, New York, vol. 104, No. 2692, 1917, 132.

38. *The Tablet*, London, vol. 115, Issue 3,651, April 30, 1910, 677.

39. *The Independent*, New York, vol. LXIX, Issue 3216, July 21, 1910, 156.

40. Benet Wellums, "Roundelay 2," *Pastoral Music*, Washington, DC, National Association of Pastoral Musicians, vol. 15.1, October–November 1990, 55–6. See page 55.

41. Jane Bell Kiester, *Giggles in the Middle: Caught'ya! Grammar with a Giggle for Middle School* (Gainesville, FL, Maupin House, 2006), 42. The author kindly replied to my query, explaining that she had been told this information by a reliable source, and had also come across a confirmatory reference during research into the limerick form; alas, neither source nor reference had been recorded.

42. Frank Martinus Arion, "Creole influences in European Limericks," abstract, *Unity and Diversity in the Caribbean: Abstracts of Papers Presented at the Fifth Annual Conference, Willemstad, Curaçao* (July 12–14, 1983, vol. 5), 32–3.

43. Frank Martinus Arion, "Krioolse Kinderrijmen in het Nederlands en de oorsprong van de Limerick," in *Homenahe na Raúl Römer*, edited by Frank Martinus Arion (Willemstad, Curaçao, Instituto Lingwístiko Antiano, 1989), 119–141, see 139–141.

44. Frank Martinus Arion, "The Victory of the Concubines and the Nannies," in *Caribbean Creolization; Reflections on the Cultural Dynamics of Language, Literature and Identity*, edited by Kathleen M. Balutansky and Marie Agnès Sourieau (Gainesville, University Press of Florida, 1998), 110–117.

45. For example: https://www.youtube.com/watch?v=uDgXUiEzARw and https://www.youtube.com/watch?v=yXeunyN13uQ.

46. Langford Reed, *The Complete Limerick Book* (London, Jarrolds, second edition, 1926), 21. Baring-Gould (page 30) explains what the limerick means. Bibby (page 34) tells us who the protagonists were.

47. Langford Reed, *The Complete Limerick Book*, 1926, 22.

48. Gershon Legman, *The Limerick*, vol. 1 (St. Albans, Herts, Panther Books, 1976), 60.

49. Mason Long, *Poetry and its forms* (Ann Arbor, MI, Edwards Brothers Inc., 1935) 201. Also G.P. Putnam's Sons (New York, 1938).

50. Richard Linn Edsall, "The

Limerick," *The Atlantic Monthly*, July 1924, 134–137; see page 134.

51. Clement Wood, ed., *A Book of Humorous Limericks, Little Blue Book No. 1018* (Girard, KS, Haldeman-Julius Company), 1926.

52. Clement Wood, *Wood's Unabridged Rhyming Dictionary* (Cleveland, World Publishing Company, 1943), 1028.

53. Louis Untermeyer, *The Pursuit of Poetry: A Guide to Its Understanding and Appreciation with an Explanation of Its Forms and a Dictionary of Poetic Terms* (New York, Simon and Schuster, 1969), 220.

54. *The Times*, London, Friday, December 12, 1924, 20.

55. William H. Whitmore, *The Original Mother Goose's Medley, as First Issued by John Newbery, of London, about A.D. 1760* (Albany, Joel Munsell's Sons, 1889).

56. *The New York Times*, February 4, 1899. Article by Joel Benton for the Saturday Review section.

57. *The New York Times*, April 24, 1909.

58. Iona Opie and Peter Opie, eds., *The Oxford Dictionary of Nursery Rhymes* (London, Oxford University Press, 1951), 38–42.

Chapter 2

1. Ralph A. Lyon: *A Pocketful of Limericks* (Boston, Mayhew Publishing, 1908).

2. Stephenson Browne, *Boston Gossip of Latest Books*, a review in *The New York Times*, June 13, 1908.

3. Wallace Rice and Frances Rice, *The Little Book of Limericks* (Chicago, Reilly & Britton, 1910) 4.

4. Wallace Rice and Frances Rice, *The Humbler Poets; a Collection of Newspaper and Periodical Verse 1885–1910* (Chicago, A.C. McClurg, 1911), xiv.

5. Walter Graham, *English Literary Periodicals* (New York, T. Nelson & Sons, 1930), 53–4. Much the same information can be found in Walter James Graham, *The Beginnings of English Literary Periodicals: A Study of Periodical Literature, 1665–1715* (New York and London, Oxford University Press, 1926), 42–3.

6. Hester Lynch Piozzi, *Thraliana, The Diary of Mrs. Hester Lynch Thrale (later Mrs. Piozzi) 1776–1809*, vol. 2 (Oxford, Clarendon Press, 1951), 1075.

7. Piozzi, *Thraliana*; *ibid.*; states this in footnote 3 on page 1075. Other sources I have seen suggest 10–12 April for the newspaper publication. I have not been able to find the original newspaper entry.

8. Cyril Bibby, *The Art of the Limerick* (London, Research Publishing Company, 1978), 42.

9. George N. Belknap, *History of the Limerick*, Papers of the Bibliographical Society of America (New York, vol. 75, no. 1, 1981), 1–32. See 12–13.

10. Belknap, *ibid.*, page 14.

11. Marco Graziosi, "The Limerick (Part 1)," *Pentatette* (Moffett, CA, November 1996), 4–6; "The Limerick (Part 2)," *Pentatette*, December 1996, 4–6; "The Limerick (Part 3)," *Pentatette*, January 1997, 4–6. These articles are online at Nonsenselit.org.

12. Gershon Legman, *The Limerick*, vol. 1, (St. Albans, Herts, Panther Books, 1976). Page 31 states: "Sufficient has been shown, however, to justify the opening statement that the limerick is, and was originally, an indecent verse-form." This refers back to the second paragraph on page 7. Legman then goes on to say that public morals and bowdlerization put the limerick out of business in the early 18th century. No evidence is given, just conjecture.

13. Blog entitled http://stylisticienne.com/notalimerick/, by Dr. Jenni Nuttall of St. Edmund Hall, Oxford, January 12, 2016.

Chapter 3

1. *The Times Literary Supplement*, April 22, 1944, 204.

2. *The New York Times*, July 26, 1944.

3. *The New York Times*, August 9, 1944.

4. Robert Herbert, "How Form of Jingle Got Its Name. Word 'Limerick' as Applied to Verse. Theory as to Its Origin," *The Limerick Leader*, November 27, 1943.

5. Robert Herbert, "There Was a Young Man from … The Origin of 'Limericks,'" *The Limerick Leader*, July 25, 1955.

6. Robert Herbert, "Limericks were born in—Limerick. O'Tuomy's Liquor Made Everyone Sicker," *The Irish Digest*, vol. LX, no. 4, October 1957, pages 31–33.

7. H.I. Brock, "A Century of Limericks," *The New York Times Magazine*,

Notes—Chapter 3

November 17, 1946, 19 and 53. H.I. Brock, "Limerick Addenda," *The New York Times Magazine*, December 8, 1946, 38–39.

8. *The New York Times Magazine*, May 4, 1947.

9. *American Notes & Queries*, May 1947, 31. Letter entitled "One of the first limericks?" by J. Lynch.

10. Kathleen Hoagland, *1000 Years of Irish Poetry* (New York, Devin-Adair, 1947), 186–189. Also 790 and xlvi–xlvii.

11. Morris Bishop, "Speaking of Books: Limericks." Review of Conrad Aitken's *A Seizure of Limericks*, *The New York Times Book Review*, January 3, 1965, 2.

12. *The Observer*, December 17, 1967, 21. Review of several books by Chaim Bermant entitled *From Bawd to Verse*. The book which sparked the comment was *An Explosion of Limericks*, by Vyvyan Holland.

13. *The Observer*, December 24, 1967, 11. Letter from E.T. Hanrahan, ME, PhD, of Dublin. In the example given, "your liquor" is misquoted as "good liquor."

14. Vivien Noakes, *Edward Lear: The Life of a Wanderer* (London, William Collins Sons, 1968), 324.

15. Vivien Noakes, *Edward Lear: The Complete Nonsense & Other Verse*, London, Allen Lane, 2001), xxiii. Also Penguin Classics, London, 2006, xx.

16. Cyril Bibby, *The Art of the Limerick* (London, Research Publishing Company, 1978), 37–38.

17. David Stewart, "The Limerick is Furtive and Mean...," *Smithsonian Magazine* (Washington, D.C., September 2002), 90–96.

18. Unpublished letter entitled "The Mirth Myth" sent by Dr. Arthur Deex to the editor of the *Smithsonian Magazine*. Published in *Pentatette* (Moffett, CA, November 2002), 4.

19. John T. Koch, ed., *Celtic Culture: A Historical Encyclopedia*: Volumes 1–5 (Santa Barbara, CA, ABC-CLIO, 2006), 1388.

20. *Pentatette* (Moffett, CA, September 1995, 8), Letter from Baz Millar, Regional Development Executive of the Shannon Development Company, Limerick, Ireland.

21. James F. Clarity, "Limerick (Stab City, No Less) Rebounds," *The New York Times*, December 18, 1998.

22. A clip was uploaded in 2007 to YouTube. It is poor in terms of video quality and pathetic in terms of limerick quality. It contains the usual claim about Maigue poets; https://www.youtube.com/watch?v=P4qJMuYsf7Y. A much clearer version was later put online at https://www.youtube.com/watch?v=o_-LeGg4vt4.

23. Clodagh O'Leary, "The limerick finds its way home," *The Limerick Leader*, June 28, 2006, 3.

24. Matthew Potter, "The Curious Story of the Limerick," (Limerick, Ireland, Limerick Writers' Centre, 2013).

25. Jean Harrowven, *The Limerick Makers*, (London, Research Publishing Company, 1976), 13–14.

26. *Proceedings of the Seventh Symposium of Societas Celtologica Nordica*, edited by Mícheál Ó Flaithearte, Uppsala University. Papers read at a conference 21–22 May 2004. Collected papers published 2007. Paper by William Mahon entitled "Eoghan Rua Ó Súilleabháin's Aisling Parody: An Phis," 119–135. See pages 124–6. Thanks to Doug Harris for alerting me to this reference.

27. *The Limerick Leader*, July 20, 1955, 1.

28. *The Limerick Leader*, July 27, 1955.

29. George Derwent Thomson, "Studies in Ancient Greek Society," (London, Lawrence & Wishart, vol. 1, 1949), 496 and 585.

30. Colm Ó Baoill, "The Limerick and Gaelic Song," *Transactions of the Gaelic Society of Inverness* (Vol. LVIII, 1993–94, printed 1995), 171–196. See 190.

31. George N. Belknap, "History of the Limerick," *The Papers of the Bibliographical Society of America* (New York, vol. 75, no. 1, 1981), 1–32. See 11–12.

32. Seamus O Cinneide, "In Limerick city no guide book to limericks," *The Limerick Leader*, August 2, 1975, 3.

33. Harrowven, *The Limerick Makers*, 22.

34. Harrowven, *The Limerick Makers*, 23–24.

35. Críostóir Ó Floinn, "The Irish origins of the 'limerick,'" (privately published, 2018). Printed and bound in Ire-land by eprint limited. The work is an enlarged version of an essay published with three others in 2014 (*Remember Limerick*), which itself was enlarged from

an essay published in a collection called *Beautiful Limerick*. Mr. Ó Floinn remarks that one reason for issuing the book was to challenge the view of Dr. Potter, whose 2013 work "had a negative opinion on the connection between Limerick and the limerick." Mr. Ó Floinn also remarks on "the audacity of all those non-Irish commentators on the origin of the limerick who do not know Irish and are therefore incompetent to investigate the possible provenance of the limerick in the poems of the Maigue poets." A fair point; however, non-experts can make advances in a subject precisely because they are not hidebound by an in-depth "knowledge" of what is and isn't possible; for example, the explanation by Linus Pauling of sickle cell anemia. He was not a medical doctor.

36. Vincent Morley, "Irish Jacobitism, 1691-1790," in *The Cambridge History of Ireland: vol. 3, 1730-1880*, James Kelly, ed. (Cambridge University Press, 2018), 35. The source cited for this is Úna Nic Éinrí, ed., *Canfar an dán: Uilliam English agus a chaidre* (Dingle: An sagart 2003), 144. This latter work comes with a CD allowing purchasers to listen to the poems being declaimed and sung.

Chapter 4

1. R.A. Peddie and Q. Waddington (editors and compilers), *The English Catalogue of Books 1801-1836*, (London, Sampson Low, Marston, 1914).

2. F.J. Harvey Darton, "Children's Books," in *The Cambridge History of English Literature*, edited by Sir A.W. Ward and A.R. Waller (Cambridge, Cambridge University Press, vol. XI, *The Period of the French Revolution*, 1914), 386, 483 and 486. The American edition and later UK editions have different page numbers.

3. For example: F.J. Harvey Darton, *Children's Books in England, Five Centuries of Social Life* (Cambridge, Cambridge University Press, 1932). Page 208 cites "the Old Woman named Towl, from *Sixteen Wonderful Old Women* (Harris, 1821; plates dated 1820)," and says: "That is said to be the first appearance of a verse form which Edward Lear made immortal a quarter of a century later, now known, for still unknown reasons, as the Limerick." There is no bibliography in the book.

4. Letter from Gershon Legman to Dr. Arthur Deex, dated July 4, 1984. Copy kindly given to me by Dr. Deex in 2006.

5. George N. Belknap, "History of the Limerick," *The Papers of the Bibliographical Society of America* (New York, vol. 75, no. 1, 1981), 1-32. See 16.

6. Willard R. Espy, *The Life and Works of Mr. Anonymous*, (New York, Hawthorn Books, 1977).

7. *Notes & Queries*, London, September 25, 1897, 247-8.

8. *The New York Times*, November 21, 1897, 22.

9. For example: *Madison County Times*, Chittenango, Madison County, New York, January 14, 1898, 1.

10. Langford Reed, "The Lure of the Limerick," *The Literary Digest International Book Review* (New York, vol. III, no. 2, January 1925), 83-86. See 84.

11. See comment in a summary of a letter from Langford Reed's daughter to the mayor of Limerick, published in *The Limerick Leader*, July 20, 1955, 1.

12. Brian Alderson, "Classics in Short No. 145, Some Old Men and Others, Books for Keeps," *The Children's Book Magazine No. 246* (London, January 2021), 36.

13. *Wallis's Improved Sixpenny Books; The Beauties of Shakspeare* [sic] (London: E. Wallis, no date). A picture of the front cover of the book can be found at https://research.ncl.ac.uk/alderson/project/poet3/.

Chapter 5

1. Richard Linn Edsall, "The Limerick," *The Atlantic Monthly* (Boston, July 1924), 134-137; see 135.

2. It took me years to find the verses in question and I am indebted to Professor Nicholas Roe for his help in locating them. They are in *The Tatler*, September 7, 1830, page 12. Leigh Hunt was the editor. Professor Roe also directed my attention to *The Poetical Works of Leigh Hunt*, edited by H.S. Milford, Oxford University Press, 1923. Pages 752-3 cite the limericks and give an explanation of them as follows: "Mr. Trevor Leigh-Hunt has a MS. version of this poem, with a footnote: 'This was an

admonition to Mr. Galt not to continue the unprovoked attacks which he made on me in the course of some absurd criticisms of his on Lord Byron. In these criticisms, not being able to express a sense which he had of something undefinable in the genius of the noble poet he described it as being "cartilaginous." Mr. Galt turned out to be a good kind of man, when you came to know him, and was author of some works of merit, but criticism and satire were things which he should not have meddled with, especially upon authors in their adversity.'"

3. *The Globe*, London, March 8, 1901, 1.

4. Carolyn Wells, *A Nonsense Anthology* (New York, Charles Scribner's Sons, 1902), xxv.

5. Harvey Peake, "The Limerick," 1908. This appeared in several U.S. newspapers in the *Illustrated Sunday Magazine*. For example *Pittsburgh Post-Gazette*, PA, August 16, 1908, 48 and 63; *The Courier-Journal*, Louisville, KY, August 16, 1908, 39 and 45.

6. Edsall, "The Limerick," 135.

Chapter 6

1. William Makepeace Thackeray, "Two humorous sketches illustrating limericks," drawing, ca. 1844, https://collections.vam.ac.uk/item/O152476/two-humorous-sketches-illustrating-limericks-drawing-thackeray-william-makepeace/.

2. Gordon N. Ray, *Thackeray: The Uses of Adversity 1811–1846* (New York, McGraw-Hill, 1955), 284.

3. *Punch*, London, December 13, 1845, 259.

4. Langford Reed, *Mr. Punch's Limerick Book* (London, Cobden-Sanderson, 1934) 7.

5. Cyril Bibby, *The Art of the Limerick* (London, Research Publishing Company, 1978), 99.

6. Frank Harris, *My Life and Loves, Volume 2* (privately printed for the author, 1925), 467.

7. David Brass Rare Books, Calabasas, California. Via abebooks. December 2016.

8. Pages from Lear's 1846 book can be seen online, for example at http://www.bl.uk/learning/timeline/large126938.html.

9. *The Haileybury Observer*, February 13, 1850, page 177: "There was a young lady of Norway ..." plus a non-limerick layout unattributed translation into Latin; *The Haileybury Observer*, May 14, 1851, page 121: "There was an old man of the isles ..." plus a non-limerick layout translation into Latin by George Henry Maxwell Batten; *The Haileybury Observer*, December 10, 1851, page 237: "There was an old man of Leghorn ..." plus a translation into Latin in an almost limerick-like layout by William Waterfield.

10. Donald Thomas, *Lewis Carroll: A Portrait with a Background* (London, John Murray, 1996), 60.

11. Donald Thomas, *Lewis Carroll*, 29–30, 61.

12. Morton N. Cohen, *Lewis Carroll: A Biography* (London, Macmillan; New York, Knopf, 1995), 13.

13. Lewis Carroll, *Useful and Instructive Poetry*, with an introduction by Derek Hudson (London, Geoffrey Bles, 1954. Also New York, Macmillan, 1954 and 1955).

14. J.T. Fowler, *College Histories. Durham University* (London, F.E. Robinson, 1904). Contains useful information about both Bishop How and Reverend Bradley.

15. *Life and MS. Letters of the late Rev. A.C. Simpson, LL.D.*, *The British Quarterly Review*, Jackson, Walford, and Hodder, London, Vol. XLVI, July and October 1867, 143–179. Quoted letter on page 167.

16. Henry Thomas Rogers (attributed), A sketch of the life and character of the Rev. A.C. Simpson, LL.D / from *The British Quarterly Review*, with additional extracts from his letters (London, Benjamin Pardon, 1867).

17. *The Belfast Comet*, No. 11, October 19, 1849, 82.

18. *The Belfast Comet*, No. 19, December 14, 1849, 148–149.

19. *The Southern Quarterly Review*, Volume 2, Issue 3, July 1842, Charleston, see 72–74.

20. *The Book of Nursery Rhymes Complete. From the Creation of the World to the Present Time* (Philadelphia, Theodore Bliss, 1846), 101, 102, 103, 107, 197, 235.

Chapter 7

1. Lucius Manlius Sargent, *Dealings with the Dead, Volume 2, By a Sexton of*

the Old School (Boston, Dutton and Wentworth, and Ticknor and Fields, 1856), 361-2.

2. *The Haileybury Observer*, December 10, 1851, 237.

3. George John Cayley, *Las alforjas; or, The bridle roads of Spain, in two volumes* (London, Richard Bentley, vol. 2, 1853), 116.

4. John Stevenson Bushnan MD, *Burton and Its Bitter Beer* (London, Wm. S. Orr, 1853), 52–53.

5. *Once a Week (New Series)*, London, Thomas Cooper, November 20, 1869, 352.

6. The limerick/letter can be found in such books as James Grant Wilson, *Thackeray in the United States, 1852-3, 1855–6* (New York, Dodd, Mead, 1904), 105. A facsimile of the letter is in Thomas F. Madigan, *Word Shadows of the Great: The Lure of Autograph Hunting* (New York, Frederick A. Stokes, 1930), 213. Brought to my attention by Doug Harris, see *Pentatette* (Moffett, CA, January 2009), 1.

7. For example: Linda Marsh, *The Wordsworth Book of Limericks* (Ware, Hertfordshire, Wordsworth Editions, 1997), 56.

8. *Exeter and Plymouth Gazette*, England, December 3, 1921, 3.

9. *Yorkshire Evening Post*, June 29, 1953, 4.

10. *Alumni Oxonienses, The Members of the University of Oxford, 1715–1886* (Oxford and London, Parker, vol. 1, 1888). Pages 252 and 253 contain details of Edward Churton and three of his sons, one of them being Joshua Watson Churton. See also: E.P. Eardley Wilmot and E.C. Streatfeild, *Charterhouse: Old and New* (London, John C. Nimmo, 1895), 181. This says Churton went to University College, Oxford, but died before he could take his degree.

11. *Western Times* (Devon, England), December 15, 1865, 5.

12. Mark Davies, "Four Limericks and a Carving, Unpublished Verses and Misattributed Panels in Alice Liddell's Oxford," *The Times Literary Supplement*, July 1, 2022, 23.

13. Charles H. Bennett (editor and illustrator), *Old Nurse's Book of Rhymes, Jingles and Ditties* (London, Griffith and Farran, 1858), 42, 44.

14. A. Funnyman (actually Cuthbert Bede), *Funny Figures* (London, James Blackwood, 1858).

15. Vicesimus Knox, ed., *Elegant Extracts: or Useful and Entertaining Pieces of Poetry, Selected for the Improvement of Youth, in Speaking, Reading, Thinking, Composing; and in the Conduct of Life; Being Similar in Design to Elegant Extracts in Prose* (London, Charles Dilly, 1789), 598.

16. *The Bear University Magazine*, No. 1, October 1858, edited by the Right Honorable George Otto Trevelyan (Trinity), printed by Mr. Williams, 98 Sidney Street, Cambridge. See page 18. This was a single-issue magazine. Reprinted twice; these reprints were confusingly called Second Edition and Third Edition.

Chapter 8

1. *Punch*, January 7, 1860, 4.

2. *Punch*, March 31, 1860, 135.

3. *Punch*, October 27, 1860, 162.

4. Original letter in National Library of Wales, Aberystwyth, Glynne of Hawarden Estate Records 4722.

5. Original document in National Library of Wales, Aberystwyth, Glynne of Hawarden Estate Records 5462.

6. John Bailey, ed., *The Diary of Lady Frederick Cavendish* (London, John Murray; New York, Frederick A. Stokes, 1927).

7. Cuthbert Bede, *Glencreggan: or A Highland Home in Cantire* (London, Longman, Green, Longman, and Roberts, vol. 1, 1861), 345.

8. A.D.P. (Arnold Danvers Power), *Four Score Limericks* (London, privately published, 1934), un-paginated, see limerick number 62.

9. George and Edward Dalziel, *The Brothers Dalziel. A Record of Fifty Years' Work in Conjunction with Many of the Most Distinguished Artists of the Period. 1840–1890* (London, Methuen, 1901), 317.

10. Vivien Noakes, *Edward Lear: The Life of a Wanderer* (Stroud, Sutton Publishing, revised ed., 2004), 163.

11. For example: *The Saturday Review*, London, December 7, 1861, in unpaginated advert section at end. *The Athenæum*, London, December 14, 1861, 793 (under the heading "Christmas Presents"). *The Daily News*, London, December

16, 1861, 8. *The Examiner*, London, December 21, 1861, 815. *The Daily News*, London, December 23, 1861, 8.

12. *The Saturday Review*, London, December 21, 1861.

13. *Manchester Times*, England, January 4, 1862.

14. An expression used in Peter Swaab, *Over the Land and Over the Sea: Selected Nonsense and Travel Writings* (Manchester, Fyfield Books, Carcanet Press, 2005), 3. What was fierce about the Old Man of Kildare is not clear to me.

15. Vivien Noakes, *Edward Lear. The Complete Verse and Other Nonsense* (London, Penguin Books, 2001), 492.

16. Peter Levi, *Edward Lear: A Biography* (London, Macmillan, 1995), 185.

17. *The Bookseller*, December 12, 1865, 1022.

18. See adverts inserted into such Warne books as *The Common Seaweeds of the British Coast and Channel Islands*, Louisa Lane, 1865; *Tales from Dreamland*, Horace Elisha Scudder, 1865; *The Huguenot Family, or, Help in Time of Need*, Catherine Douglas Bell, 1866; *Louie Atterbury*, Miriam Coles Harris, 1866; *Ella and Marian*, Catherine D. Bell, 1866.

19. Vivien Noakes, *Edward Lear, 1812–1888* (London, Weidenfeld & Nicolson, 1985), 170.

20. For example: Michael Benjamin Heyman, "Isles of Boshen, Edward Lear's Literary Nonsense in Context" (PhD thesis, University of Glasgow, June 1996).

21. Ann C. Colley, *Edward Lear and the Critics* (Columbia, SC, Camden House, 1993), 29, citing earlier references.

22. Frank Arthur Mumby, *The House of Routledge, 1834–1934, with a History of Kegan Paul, Trench, Trübner and Other Associated Firms* (London, G. Routledge & Sons, 1934), 108.

23. *The South Australian Advertiser*, February 18, 1862, 3.

24. *The Spectator*, December 28, 1861, 13–14. Article titled "The Pleasures of Astrology." This was reprinted in such newspapers as *The Welshman*, January 3, 1862, 3 and *The Worcester Herald*, January 4, 1862.

25. *Punch*, April 12, 1862, 144.

26. *South Australian Weekly Chronicle*, June 28, 1862, 3; see also *South Australian Advertiser*, June 30, 1862, 3.

27. I have not yet found the original article in the *Literary Budget*; however, several UK newspapers printed similar extracts to the Australian papers; for example, *The Hereford Times*, February 15, 1862, 6; *The Sherborne Mercury and Western Flying Post*, February 18, 1862, 7; and *The Taunton Courier*, February 19, 1862, 3.

28. Julian Hawthorne, *Nathaniel Hawthorne and His Wife* (Boston, James R. Osgood, vol. 2), 322.

29. Albert H. Smyth, *Bayard Taylor* (Boston and New York, Houghton Mifflin, 1896), 246. It is unclear which "triumvirate of friends" is being referred to. One likely group is Bayard Taylor, Richard Henry Stoddard and Fitz-James O'Brien. Taylor returned to New York in 1864 from Russia, but O'Brien had died in 1862 of wounds. So either a different group of friends is being referred to, the biographer made a mistake, or an earlier edition of Lear's book is involved. I have not been able to clarify the matter, nor find any examples of Taylor's limericks. I think it most likely that the third edition of Lear's book is being referred to (because the first two were produced in such small numbers and in the UK), and the year was 1864 or later.

30. *The Nation*, January 11, 1866, 54.

31. William Minto, ed., *Autobiographical Notes of the Life of William Bell Scott: and Notices of His Artistic and Poetic Circle of Friends, 1830 to 1882* (London, James R. Osgood, McIlvaine, vol. 2, 1892), 187.

32. Ford Madox Hueffer, "A Group of Pre-Raphaelite Poets," in *Harper's Monthly Magazine*, October 1910, 778–785, see 782.

33. T. Hall Caine, *Recollections of Rossetti* (London, Cassell, 1928), 74. (This is an expanded edition of the 1882 work, which does not contain the remark.)

34. T. Hall Caine, *Recollections of Dante Gabriel Rossetti* (London, Elliot Stock, 1882), 96. U.S. edition published by Roberts Brothers, 1883.

35. Langford Reed, *The Complete Limerick Book* (London, Jarrolds, 1924), 14.

36. Unknown, "Table-talk in a whisper," *Temple Bar: A London Magazine for Town and Country Readers*, November 1866, 538–546. See page 543.

37. *Once a Week, an Illustrated Miscellany of Literature, Popular Science and Art*, January 5, 1867, page 27.

38. Howard Payson Arnold, *The Great*

Notes—Chapter 8

Exhibition: with Continental Sketches, Practical and Humorous (New York, Hurd and Houghton, 1868), 140–141.

39. Thomas Adolphus Trollope, *What I Remember, Vol. 3* (London, Richard Bentley and Son, 1889), 81–85.

40. *Adelaide Observer*, December 25, 1869, 13.

41. *South Australian Register*, January 3, 1870, 3.

42. Paul Chapman, "A Reminiscence of Coventry Patmore," *The Nineteenth Century and After*, October 1904, 668–674. See page 672.

43. Rev. W. Tuckwell, *A.W. Kinglake: A Biographical and Literary Study* (London, George Bell and Sons, 1902), 146.

44. *The Examiner*, November 18, 1876, 1302.

45. *The Huddersfield Daily Chronicle*, November 14, 1887, 4.

46. *The Times*, London, February 6, 1888, 10.

47. For example: Arthur Prager, *The Mahogany Tree: An Informal History of Punch* (New York, Hawthorn Books, 1979), 19–20. Also Ann Monsarrat, *An Uneasy Victorian: Thackeray the Man, 1811–1863* (London, Cassell, 1980), 412.

48. Sheryl Perry, "A Chronology of People," entry for December 29, 1809, *The Erotica Bibliophile*, http://www.erotica bibliophile.com/miscellaneous_people.php.

49. M.R.D. Foot and H.C.G. Matthew, eds., *The Gladstone Diaries* (Oxford, Clarendon Press, 1968–1994, vol. 6), 146.

50. See Wikipedia entry for Mary Gladstone, daughter of William Ewart Gladstone.

51. It has been extremely difficult to date this limerick. It is obviously earlier than November 1863—the quoted letter written by Susan Lesley on November 13, 1863, proves this. Internal evidence from Higginson's autobiography (250–1) suggests very strongly November 1862. Comments in Randall Fuller's book *From Battlefields Rising, How the Civil War Transformed American Literature* (Oxford: New York, Oxford University Press, 2011), 94, also suggest the same date. The best evidence comes from *The Minneapolis Journal*, January 9, 1901, 7. This describes a lecture which Colonel Higginson was going to give, and mentions a Colonel Trowbridge, who was his lieutenant-colonel in the first Black regiment. Trowbridge says that in November 1862, while Higginson was trying to decide whether to accept the position or not, a lady "wrote this skit"—the limerick then follows.

52. Thomas Wentworth Higginson, *Army Life in a Black Regiment* (Boston, Lee and Shepard; New York, C.T. Dillingham, 1869). Republished numerous times in different editions. See for example Chapter Two, diary entry for January 14, 1863.

53. Christopher Looby, ed., *The Complete Civil War Journal and Selected Letters of Thomas Wentworth Higginson* (Chicago, University of Chicago Press, 2000), 14.

54. Thomas Wentworth Higginson, *Cheerful Yesterdays* (Boston and New York, Houghton Mifflin, 1898), 250–1. Widely reported in newspapers of the time: the limerick was especially quoted.

55. Mary Lesley Ames, *Life and Letters of Peter and Susan Lesley, vol. 1* (New York, G.P. Putnam's Sons, 1909), 477. A librarian in the Schlesinger Library kindly sent me a scan of the original letter; the verse is definitely in the letter and the letter date is November 13, 1863.

56. *Punch*, December 27, 1862, 259.

57. There is debate as to whether he was born in 1815 or 1816. While obviously of immense importance to Mr. Brooks, it is not an important matter for us.

58. George Somes Layard, *A Great "Punch" Editor; being the Life, Letters and Diaries of Shirley Brooks* (London, Sir Isaac Pitman & Sons, 1907), 202. U.S. edition is *Shirley Brooks of Punch; His Life, Letters, and Diaries* (New York, Henry Holt, 1907).

59. *The Times*, February 24, 1874, 10.

60. *The Times*, March 2, 1874, 10.

61. The eagle-eyed reader will notice that I have not included a reference which shows that Mr. Brooks actually wrote these six limericks. That is because I do not have one. I *assume* he did, for two reasons. First, they immediately precede the limericks he did write for *Punch*. Second, they are all about UK towns, and in the same style as the ones he is known to have written.

62. *The Bristol Mercury*, December 20, 1862.

63. *The Belfast News-Letter*, December 23, 1862.

64. *Trewman's Exeter Flying Post or*

Plymouth and Cornish Advertiser, December 24, 1862.

65. *The Nottinghamshire Guardian*, December 26, 1862, 7.

66. *The Hampshire Advertiser County Newspaper*, December 27, 1862, 7.

67. *Harper's Weekly*, January 24, 1863, 51.

68. Layard, *A Great "Punch" Editor*, 203.

69. For example: *Liverpool Mercury, etc.*, January 3, 1863; *Wrexham and Denbighshire Advertiser, and Cheshire, Shropshire and North Wales Register*, January 31, 1863, 2. See also February 4, 1863, 2; *The Hampshire Advertiser*, February 21, 1863, 7.

70. *Halifax Morning Sun*, April 17, 1863, gives five limericks on Nova Scotia towns, called "Nursery Rhymes, after the manner of Punch."

71. For example: *The Manaro Mercury, and Cooma and Bombala Advertiser*, June 19, 1863, 3; *Bell's Life in Sydney and Sporting Chronicle*, October 8, 1864, 3. Article titled "Nurseryversey Rhymes." Gives 17 limericks on Australian towns.

72. *The Carmarthen Chronicle, and Haul Advertiser*, February 28, 1863, 2–3. Letter by Rhobin Goch of Glan Tywi.

73. *Punch*, February 21, 1863, 77.

74. *Punch*, October 5, 1872, 137.

75. Langford Reed, *Mr. Punch's Limerick Book* (London, Cobden-Sanderson, 1934), 111.

76. For example: Glyn Rees, *The Mammoth Books of Limericks* (London, Robinson, 2008), 21. The author also states that *Punch* regularly ran innocuous limerick competitions in the 1860s: *Punch* never ran limerick contests in the 1860s. See also: Matthew Potter, *The Curious Story of the Limerick* (Limerick, Limerick Writers' Centre, 2013), 44. Author states this was the "first ever limericks competition."

77. Gershon Legman, *The Horn Book, Studies in Erotic Folk-Lore* (London, Jonathan Cape, 1970), 429. (Original U.S. publication of this book was 1964; it collected together Legman's writings from the 1950s and '60s.) Probably more accessible in Legman, *The Limerick*, preface to Panther edition of 1974, page 9.

78. Bibby, *The Art of the Limerick*, 80. Uses part of Legman's expression: "submission of a disconcerting number of bawdy and sacrilegious limericks." See also Rees, *The Mammoth Books of Limericks*, 21. Rewrites Legman's expression to read: "anonymous submission of a disconcerting number of bawdy and sacrilegious limericks."

79. William S. Baring-Gould, *The Lure of the Limerick* (New York, Clarkson N. Potter, 1967), 48.

80. Bibby, *The Art of the Limerick*, 77.

81. S.M. Ellis, ed., *Letters and Memoirs of Sir William Hardman, Second series, 1863–1865* (London, C. Palmer, 1925), 138.

82. Barry Feinberg, *The Collected Stories of Bertrand Russell* (London, George Allen & Unwin, 1972), 299.

83. Feinberg, *The Collected Stories of Bertrand Russell*, 299.

84. Victor Shea and William Whitla, eds., *Essays and Reviews: The 1860 Text and its Reading* (Charlottesville, University Press of Virginia, 2000), 848.

85. George Augustin Macmillan, *Letters of Alexander Macmillan* (London, Macmillan, 1908), 131.

86. George John Worth, *Macmillan's Magazine, 1859–1907: "No flippancy or abuse allowed"* (Aldershot, UK; Burlington, VT, Ashgate Publishing Limited, 2003), 35.

87. S.M. Ellis, ed., *A Mid-Victorian Pepys: The Letters and Memoirs of Sir William Hardman* (London, C. Palmer, 1923), 245. Letter written January 1863.

88. Robin is identified as George Meredith on page v of the preface to *Letters and Memoirs of Sir William Hardman, Second Series, 1863–1865*, annotated and edited by S.M. Ellis (London, C. Palmer, 1925).

89. *Notes and Queries*, 8th S. II. October 22, 1892, page 324.

90. Right Hon. Sir Mountstuart E. Grant Duff, *Notes from a Diary, 1851–1872*, Vol. 1 (London, John Murray, 1897), 222, entry for February 4, 1863.

91. Duff, *Notes from a Diary*, 119–120, entry for September 26, 1875.

92. See for example Lewis Melville, *William Makepeace Thackeray; a Biography including hitherto uncollected letters & speeches & a bibliography of 1300 items*, in two volumes (London, Bodley Head, 1909), vol. 1, 278.

93. *The Living Age*, vol. 76, No. 980, March 14, 1863, page 527. (Magazine sometimes called *Littell's Living Age*.)

94. Charles Meeker Kozlay, *Stories and

Poems and Uncollected Writings by Bret Harte (Boston and New York, Houghton Mifflin, 1914), 327. A footnote states the poems are from *The Golden Era*, June 14, 1863.

95. Jeff Guy, "Class, Imperialism and Literary Criticism: William Ngidi, John Colenso and Matthew Arnold," *Journal of Southern African Studies*, Vol. 23, No. 2, June 1997: 219-241. See page 219. See also Alison Blunt and Cheryl McEwan, *Postcolonial Geographies* (London, Continuum, 2002), 42. The following claims Dean Disney wrote the limerick: James Ewing Ritchie, *Brighter South Africa: or Life at the Cape and Natal* (London, T. Fisher Unwin, 1892), 184. Naturally, *Punch* magazine has been claimed as the originator: S.D. Connell, "What are the Churches to do?" *The North American Review*, Vol. 205, No. 736, March 1917, 421-428. Page 421 gives the limerick and says: "as flippantly recorded by *Punch*."

96. David Laing Purves, *Epigrams and Literary Follies* (Edinburgh, William P. Nimmo, 1868), 85.

97. Horace Smith, *Interludes (Second series) being two essays, a farce, and some verses* (London and New York, Macmillan, 1894), 124. Not in the first series of 1892.

98. *The Sunday Times*, July 29, 1923; 6; August 5, 1923; 6; August 12, 1923, 6, letter from Sir Frederick Fison; August 19, 1923, 6; August 26, 1923, 7; September 2, 1923, 6.

99. G.A.C. (identity unknown) and Franklin Thomas Baker, eds., *Poema Militare: Seu Equitum Auratorum Cohortis Secundae Historia Pseudo-comica Nec Non; Veracissima: Carminibus, Caninis, Reddita* (London, privately printed, 1863). Said to be 39 pages long, but actually 41 as the last page is misnumbered as 37. Two known copies. In Bodleian at Vet. A7 e.415. In University of California, Davis, at Shields Special Collections II:206. UCDavis also has a microfiche copy of their book. The UC copy is the same as the Bodleian copy, including the misnumbered last page; it is not a different edition. It contains a loose piece of paper on which are written exactly the same six limericks which are handwritten in the Bodleian copy. The handwriting is similar but I think the writers are different people. These handwritten verses are called "Extra verses not printed."

100. Copies of *The New York World* for 1863 are unavailable. Contemporary American newspapers refer to the *World* as the origin and cite April 15 and April 18. These dates may indicate two appearances of the verses or may be a typographical error.

101. For example: *Southern Literary Messenger*, June 1863, 382-4; *Wilmington Journal*, June 18, 1863, 2; *Galveston Weekly News*, June 24, 1863, 2; *SONGS AND BALLADS OF FREEDOM. A Choice Collection: inspired by the INCIDENTS AND SCENES OF THE PRESENT WAR* (New York, J.F. Feeks, 1864), 18-20. There are only nine limericks—the Governor Andrew verse is omitted.

102. Hilda Bohem, "We're all mad here: A personal view of Carrolliana," *UCLA Librarian*, vol. 35, 1982, 36-38. See page 37.

103. The New York Public Library catalogue; evidence seems to be a handwritten date on the cover. Yale University library catalogue; unknown reason for dating.

104. *American Literary Gazette and Publishers' Circular*, Vol. 3, No. 9, September 1, 1864. Page 268 carries an ad for Hurd & Houghton, Publishers and Booksellers, 401 Broadway, Corner of Walker St., New York. Under the heading "Ready September 15," one entry reads: "Rummical Rhymes, with Pictures to Match. Set fourth [sic] in fayre prospect alphabetically & geographically. Profusely illustrated with well executed humorous pictures, printed in oil colors. Cover in colors. Price 25 cents. *(Entirely New)*."

105. For example: *New York Daily Tribune*, October 11, 1864, 2, advertisement headed: "DON'T forget THE CHILDREN. Hurd & Houghton have just published ..." The list includes *Rummical Rhymes* at 30 cents.

106. *Nonsensical Rhymes with Absurd Pictures in Red and Black*, Hurd and Houghton, 459 Broome Street, New York. Often catalogued as 1870?—but actually 1866; see next reference.

107. *American Literary Gazette and Publishers' Circular*, Philadelphia, Vol. 7, No. 11, October 1, 1866. Page 272 carries an ad for Hurd and Houghton's books, including *Nonsensical Rhymes*, which is described as "Nearly ready."

108. In my copy the F illustration is

opposite Gravesend limerick; I opposite Frome; G opposite I/J, and limericks for U and V have V above U.

109. Several library catalogues suggest this. Also, *The Reader* (London), on page 846 of December 31, 1864, carries an ad for *Rummical Rhymes* with the remark: "by J V Barret." *The Bookseller* (London), on page 1118 of December 31, 1864, carries the same ad but spells the name as Barrett.

110. *The Bookseller: The Organ of the Book Trade*, December 10, 1863, 743.

111. *The Nation*, January 11, 1866, 54.

112. See for example page 14 of the advertising section of *Dame Nature and Her Three Daughters* (New York, Hurd and Houghton, 1869).

113. For example: *The Sydney Morning Herald*, February 13, 1864, 9.

114. *The Musical Standard*, August 15, 1863, 27.

115. Joseph Bennet, *Forty Years of Music, 1865-1905* (London, Methuen, 1908), 185.

116. George Somes Layard, *A great "Punch" editor, being the life, letters, and diaries of Shirley Brooks* (London, Sir Isaac Pitman & Sons, 1907), 38.

117. *Wilkes' Spirit of the Times*, Vol. 8, No. 9, May 2, 1863, 130.

118. Legman, *The Horn Book*, 428. Probably more accessible in Legman, *The Limerick*, preface to Panther edition of 1976, page 8. By the time we get to references like Bibby, *The Art of the Limerick*, 78, we are told the letters "probably stood for the surname of Charles Godfrey Leland."

119. C. Grant Loomis, "Names in American Limericks," in *Names: A Journal of Onomastics*, Vol. 2, Issue 4, December 1954, 229-233. See page 232. See also C. Grant Loomis, "American Limerick Traditions," in *Western Folklore*, Vol. 23, No. 3, July 1963, 153-157. See page 154.

120. Anonymous, *Sights and Notes: by a Looker on in Vienna: Dedicated to the Union Army!* (Washington, no publisher stated, 1864). Un-paginated; see last three pages.

121. *American Literary Gazette and Publishers' Circular*, May 1, 1863, 61.

122. *American Literary Gazette and Publishers' Circular*, June 15, 1863, 185.

123. See copy described in nonsenselit.org, at http://www.nonsenselit.org/pictures/the-first-american-edition-of-the-book-of-nonsense/.

124. James Kelly, *The American catalogue of books comprising books published in the United States from Jan., 1861, to Jan., 1866* (New York, John Wiley and Son, 1866), 22 and 116.

125. The earliest references I know for the James Miller edition both say "James Miller has now ready for the holidays, 70, '71" followed by several book titles and descriptions. *The Literary World*, No. 7, Vol. 1, December 1, 1870, 112. *American Literary Gazette and Publishers' Circular*, December 1, 1870, 13.

126. David Homer Bates, *Lincoln in the Telegraph Office* (New York, Century, 1907), 202–204.

127. Frazar Kirkland (pseudonym of Richard Miller Devens), *The pictorial book of anecdotes and incidents of the war of the rebellion, civil, military, naval and domestic ... With famous words and deeds of woman, sanitary and hospital scenes, prison experiences, &c.* (Hartford, CT, Hartford Publishing Company, 1866), 108.

128. Benson J. Lossing, *A Biography of James A. Garfield, Late President of the United States* (New York, Henry S. Goodspeed, 1882), 288 and 304–5.

129. Morris Schaff, "The Battle of the Wilderness, Part I," *The Atlantic Monthly*, June 1909, 721–731. See page 731. Subsequently published as a book with the same title.

130. Charles Godfrey Leland, *Memoirs, Vol. 2* (London, William Heinemann, 1893), 44.

131. Charles Godfrey Leland, *Abraham Lincoln and the Abolition of Slavery in the United States* (New York, G.P. Putnam's Sons, 1879), 236–7.

132. Albert Barrère and Charles C. Leland (compilers and editors), *A dictionary of slang, jargon and cant. Vol. 1.* (Edinburgh, Ballantyne Press, 1889), 90.

133. *The Saturday Review*, December 19, 1863, page 805. Ad says: "This day is published ... Ye Book of Sense; 'Is it true, think you?'"

134. *The Morning Post*, December 18, 1863, 6. Anonymous article titled "Illustrated Books for Christmas."

135. For example: Carolyn Wells, *A Nonsense Anthology* (New York, Charles Scribner's Sons, 1902), 263; Barbara Ire-

son, *The Faber Book of Nursery Verse* (London, Faber & Faber, 2nd edition, 1965), 221.

136. Carolyn Wells, *Carolyn Wells' Book of American Limericks* (New York & London, G.P. Putnam's Sons, 1925), 85.

137. For those who don't, try limerick number 843 in vol. 2 of *The Limerick*, Gershon Legman, 1976, Panther paperback edition.

138. *The Sydney Morning Herald*, September 14, 1864, 8.

139. Bob Turvey, "Making sense of Ye Book of Sense," *Pentatette* (Moffett, CA, January 2007), 5–7.

140. See for example, ad in: *American Literary Gazette and Publishers' Circular*, Volumes 17–18, October 2, 1871, 331. Also *The Literary World*, Volumes 1–2, January 1, 1872, 350.

141. Adrian Lane-Mullins, *Limericks for Laughs, An Anthology of Ring-A-Ding-Dingers! Vol. 3* (Brisbane, Customercorp, 2013), 99. (The page bearing the cards is reproduced as if it was part of the original book.)

142. Sidney George Fisher, "The Diary of Sidney George Fisher 1865," in *The Pennsylvania Magazine of History and Biography*, Vol. 89, No. 2, April 1965, 207–227. See 220–221 and 226. The same information is in Jonathan W. White, ed., *A Philadelphia Perspective: The Civil War Diary of Sidney George Fisher* (New York, Fordham University Press, 2007), 263–264 and 269–270.

143. *Judy*, London, October 2, 1867, 300.

144. *Carmina et Epigrammata in Aula Collegiata apud Westmonasterienses coram Electoribus Recitata, QUINT. NON. MAI. MDCCCLXIX* (London, Spottiswoode, Election 1869), 10.

145. Several sources say the fellowship was awarded in 1869. The assistant archivist at Trinity tells me it was awarded on October 1, 1869. Quiller-Couch (see next reference, *Memoir of Arthur John Butler*, page 42) records October 11, 1869. The congratulatory letter from Stephen Fremantle would have been around this time. I have not seen the original letter.

146. A snippet from the letter from Stephen Fremantle is quoted in Sir Arthur Quiller-Couch, *Memoir of Arthur John Butler* (London, John Murray, 1917), 70.

147. Charles L. Graves, *The Life and Letters of Sir George Grove, C.B.* (London and New York, Macmillan, 1903), 243.

148. SCRAWLS BY XIT, published (for the Author) by W.P. Spalding, 43 Sidney Street, Cambridge. Un-paginated. Undated. Anonymous. The publication date of this extremely rare book has been suggested to be 1881 (NLS and BL) or 1882 (Bodleian). The contents show it was almost certainly written by an Oxford man.

149. "There was a young fellow from Trinity ..." See all over the internet.

150. George Gamow, *One, Two, Three ... Infinity: Facts and Speculations of Science* (New York, Viking Press, 1947). Many reprints and editions.

151. Library and Archives Canada, "Diary of an Irish immigrant woman," 1869. Former archival reference no. MG55/29-No131. Mrs. Froster was an emigrant making her tortuous journey from Dublin to Quebec with her family aboard *The Lady Seymour*. Pages 7 and 9 record two Lear-like limericks written during the voyage. Brought to my attention by Doug Harris.

Chapter 9

1. Horace Gregory, *The World of James McNeill Whistler* (New York, Toronto, Edinburgh, Thomas Nelson and Sons, 1959), 92.

2. William E. Fredeman, ed., *The Correspondence of Dante Gabriel Rossetti: The Chelsea years, 1863–1872* (Cambridge, D.S. Brewer, 2004), 461. See also rossettiarchive.org.

3. Roger Lancelyn Green, *Authors & Places: A Literary Pilgrimage* (London, B.T. Batsford, 1963), 138.

4. Roger Lancelyn Green, *The Book of Nonsense* (London, J.M. Dent & Sons, 1956), 248. Gives limerick; only cites "Oral tradition."

5. S.M. Ellis (editor and annotator), *The Hardman Papers, A Further Selection (1865–1868) from the Letters and Memoirs of Sir William Hardman* (London, Constable, 1930), 7. In a letter written April 1865.

6. See for instance Vivien Noakes, *Edward Lear: The Complete Verse and Other Nonsense* (London, Penguin Books, 2001), 519.

7. Anonymous, *The Limerick, A Facet of Our Culture* (Mexico City, privately printed, 1944), 18. Actually A. Reynolds Morse, Cleveland, Ohio, 1948. Amusingly, Morse states that *The Light Green* appeared at "Cambridge College," whatever and wherever that might be! See also William S. Baring-Gould, *The Lure of the Limerick* (New York, Clarkson N. Potter, 1967), 50. Probably quoting Morse.

8. Sir Robert P. Edgcumbe, *The Works of Arthur Hilton, Together with His Life and Letters* (Cambridge, Macmillan and Bowes, 1904), 57. Edgcumbe quotes two other limericks from this time.

9. It was actually published in London. See for example G.W.E. Russell, *Collections and Recollections* (London, Smith Elder, 1904), 304.

10. For example: Anonymous, *The Limerick, A Facet of Our Culture*. Roger Lancelyn Green, ed., *A Century of Humorous Verse* (London, J.M. Dent & Sons, 1959), 282; E.O. Parrott, *The Penguin Book of Limericks* (London, Viking, 1983), 35; Linda Marsh, *The Wordsworth Book of Limericks* (Ware, Hertfordshire, Wordsworth Editions, 1997), 48.

11. C.L. Graves, "The Cult of the 'Limerick,'" *Cornhill Magazine*, Vol. XLIV, 1918, 158–166.

12. *Punch*, Vol. 64, January 25, 1873, 31.

13. I say undoubted gems because they were thought good enough to be reprinted over a century later: Paul Jennings, *The Book of Nonsense* (London, Raven Books (Macdonald), 1977), 298–299.

14. Reginald Shirley Brooks, ed., *Wit and humor: poems from "Punch" by Shirley Brooks* (London, Bradbury, Agnew, 1875), 309–10. This book, edited by Shirley Brooks's son, has the *Punch* letter and limericks standing above the date 1871, and in the correct chronological sequence relative to other poems in the book. However, as this letter was published in *Punch* on January 25, 1873, I have used this date in the main text. It might have been written in 1871, or Brooks's son might have made a mistake.

15. The limerick is included in several books about Roosevelt. For example: Edmund Morris, *The Rise of Theodore Roosevelt* (New York, Coward, McCann & Geoghegan, 1979), footnote 45 to Chapter 2. Also Peter Collier and David Horowitz, *The Roosevelts: An American Saga* (New York, Simon & Schuster, 1994), 41. See also Harry Themal, "On Presidential Limericks," *Pentatette* (Moffett, CA, January 2007), 5.

16. Charles L. Graves, *The Life and Letters of Sir George Grove, C.B.* (London and New York, Macmillan, 1903), Prefatory Note, 201, 243, 460.

17. *The Spectator*, April 3, 1915, 475.

18. Right Hon. George W.E. Russell, *One Look Back* (London, W. Garner, Darton, 1911), 83–4, 94.

19. Adon (actually William Frederick Traill), *Lays of Modern Oxford* (London, Chapman and Hall, 1874), 32–40. See 39.

20. For this and other reviews, see advertising in front pages of the author's next book: Adon, *Through Storm and Sunshine* (London, Henry S. King, 1875).

21. Prof. Chaucer Jones, W.H.B., with illustrations by Sir Michael Angelo Raphael Smith, C.G.B. (actually William H. Beckett and Charles G. Bush), *Rhymes of Nonsense Truth & Fiction* (New York, G.W. Carleton, 1874).

22. *The Spokesman-Review*, Spokane, Washington, July 5, 1958. See Bennet Cerf's "Out on a Limerick" column, un-paginated in *This Week Magazine*, July 6, 1958. This is *The National Sunday Magazine*, which formed part of this (and several other newspapers).

23. The London Hermit (actually Walter Parke), *Songs of Singularity, or, Lays for the Eccentric* (London, Simpkin, Marshall, 1875).

24. Walter Parke, *The Merry Muse, with Graver Moments: A Collection of Poems, Humorous and Serious, for Reading or Recitation* (London, Ward and Downey, no date), 45–46. Copyright library catalogues state 1890. Newspaper reviews confirm Sept/Oct 1890.

25. *The Spectator*, December 25, 1875, 1636, lists this book as being published for 3/-.

26. Anonymous, *Christmas Chimes and New Year Rhymes, serious and comic. With a gallery of not-ables drawn and quartered in various verse, sense, and nonsense* (London, Basil Montagu Pickering, 1876).

27. A. Norman Jeffares, ed., *The Poems and Plays of Oliver St. John Gogarty* (Gerrards Cross, Buckinghamshire, Colin Smythe Limited, 2001), 352. See also com-

ments on page 724 and on surrounding pages; Gogarty did sometimes crib and "improve" old limericks; see pages 842–4.

28. *The Graphic*, March 4, 1876.

29. *Punch*, March 10, 1877, 98; March 17, 1877, 110; March 24, 1877, 130; March 31, 1877, 142; April 28, 1877, 191; May 5, 1877, 202; May 12, 1877, 215; May 19, 1877, 218.

30. George Louis Palmella Busson du Maurier, *A Legend of Camelot, Pictures and Poems, &c.* (London, Bradbury, Agnew, 1898), 25–40.

31. Rudyard Kipling, "The Propagation of Knowledge," *Strand Magazine*, January 1926; *McCall's Magazine*, January 1926. This story forms a chapter in *Debits and Credits* (London, Macmillan; New York, Doubleday, Page, 1926), 230–253, see 232. In 1929 it formed one of five new chapters in *The Complete Stalky & Co*. The character Beetle quotes a limerick written by George du Maurier from *Punch* magazine, May 5, 1877, 202.

32. *The Spectator*, September 30, 1916, 12–13. Part of a letter by the cryptic J.D.A.

33. Gershon Legman, *The Horn Book, Studies in Erotic Folklore and Bibliography* (New York, University Books, 1964; London, Jonathan Cape, 1970). Chapter entitled "The Limerick: a History in Brief," pages 427–453; see page 447.

34. John Payne Collier to J.W. Ebsworth, letter of July 11, 1877. Formerly in the collection of Arthur and Janet Freeman, now at Johns Hopkins University, Baltimore. Initially brought to my attention in Arthur Freeman and Janet Ing Freeman, *John Payne Collier: Scholarship and Forgery in the Nineteenth Century* (New Haven, CT, Yale University Press, 2004), 919. Subsequent correspondence from Professor Janet Freeman gave me the full relevant text.

35. Sheet music titled NURSERY RHYMES, Written, Composed and Sung With unbounded applause by Arthur Lloyd (London, H. D'Alcorn, 1878), price 3/-.

36. *The Sporting Times*, September 10, 1887, 1.

37. Eric Partridge, *Routledge Dictionary of Historical Slang* (London, Routledge (Taylor & Francis group), 2003), 3726. Seemingly quoting a *Sporting Times* definition of 1891, referring to "some twenty years ago."

38. TAURUS and ORION, *THE BOOK OF LIMERICKS* (London, *The Daily Express*, 1916), 6. A book compiled to raise money for the Armed Forces in World War I.

39. Nosti, *A Collection of Limericks* ("Privately printed in Switzerland, 1944"), 17.

40. Sidney Hook, *Out of Step: An Unquiet Life in the 20th Century* (New York, Harper and Row, 1987), 371.

41. Hook, *Out of Step*, 358–359. Hook relates a story in which magazine editor V.F. Calverton's daughter had seen both Calverton and Russell peeing, and had told her father that: "Uncle Bertie's wee-wee is larger than yours." On being told this: "Bless her little heart," Russell responded without turning a hair, "for her generous commendation."

42. Bob Turvey, "The Limericks of Algernon Swinburne," *The Journal of Pre-Raphaelite Studies* (Toronto, Canada, New Series 20: Fall, 2011), 63–71.

43. *The Sydney Once a Week Magazine*, Series 1, Vol. 1 (January 19–June 29, 1878). See pages 378 and 664.

44. "'LIMERICKS': AS THEY ARE WRITTEN AND AS THEY ARE SUNG," *The Musical Home Journal*, Vol. VI, No. 140, July 2, 1907. Reprinted in several New Zealand newspapers, for example: "What is a 'Limerick'?" *Evening Post*, September 21, 1907, 19.

45. *Hertford Mercury and Reformer*, August 10, 1878. This also quotes the Cyprus limerick.

46. *The Burnley Express*, August 24, 1878, 7.

47. *The New York Times*, August 25, 1878.

48. *The Buffalo Daily Courier*, August 26, 1878, 1.

49. *Tichborne Comicalities*, 1871. Nine colored prints with captions in verse published during the civil lawsuit. One is a limerick. A seemingly unique copy is in the Hartley Library at the University of Southampton.

50. *The Sporting Times*, October 19, 1878, 7.

51. *The Chronicle*, Vol. 10, Issue 14, 1879, 223 (preceding text shows it is taken from ACTA). *The Virginia Spectator*, Vol. XVIII, No. 9, June 1879, 600 (stands over word ACTA). *The Rochester Campus*, Vol.

VI, No. 10, July 1879, 188 (in its Clippings column). The limerick probably comes originally from *The Acta Columbia*. Copies of this are not available to me.

  52. See ad on the back cover of G. Finch Mason, *My day with the hounds: and other stories* (Cambridge, W.P. Spalding, 1920).

  53. "There was an old fellow …," Anonymous review of three limerick books in *The Times Literary Supplement*, February 6, 1969, 133–4, see page 134, second column. Also in Robert Conquest, *The Abomination of Moab* (London, Temple Smith, 1979), 91. Also in Jeff Chaucer (a pseudonym of Robert Conquest), *A Garden of Erses* (Washington, Orchises Press, 2010), see pages 10-11 of the introduction by Robert Conquest.

  54. *The Sporting Times*, September 30, 1899.

  55. For example, at www.Horntip.com.

Chapter 10

  1. Mary H. Krout, "English Journalism," in *The Chautauquan. A Monthly Magazine*, Vol. XXVIII—New Series, No. 4, January 1899, 345–350, see page 346. Reprinted in *Printers' Ink*, New York, February 15, 1899, 51–55, see page 52.

  2. *Truth*, Vol. 7, June 3, 1880, 729. Entries called "Assorted specimens—good and otherwise" were given on June 17, 1880, 793–794.

  3. *Truth*, Vol. 8, July 1, 1880, 29. This announced the winner.

  4. *Truth*, Vol. 10, September 15, 1881, 369.

  5. "Assorted specimens—good and otherwise" can be read in *Truth*, Vol. 10, September 15, 1881, 337–338.

  6. On page 142 of the second edition of Langford Reed's *The Complete Limerick Book*, three limericks are given which are stated to be nearly a hundred years old. Since the book was published in 1926, this would suggest around 1830. The third limerick: *There was a maid-servant of Fife, Whose corns were the plague of her life; For boots she wore Master's But with Alcock's corn plasters She now gets on those of his wife!* The footnote on the page reads: "[This] is probably the oldest of all advertising limericks. Mr. Alcock [sic], who was famed for his corn-plasters, offered a prize for a verse which should advertise them, and this was the winning effort." Note that page 32 of the introduction notes: "An advertising Limerick well known seventy years ago will be found in Chapter XVIII." Presumably the above is this limerick, which is thus put at 1856 (or 1855 if Reed wrote in 1925). This fits with the comment in the footnote; "middle fifties of the last century."

  7. *Liverpool Mercury*, December 9, 1880, 3. Also *The Standard*, December 14, 1880, 3.

  8. *Anthony's Photographic Bulletin*, Vol. 15, 1884. See page 19 (in the front of the volume—not in the regular pages). The hydrofluoric acid method is on pages 415–6 if you are really interested.

  9. *The Pall Mall Gazette*, April 27, 1885. Also in subsequent issues, and in several issues of the *Daily News*, 1886.

  10. *Huddersfield Chronicle*, October 15, 1887, page 2.

  11. *The Graphic*, September 30, 1893, and in several subsequent issues.

  12. P.H. Erbes, Jr., "A line on the limerick," *Printers' Ink, A Journal for Advertisers*, December 29, 1938), 25 and 28.

  13. *Columbia Encyclopedia*, Columbia University Press, 6th ed., 2000, see entry under Limerick.

  14. C. Grant Loomis, "Names in American Limericks," *Names: A Journal of Onomastics*, Vol. 2, Issue 4, December 1954, 229–233.

  15. C. Grant Loomis, "American Limerick Traditions," in *Western Folklore*, Vol. 23, No. 3, July 1963, 153–157. See 155–6.

  16. *The Argonaut*, Vol. 4, No. 1, January 4, 1879, 14. Perplexingly, the same limerick appears later in the same magazine: Vol. 4, No. 13, March 29, 1879, on page 14, standing over the words "Truth Seeker," which seems to indicate its source. Loomis "American Limerick Traditions" (*ibid.*—page 155) records the same limerick from *Puck*, Vol. IV, No. 96, 1879, 13. I have not been able to check this reference.

  17. Joseph G. Brown, ed., *A Little Book of Tribune Verse: A Number of Hitherto Uncollected Poems, Grave and Gay* (New York, Grosset and Dunlap, 1901). A collection of poems by Eugen Field, associate editor of the Denver *Tribune*. A Sioux limerick, dated August 16, 1881, appears on page 241. See also *Puck*, Vol. IX, No. 234, August 31, 1881, 433.

18. *The Leeds Mercury*, September 3, 1881.

19. *Scribner's Monthly*, October 1881, 960. Note: this magazine was sold to the Century Company in 1881 and was retitled *The Century Illustrated Monthly Magazine*. Confusingly, this particular year is sometimes cited by either title.

20. Charles Follen Adams, *Dialect Ballads* (New York, Harper and Brothers, 1888), 95–6. See also Charles Follen Adams, *Yawcob Strauss and Other Poems* (Boston, Lothrop, Lee & Shepard, 1910), 100–1.

21. *The Marlburian*, Marlborough College, Wilts., 1882, 88.

22. See a 1903 pamphlet held at the University of California in a collection called *Pamphlets on German Phonetics*. Can be read at HathiTrust.

23. *The Boston Journal* is almost impossible to find copies of. However, several U.S. newspapers in March and April 1882 cited the limerick above the source: *Boston Journal*. For example, the *Jamestown Evening Journal*, March 31, 1882. A number of UK newspapers from May 1882 onward printed a similar story about the limerick.

24. For example this appears with an apposite illustration in Louis Untermeyer (editor) and R. Taylor (illustrator), *The Pan Book of Limericks* (London, Pan Books, 1963), 101. In the second edition of Langford Reed, *The Complete Limerick Book* (London, Jarrolds, 1926), 98, this limerick is attributed to E. Muirhead Little.

25. "'Puck'-ery Poems," *Columbia Spectator*, Vol. IX, No. 1, October 3, 1881, 4.

26. E.V. Knox, "Limericks," in the 1929 *Encyclopedia Britannica*, Vol. 14, 130. In the second edition of Reed, *The Complete Limerick Book*, 98, this limerick is attributed to A.P. Trotter (1904).

27. Gershon Legman, *The Limerick*, vol. 1, (St. Albans, Herts, Panther Books, 1976), 44.

28. *The Outlook*, August 27, 1919, 654. In column called "By the Way."

29. I believe the first printing was in the *Houston Daily Post*, November 27, 1895. See for example C. Alphonso Smith, *O. Henry Biography* (New York, Doubleday, Page & Company, 1916), 133.

30. *The Sporting Times*, September 10, 1887, 1.

31. Reed, *The Complete Limerick Book*, 43.

32. Langford Reed, "The Lure of the Limerick," in *The Literary Digest International Book Review*, January 1925, 83–86. See last comment on page 86.

33. John Letts, *A Little Treasury of Limericks Fair and Foul* (London, Pan Books, 1973), 55. Also in Bibby, 150. "Our Vicar's an absolute duck—/ But right now, he's down on his luck. / At the Sunday School treat / He tripped over his feet, / And all of us heard him say 'Now children, let us stand up and say Grace.'"

34. *Taranaki Herald*, November 15, 1881, 4. Probably stolen from a *Truth* magazine competition, reported on September 8, 1881. See page 337, limerick by TODDY.

35. *Life*, May 24, 1883, 250. Also in a book compilation called *The Good Things of Life* (New York, White, Stokes, & Allen, 1884), un-paginated.

36. *St. Nicholas: An Illustrated Magazine for Young Folks*, March 1887, 333.

37. A review in *The Graphic*, December 4, 1886, 598, starts: "Then, for the little ones, Mr. W, Crane provides "The Baby's Own Æsop" (Routledge) ..."

38. Horst Dölvers, "Depiction vs. picturing: subversive illustrations in a Victorian picture-book," *Word & Image, a Journal of Verbal Enquiry*, Vol. 7, No. 3, July–September 1991, 201–222.

39. Thomas Frank Bignold, BA, Late Scholar of Caius College, Cambridge, and of Her Majesty's Bengal Civil Service, *Leviora; Being the Rhymes of a Successful Competitor* (Calcutta, Thacker, Spink, 1888), 143.

40. *Journal of Education*, February 1, 1888, 100 and 102.

41. Jean Pfaelzer, *Driven Out: The Forgotten War Against Chinese Americans* (Berkeley, University of California Press, 2008).

42. For example: *The Daily Republican*, September 6, 1888, 3; *Fisherman and Farmer*, September 7, 1888, 3; *The Daily Review*, September 13, 1888, 2.

43. *Hampshire Telegraph and Sussex Chronicle*, September 15, 1888, 12.

44. *The Sporting Times*, March 9, 1889, 1.

Chapter 11

1. *The Isis*, May 27, 1893, 192.

2. *The Sporting Times*, February 5, 1898, 5.

3. Geoffrey Body, *The A–Z of Curious Somerset: Strange Stories of Mysteries, Crimes and Eccentrics* (Stroud, Gloucestershire, History Press, 2013), 103.

4. *South Wales Weekly Post*, August 3, 1918, 3.

5. Reverend E.D. Stone, *Herbert Kynaston, A Short Memoir, With Selections from his Occasional Writings* (London, MacMillan, 1912), 75.

6. *The Sporting Times*, March 12, 1892, 5.

7. *Truth*, September 15, 1898, 690.

8. *Mixer and Server*, Hotel and Restaurant Employees' International Alliance and Bartenders' International League of America, Vol. 13, 1904, 46. Limerick stands over *Ohio State Journal*, a currently inaccessible newspaper.

9. William Haig Brown, *Carthusian Memories and Other Verses of Leisure* (London, Longmans, Green, 1905), 212–213.

10. Charles Knowles Bolton, *The Smile on the Face of the Tiger* (Boston, Bacon and Brown, 1908), limerick number IV.

11. *The St. Louis Republic*, March 31, 1901, magazine section, is an early example. In later U.S. magazines and newspapers.

12. *Taunton Courier and Western Advertiser*, March 19, 1924, 2. Here we have a "young laddie" risking it as a biscuit and a pup doing the eating. Sent in by a child.

13. Wallace Rice and Francis Rice, *The Humbler Poets (Second Series): A Collection of Newspaper and Periodical Verse 1885–1910* (Norwood, MA, A.C. McClurg, 1911), 410.

14. "Foolish Limericks Now and Then are Relished by the Best of Men." An illustrated series of limericks in the *Chicago Tribune*, May 8, 1910. See panel 4.

15. W.S. Baring-Gould, *The Lure of the Limerick* (New York, Clarkson N. Potter, 1967), 123. Possibly a variant of the limerick given in Legman.

16. Gershon Legman, *The Limerick*, vol. 1 (St. Albans, Herts, Panther Books, 1976), endnote to limerick 218.

17. Norman Douglas, *Some Limericks* (Florence, privately printed, 1928), 50.

18. Legman, *The Limerick*, Vol. 1, limerick 218.

19. R.D. (Randall Davies), *A Lyttel Booke of Nonsense* (London, Macmillan, 1912), 88.

20. *The Sporting Times*, February 28, 1891, 1.

21. For example *Truth*, October 13, 1887, 622. Also the *Supplement to the Hampshire Telegraph and Sussex Chronicle*, October 22, 1887, 12.

22. *The Sporting Times*, March 14, 1896, 1.

23. *Punch's Almanac for 1863*, eighth page, under heading "Nursery Rhyme."

24. *Judy*, February 21, 1894, 86.

25. *The K.P.*, November 1, 1893, 118.

26. *The Isis*, November 25, 1893, 93.

27. *The K.P.*, November 29, 1893, 145. I suggest the limerick response refers to the Rio limerick printed in *The Isis* because this was the only limerick printed in *The Isis* between November 1, 1893 (when it appeared in *The K.P.*) and the date of the limerick response in *The K.P.*

28. *The Gentlewoman*, December 24, 1892, 850.

29. *The Hull Daily Mail*, September 17, 1894, 2.

30. *Judy*, February 26, 1896, 414.

31. *Buffalo Evening News*, March 17, 1896, 3, limerick stands over *Judy*.

32. *Truth*, September 9, 1897, 685.

33. *Truth*, September 30, 1897, 861.

34. Newton Mackintosh, *Precious Nonsense* (New York, Francis and Newton, 1895), un-paginated, near end, unattributed. Interestingly the middle lines read: To the man at the gate / He said: "I'm not late."—which are closer to the 1881 limerick than the others quoted in this chapter. Also, the people trying to catch the train are men in both this and the 1881 verse.

35. *Public School Magazine*, Vol. 1, 1898, 466. See also *Public School Magazine*, Vol. 2, 1898, 77, which prints a letter saying the Kew rhyme is wrong and it should be Crewe.

36. *L.A.W. (League of American Wheelmen) Bulletin and Good Roads, A Weekly Journal*, March 24, 1899, 430.

37. *The Railway Magazine*, Vol. IV, 1899, 146.

38. Anon., *The notebooks of a spinster lady, 1878–1903* (London, Cassell and Company, 1919). Page 282 refers to a diary entry in July 1901, which contains the cited limerick, as well as the Tait limerick.

39. *St. Johnsbury Caledonian*, July 26, 1905, 1. The heroine is "an aged lady." Somehow she seems to be advertising Moore & Co.'s coal.
40. Bolton, *The Smile on the Face of the Tiger*, limerick number XI.
41. Lettie Cook Van Derveer, *A Day at Happy Hollow School* (Lebanon, Ohio, March Brothers, 1901), 15.
42. P.G. Wodehouse, *Indiscretions of Archie* (London, Herbert Jenkins; New York, George H. Doran, 1921), 98.
43. McMillan Lewis, *Woodrow Wilson of Princeton* (Narbeth, PA, Livingston Publishing Company, 1952), 9.
44. *Truth*, September 1, 1898, 573.
45. *The Independent*, December 1, 1898, 1617. Limerick stands over the words *Kalamazoo Telegraph*. See also *The Sporting Times*, December 10, 1898, 1; *Pearson's Weekly*, December 31, 1898, 431.
46. *The Youth's Companion*, May 11, 1899, 244. This source is quoted by the following magazine when it reprinted the verse: *Life*, May 25, 1899, 448.
47. Bolton, *The Smile on the Face of the Tiger*. See Limerick XI and List of Sources at end. The Tait limerick is number XII and is also claimed to be by Carolyn Wells.
48. David McCord, *What Cheer* (New York, Coward-McCann, 1945), 213.
49. *Life*, January 28, 1946, 19–20. See page 20.
50. *The Sporting Times*, August 6, 1898, 3.
51. St. John E.C. Hankin, "Nonsense Verses, New and Old," *The Idler*, August 1898, 90–98.
52. *Truth*, October 6, 1898, 873.
53. G.L. MacKenzie, *Brimstone Ballads and Other Verse: Bible Bosh; or Jingles of Christian Nonsense* (London, R. Forder, 1899), 122–123.

Chapter 12

1. *Buckingham Advertiser and North Bucks Free Press*, November 28, 1903, 5.
2. *Northampton Mercury*, February 26, 1904, 2. See also *Bucks Herald*, February 27, 1904, 3.
3. Many thanks to the Winslow History website for this explanation.
4. *Today*, December 31, 1898, 267.
5. *Today*, January 21, 1899, 363.
6. For example *The Isle of Man Times and General Advertiser*, February 11, 1899, 6.
7. *The London Opinion* is a difficult paper to find. There are copies in a handful of UK and U.S. libraries. No digitized copies currently exist online. Other newspapers would sometimes report limerick competitions held by the *Opinion*, often when a local person won, and these are easier to locate. Descriptions of pre-1907 limerick competitions in the *London Opinion* can be found in the following: *The Bedfordshire Times and Independent*, August 26, 1904, 5; *The Cambrian*, June 30, 1905, 4; *The Hull Daily Mail*, July 13, 1905, 1; *The Portsmouth Evening News*, July 26, 1905, 4; *The Chelmsford Chronicle*, December 8, 1905, 5.
8. A précis of this competition can be read in the *North Wales Express*, May 5, 1905, 8.
9. "The Annual RPI and Average Earnings for Britain, 1209 to Present (New Series), Measuring Worth website, www.measuringworth.com/ukearncpi/.
10. Lincoln Springfield, *Some Piquant People* (London, T. Fisher Unwin, 1924), 241–243.
11. James Scott Duckers, *Newspaper Gambling Schemes: An Examination of Limerick Lotteries*. Issue 3 of Popular Pamphlets, circa November 1907, 15 pages. This was mentioned in several contemporary newspapers and figures were quoted from it. Some later books also mention it. Despite extensive searching I have not located a copy.
12. *Punch*, October 30, 1907, 307.
13. Section 570 of the *Report from the Joint select committee on lotteries and indecent advertisements, together with the proceedings of the Committee, minutes of evidence, and appendices. Ordered, by the House of Commons, to be Printed 29th July, 1908*. London, HMSO. (Evidence had been taken between March 23 and May 14, 1908.)
14. *Weekly Mail*, October 26, 1907, 7.
15. For example: *Western Gazette*, December 6, 1907, 5. *Hastings and St. Leonard's Observer*, December 7, 1907, 11.
16. *Truth*, March 18, 1908, 688.
17. *The Sphere: An Illustrated Newspaper for the Home*, May 30, 1908, VI.
18. *The Sphere: An Illustrated Newspaper for the Home*, June 1908, 252.

19. *The Mercury*, June 24, 1907, 2.
20. For example: "GREAT BRITAIN IS LIMERICK-CRAZY; Millions Competing for Prizes Offered by Almost Every Popular Paper in England. $1,225 FOR ONE SILLY LINE Eight Weeklies Paid Out $61,985 In a Single Week to the Winners in Their Competitions." Headline in *The New York Times*, September 29, 1907, C3.
21. John Harrison, "Limerick Contest Advertising," *Printers' Ink, a journal for advertisers*, August 5, 1908, 14–15.
22. *The Metropolitan Magazine*, April 1908, 119.
23. P.H. Erbes, Jr., "A line on the limerick," *Printers' Ink, A Journal for Advertisers*, December 29, 1938, 25 and 28.
24. See Wikipedia article entitled "Panic of 1907" for a full explanation.
25. Advertisements are often missing from bound volumes of magazines. Sometimes ads are bound in the back of collected volumes and are detached from the issue they were published in. An example of the May ad can be found via archive.org in *The Century Illustrated Monthly Magazine*, May 1908, 68–9, bound in the back.
26. *Herald and News*, July 16, 1908, 1. These figures are also given in many ads in magazines and newspapers for the monthly competitions.
27. Much of the information for this section comes from John Harrison, "Limerick Contest Advertising," *Printers' Ink, a journal for advertisers*, August 5, 1908, 14–15.
28. "Prize contest for the best and most original limericks on Pantasote Leathers," https://www.historicnewengland.org/explore/collections-access/gusn/195552/.
29. *The Pembrokeshire Herald and General Advertiser*, September 6, 1907, 4. Also *Cardiff Times*, September 7, 1907, 4.
30. *Yorkshire Evening Post*, September 16, 1907, 4.
31. From *The Daily Express*, unknown date. Copies of this newspaper are very difficult to find. Reprinted in the *West Coast Times*, November 25, 1907, 2.
32. *Yorkshire Evening Post*, September 30, 1907, 4.
33. C.L.G., "Anecdotage," in *Chambers's Journal*, 1918, 212–217. Contemporary journals identify C.L.G. as Charles Larcom Graves.
34. *The Pall Mall Magazine*, Vol. 49, 1912, 693.

Chapter 13

1. ANTHROPOPHYTEIA, *Jahrbücher für Folkloristische Erhebungen und Forschungen zur Entwicklunggeschichte der geschlechtlichen Moral*, 1910, VII. Band, 375.
2. ANTHROPOPHYTEIA, *Jahrbücher für Folkloristische Erhebungen und Forschungen zur Entwicklunggeschichte der geschlechtlichen Moral*, 1911, VIII. Band, 374.
3. Anonymous, *The Book of William: with Apologies to Edward Lear Author of the Book of Nonsense* (London and New York, Frederick Warne). No date given but mentioned/reviewed in several UK newspapers in November 1914. For instance mentions in *Yorkshire Post and Leeds Intelligencer*, November 4, 1914, 3; *Birmingham Daily Post*, November 6, 1914, 3. Reviews in *Aberdeen Press and Journal*, November 9, 1914, 2; *Dundee Courier*, November 18, 1914, 6.
4. Month from mentions/reviews in UK newspapers. For instance mentions in *Yorkshire Post and Leeds Intelligencer*, August 30, 1916, 3; *The Globe*, August 30, 1916, 6; *Belfast News-Letter*, August 31, 1916, 6. Short reviews in September and October newspapers.
5. The "coast" limerick, the "supposed" limerick, the "well/bell" limerick.
6. *The Spectator*, September 16, 1916, 317–318. Review anonymous but has a C.L. Graves feel to it.
7. *The Spectator*, September 23, 1916, 331.
8. *The Journal of the American Statistical Association*, Vol. 38, 1943, 4.
9. John St. Loe Strachey, *The River of Life* (London, Hodder and Stoughton, 1924), 189.
10. E.O. Parrott, *The Penguin Book of Limericks* (London, Viking, 1983). Page 7 records: "In a letter written to me soon after I began work on this collection [of some 800 limericks] Dr. Robert Conquest said that another distinguished English publishing house had abandoned as similar project some years ago on the grounds that there were no more than a couple of

hundred verses worthy of inclusion." In *The Life of Kingsley Amis*, Zachary Leader (London, Jonathan Cape, 2007), page 685, records: "In March 1978 he agreed to compile a Faber 'Book of Limericks', then backed out, on the grounds that he wouldn't find enough good ones and that those that he liked would be impossible to illustrate." Amis and Conquest were friends, so this may be what Parrott is referring to.

Bibliography

Online Sources

1. The most comprehensive bibliography relating to limericks was created by Dr. Arthur Deex between the late 1970s and 2010. This can be found online in two archival sites:

https://www.horntip.com/html/books_&_MSS/2010s/2010-08-23_limerick_bibliography__arthur_deex_(digital_database)/index.htm

http://www.limeryki.pl/pochodzenie/Limerick%20Bibliography%20by%20Arthur%20Deex%20(2010).htm

It lists about 2,930 books, 210 periodicals and 72 other sources which contain limericks or relate to the limerick verse form. Depending on how a limerick book is defined, approximately 2,200 different books in English are described.

Items owned by Dr. Deex (1930–2014) were bequeathed to the San Francisco Public Library, where they reside in the Deex Repository of Lyrical Limericks Collection (DROLL). It contains more than 1,300 books, periodicals, recordings, and ephemera.

2. Professor Karl Dilcher's Bibliography of Limerick Books, last updated April 12, 2000, is still online at https://www.mscs.dal.ca/~dilcher/limericks.html. There are 363 entries in the book section, plus 32 in the "not exclusively limericks" section.

3. Dr. Richard Buenger (1922–2010; Princeton 1944) donated his collection of 170 books of and relating to limericks to Princeton in 1996. The catalogue of this collection is at https://catalog.princeton.edu/catalog?search_field=all_fields&q=Buenger+collection&utf8=%E2%9C%93.

Printed Sources

Armstrong, John: *There Was a Young Lady Called Alice, and Other Limericks*, Dell Publishing, New York, 1963.

Baring-Gould, William S.: *The Lure of the Limerick, an Uninhibited History*, Clarkson N. Potter, New York, 1967. Many U.S. and U.K. editions.

Belknap, George N.: "History of the Limerick," *The Papers of the Bibliographical Society of America*, Volume 75, Number 1, 1981, 1–32.

Bibby, Cyril: *The Art of the Limerick*, Research Publishing Company, London, 1978.

Billington, Ray Allen: *Limericks Historical and Hysterical, Plagiarized, Arranged, Annotated, and Some Written (by the author)*, W.W. Norton, New York, 1981.

Bishop, Morris: "Speaking of Books: Limericks," *The New York Times Book Review*, January 3, 1965, 2.

Bolton, Charles Knowles: *The Smile on the Face of the Tiger*, Bacon and Brown, Boston, 1908.

Brock, H.I.: "A Century of Limericks," *The New York Times Magazine*, November 17, 1946, 20 & 53.

Brock, H.I.: "Limerick Addenda," *The New York Times Magazine*, December 3, 1946, 38–9.

Brock, H.I.: *The Little Book of Limericks*, Duell, Sloan and Pearce, New York, 1947.

Cerf, Bennett: *Out on a Limerick: A Collection of Over 300 of the World's Best Printable Limericks: Assembled, Revised, Dry-Cleaned and Annotated by Mister Cerf*, Harper, New York, 1960. Cassell, London, 1961.

Chaucer, Jeff (actually Robert Conquest): *A Garden of Erses*, Orchises Press, Washington, 2010.

Crist, Clifford: *Playboy's Book of Limericks*, Playboy Press, Chicago, 1972. Paperback edition, 1973.

Dies, Nefastus: "Column," a review of Baring-Gould's *Lure of the Limerick*, Encounter magazine, January 1969, 55–57.

Edsall, Richard Linn: "The Limerick," *Atlantic Monthly*, July 1924, 134–137. This article is an unattributed "Contributors' Club" opinion piece. The author is identified as Richard Linn Edsall by Gershon Legman, 1974, page 16. The author is stated to be Richard L. Edsall by Philip B. Eppard and George Monteiro in *A Guide to the "Atlantic Monthly" Contributors' Club. A Reference Publication in Literature*, G.K. Hall, Boston, 1983, 169.

Fadiman, Clifton: *Any Number Can Play*, World Publishing Company, Cleveland, OH, 1957. Chapter titled "There Was an Old Man of Tobago," 267–279.

Funnyman, A. (actually Cuthbert Bede): *Funny Figures*, James Blackwood, London, 1858.

Graves, Charles Larcom: "The Cult of the 'Limerick,'" *The Cornhill Magazine*, February 1918, 158–166.

Hankin, St. John E.C.: "Nonsense Verses, New and Old," *The Idler*, August 1898, 90–98.

Harrowven, Jean: *The Limerick Makers*, Research Publishing Company, London, 1976. Paperback reprint by Borrowdale Press, Norwich, 2000.

Legman, Gershon: *The Horn Book, Studies in Erotic Folk-Lore*, University Books, New York, 1964. Jonathan Cape: London, 1970. Chapter titled "The Limerick. A History in Brief," 427–453.

Legman, Gershon: *The Limerick*, Panther Books, St. Albans, Hertfordshire, 1976. A two-volume paperback set.

Legman, Gershon: *The Limerick*, privately published, Paris, 1953. (Several editions published openly after U.S. and U.K. censorship was relaxed. Most later editions contain an enhanced version of a chapter describing the development of the limerick which was first published in *The Horn Book*.)

Legman, Gershon: *The New Limerick*, Bell Publishing, New York, 1977. Later titled *More Limericks*.

Letts, John: *A Little Treasury of Limericks Fair and Foul*, Pan Books, London, 1973.

Loomis, C. Grant: "American Limerick Traditions," *Western Folklore*, Vol. 23, No. 3, July 1963, 153–157.

Loomis, C. Grant: "Names in American Limericks," *Names: A Journal of Onomastics*, Vol. 2, Issue 4, December 1954, 229–233.

Lyon, Ralph A.: *A Bunch of Limericks and Foolish Verse*, J.S. Ogilvie Publishing, New York, 1907.

Lyon, Ralph A.: *A Pocketful of Limericks*, Mayhew Publishing, Boston, 1908.

Marillier, Harry Currie: *University Magazines and their Makers*, enlarged second edition, Howard Wilford Bell, London, 1902.

Marsh, Linda: *The Wordsworth Book of Limericks, A Comprehensive Anthology of Over 1800 Risqué, Rude and Comical Verses*, Wordsworth Editions, Ware, U.K., 1997. U.S. edition as *Limericks for All Occasions*, Welcome Rain Publishers, New York, 1999.

Morley, Christopher: *Hostages to Fortune, A Collection of Poems, Essays, and Short Stories, Written for the* Haverfordian *by Christopher Morley During His College Days*, Haverford, Pennsylvania, *The Haverfordian*, 1925. Chapter titled "The Limerick," 10–21.

Morse, A. Reynolds: *The Limerick, A Facet of our Culture*, privately printed, stated to be Mexico City, 1944. Actually Cleveland, OH, 1948. (The author is Anonymous; the attributions are from Ren Morse's letters to Dr. Arthur Deex.)

Ogden, James: "From Lyric to Limerick," *Notes and Queries*, December 1994, 529–531.

Ó Floinn, Críostóir: *The Irish origins of the "limerick,"* privately published, 2018. Printed and bound in Ireland by eprint limited.

Opie, Iona, and Peter Opie: *The Oxford Dictionary of Nursery Rhymes*, Oxford University Press, London, 1951.

O'Sullivan, D.J. (editor): "The Bunting Collection of Irish folk music and songs, edited from original manuscripts," *Journal of the Irish Folk Song Society*, Volumes 22–23, 1927, 26–35.

Parrott, E. O.: Illustrations by Robin

Jacques: *The Penguin Book of Limericks*, Viking, London, 1983. U.S. edition, Viking, New York, 1986.

Pentatette: a monthly magazine created by Dr. Arthur Deex and edited by him for the first 360 of the 363 issues produced. Contained limericks, reviews of limerick books, articles on matters limerickal, etc. First issue October 1981; last issue December 2011. It arose from a special interest group within American Mensa, and was initially called *Limerick SIG Newsletter* Number [...]. In December 1986, the name was changed to *The Pentatette*. Originally in print form, then both print and digital. Complete runs exist in private hands.

Potter, Matthew: *The Curious Story of the Limerick*, Limerick Writers' Centre, Limerick, Ireland, 2013. Revised and updated 2017.

Reed, Langford: *The Complete Limerick Book*, Jarrolds, London, first U.K. edition 1924.

Reed, Langford: *The Complete Limerick Book*, U.S. edition, G.P. Putnam's Sons, New York, 1925.

Reed, Langford: *The Complete Limerick Book*, Jarrolds, London, second U.K. edition 1926.

Reed, Langford: *The Indiscreet Limerick Book, 200 New Examples*, Jarrolds, London, 1928.

Reed, Langford: "The Lure of the Limerick," *The Literary Digest International Book Review*, Funk & Wagnalls Company, January 1925, 83–6.

Reed, Langford: *Mr. Punch's Limerick Book*, Cobden-Sanderson, London, 1934.

Reed, Langford: illustrated by Joyce Dennys: *My Limerick Book*, Thomas Nelson and Sons, London, 1937.

Reed, Langford: illustrated by Joyce Dennys: *There was a Young Lady ... and other limericks*, Collins, London, 1937.

Reed, Langford: illustrated by Rupert Fishwick: *Limericks for the Beach, Bathroom, and Boudoir, 120 Examples*, Jarrolds, London, 1933.

Reed, Langford: with forty illustrations by Batchelor: *The New Limerick Book*, Herbert Jenkins, London, 1937.

Rees, Glyn: illustrations by Gray Jolliffe: *The Mammoth Book of Filthy Limericks*, Constable & Robinson, London, 2009. U.S. edition Running Press, Philadelphia, 2009.

Rees, Glyn: illustrations by Tim Archbold: *The Mammoth Book of Limericks*, Constable & Robinson, London, 2008. U.S. edition Running Press, Philadelphia, 2008.

Rice, Wallace, and Frances Rice: *The Humbler Poets; A Collection of Newspaper and Periodical Verse 1885–1910*, A.C. McClurg, Chicago, 1911.

Rice, Wallace, and Frances Rice: *The Little Book of Limericks*, Reilly & Britton, Chicago, 1910.

Rider, Cowl: "What has become of the Limerick?" *The Saturday Review of Literature*, February 5, 1944, 12–14.

Russell, Rev. Matthew (editor): *The Irish Monthly*, February 1898. Article by Matthew Russell titled "A Batch of Irish Learics," 87–89.

Swann, Robert, and Frank Sidgwick: *The Making of Verse: a Guide to English Metres*, Sidgwick and Jackson, London, 1934.

Tigges, Wim (editor): *Explorations in the Field of Nonsense*, Rodopi, Amsterdam, 1987. Chapter by Wim Tigges titled "The Limerick: The sonnet of Nonsense?" 117–133.

Treglown, Jeremy: "Literature's tickling sticks," *Books and Bookmen*, January 1979, 48–49.

Turvey, Bob: "For better, for verse (A description of the Great Limerick Competition Boom of 1907)," *Financial Times Magazine*, May 5, 2007, 22–23.

Turvey, Bob: "Kipling and the Limerick," *The Kipling Journal*, March 2003, 8–20.

Turvey, Bob: "The Limericks of Algernon Swinburne," *The Journal of Pre-Raphaelite Studies*, New Series 20: Fall 2011, 63–71.

Turvey, Bob: *The Secret Life of Limericks*, The Mad Duck Coalition, New York, 2024.

Untermeyer, Louis: "The Lure of the Limerick," *The Holiday Reader*, edited by Bernard Smith and Philip Van Doren Stern, Simon & Schuster, New York, 1947, 327–334.

Untermeyer, Louis: illustrated by R. Taylor: *The Pan Book of Limericks*, Pan Books, London, 1963.

Vaughn, Stanton: *700 Limerick Lyrics*, Carey-Stafford, New York, 1906.

Wells, Carolyn: *Book of American Limericks*, G.P. Putnam's Sons, New York, 1925.

Wells, Carolyn: *Limericks, Frank Leslie's Popular Monthly*, March 1903, 532–5. (See note describing Wells's article in *Pearson's Magazine*, 1903.)

Wells, Carolyn: "Limericks: A Selection of Humorous Verse from all Sorts and Conditions of Writers," *Pearson's Magazine*, May 1903, 565–568. Text is almost identical—but not quite—to Wells's article in Frank Leslie's magazine, 1903. Illustrations are different in each article. Six limericks in the U.S. article are ascribed to authors, but not in the U.K. article. There is one extra limerick in the U.S. article (goat) and five extra limericks in the U.K. article (Colquhoun, Cholmondeley, Carr, Tate, Lulu).

Wells, Carolyn: *A Nonsense Anthology*, Charles Scribner's Sons, New York, 1902.

Wells, Carolyn: *The Rest of My Life*, J.B. Lippincott, Philadelphia, 1937.

Wells, Carolyn: "A Vindication of the Limerick," *Harper's Monthly Magazine*, October 1906, 803–6.

Wells, Carolyn: *A Whimsey Anthology*, Charles Scribner's Sons, New York, 1906.

Werner, Jack: *Small Latin and Less Greek*, Dennis Dobson, London, 1954.

Wood, Clement: *A Book of Humorous Limericks*, Little Blue Book No. 1018, Haldeman-Julius Company, Girard, KS, 1926.

Index

Numbers in **_bold italics_** indicate pages with illustrations.

abbreviated words 156–157
Aberdeen 3
Aberistwith 142
Aberystwith 142
Aberystwyth 141, 142, 143
abuse 109, 198
abuse by dogs 165
acquitted 160
Act of Parliament 73
Adelaide 93
advertisements in limerick form 151, 153–154, 181–190
ale 16
Allcock's Corn Plasters 153
Allegro con brio 120
Allison-Shelley collection 32, 85
America: suggested birthplace of limericks 27–28; early interest in limericks 71–72, 73, 90, 91, 92, 97–98, 99, 107, 108, 112–114, **_115_**, 117, **_118_**, 118–119, 131–132, 134–135, 137–138
American braggadocio 72
American Civil War 82, 113, 118
American Notes & Queries 40
Ancient Egypt: suggested birthplace of limericks 13
Ancient Greece: suggested birthplace of limericks 17–19
Ancient India: suggested birthplace of limericks 14
Andante 120
Andy 39
Anecdotes and Adventures of Fifteen Gentlemen 28, 55, 56, 57, **_59_**, 64, 65, 67, 72, 79, 85
Anecdotes and Adventures of Fifteen Young Ladies 55, 56, 58
Anecdotes of Seven Curious Old Couple [sic] of England 62

Antietam 111
Anti-Gambling League *see* National Anti-Gambling League
Anzac 199
apples 14
Aquinas, Saint Thomas 20–23
Arion, Frank Martinus 24, 25
Aristophanes 17, 18
arithmetical 103
arsenic 83
arsenic soap 131
The Art of the Limerick 5
Arundines Cami 60, 65, 72, 73, 139
Ashbee, Herbert Spencer 126
ass 120, 139
Attaboy! 141
Australian limericks 89–90, 93, 143–144, 186–187, 191–192
Avon 67

babe at the breast 66
baboon 162
The Baby's Own Æsop 159–160
the Backs 129
Bainbridge 33–34
baker 154
bald headed man of May Fair 86
baldness 86
ball 77, 116, 126, 160, 164–166
Barbadoes 74
Baring-Gould, William 5, 17, 40, 100, 206, 228
barrow 167
beadle 99
bear grease 86
beard 152
The Beauties of Shakspeare [sic] 61
bedding 66, 132, 133
Bede, Cuthbert 69, 70, 79, 84, 85

261

Beecher, Henry Ward 135
beer 75–75, 198
The Beggar's Opera 50, 222
Belgrade 160
Belknap, George 4, 29, 36, 47–48, 56, 66, 216
Bellows, Isabel Frances 158, *159*
Bell's Life 80
Bengal 164, 165, 166
benighted 135
berry 34
best limerick 43, 157, 192
Bhagavad Gita, suggested origin of limericks 14
Bibby, Dr. Cyril 5, 17, 22, 29, 36, 41, 67, 100, 204, 205, 206, 209, 210, 213, 215, 216, 225, 228, 229, 230, 232
Bibliography of Forbidden Books 126
Bicester 57, 82, 101, 149; *see also* Bister
biscuit 65, 165
Bishop of Chichester's britches 139
Bishop of Limerick 35
Bishop of Natal 102, 104, 105
bisle 154
Bister 27, 28, 67, 79; *see also* Bicester
bitches 126
bitten 136
bladder 96
blind as a bat 190
bliss 57
blisters 138
Blitz 158
bluster 34
boat captain of Downing 129
boiler 190
bollocks 126
The Book of Bubbles 118
Ye Book of Copperheads 113–114, *115*
The Book of Limericks 196
The Book of Nonsense 60, 69, 75, 85, 86–94, 112, 122, 126, 152, *197*
Book of Nursery Rhymes Complete. From the Creation of the World to the Present Time 72
Ye Book of Sense 114–117, *116*, *118*
*The Book of Williamen}196, *197*
Borwick's powder 154
Bosnia 125
Boston 27, 28, 31, 97, 98, 122
Boswell, James 26, 34
Bourse 137
Bozz up 34
Bradley, Edward *see* Bede, Cuthbert
brandy 39
Bray 119, 150
bread 126–127, 154

breast 66
breasts 66, 139
breeches 49, 126
brick 149, 150
brickworks 158
Bright 192
Brighton 139, 158
britches 49, 139
British Parliament 62, 67, 73, 83
The British Quarterly Review 76
Briton 84, 85, 136
Brock, H.I. 17
Brooks, Mr. Shirley 96, 99, 107, 110, 120, 123, 131
broom 67, 83
broom of St. Stephen's 67
Brougham and Vaux, Henry Lord 67
Broughton 97
buckskin 155
bugger 195
buggered 126, 195
bum 126
bun 164, 165
Bunting collection 46, 219, 222, 227
burnt 191
bursted at sea 190
Bute 83, 84
butterfly net 129
buzz 89

Cadiz 93, 199
Caffre 105
Caine, Hall 92
Caius 80, 129, 156
Calcutta 83, 84, 160
Caliste 26
Cape 166
Carlisle 154
Carroll, Lewis 69, 79
Carter's pills 154
cats 136
Cavendish, Lucy 82–84
ceiling 58
Cerf, Bennett 14, 135
chair 99
chairs 189
chancre 195
chapel 130
Chaplin, Charlie 199
Chatham 158
Cheadle 84, 99, 145
cheating in limerick competitions *see* dishonesty in limerick competitions
Cheedle 83
Chelsea 103
cherry 34

Index

Chester 92, 126, 149
Chichester 139
chin 117
China, suggested birthplace of limericks 24
Chinaman touring the Nile 14
Chinese 161
chirurgeon 96
Cholmondeley 156, 162
Christ Church 79
Christmas Chimes and New Year Rhymes 138–139
church 167
churches 83, 167
Churchill 83
Churston 163
Churton, Joshua Watson 77–78
Chutney 120
cider 14
cigars 132, 133
clap 195
The Classical Journal 19
claws 84
clay 149, 150
Cleo 120
clients 13
cliff 90
cloak 93
clover 139
cluster 34, 35
Clyde 14
Colenso, Bishop John William 102–106
Colley, Ann C. 88
Collier, John Payne 142, 143
Colonel 155, 156, 157
Colquhoun 162
Columbia Encyclopedia 154
committed 160
Como 75
competitions 146, 151–152, 172–173, 175–192, 201
The Complete Limerick Book 3, 22, 44, 60
conductor 126
constructor named Eiffel 161
coon 181
Cork 109
corks 136
Council of Trent 23–24
Countess of Bray 150
cow 112, 113, 128
coxswain 156
crabs 195
crape 166
create a limerick competition *see* limerick competitions
creole 24, 25

Crewe 153, 168, 169, 170, 171, 178
Crimean War 78, 94, 118
Cromer 90
Croom poets *see* Maigue poets
Cruickshank, Robert 56, 59
crumb 126
crust 126
cucumber 147
cunt 104, 147, 149, 150, 166
cygnets 129
Cyprus 145, 146
Cythera's Hymnal 125–126, 144, 149

Dagmar 120, 126
Daily Express 191, 196
Dallas, Eneas Sweetland 125
Dalziel, George and Edward 86, 87, 97
Dame Trott 60
The Dark Blue 128
Dean Inge *see* Inge, William Ralph
Dean of Derry 35
Dean's door 129
Deex, Dr. Arthur 56, 257
degree 134
Denbigh 100, 152
de Polis et Axis 33
devices 167
devil 25
Dey of Algiers 195
Dickery Dickery Dock 28, 61
digestions 139
digits 121
Dilettante Curtainlifter 110
di'monds 77
Dingo, Professor 133–134
Dinneen, Father Patrick 45
dinner 69, 74, 195
dirty limericks, early examples of 96, 101, 120, 125, 141–143, 146–147
dishonesty in limerick competitions 100, 152, 172–173, 177
diversion 16, 66
Divinity 121, 129
dog 164, 165, 166
doorway 90
Dover 139
Down Under 199
Downing 129
drinking 129
Drucker, Mr. Scott 182
Duchess of Como 75
duck's bridge 128
Dumbarton 198
Durston 163
Dutch limericks 24–25

Ealing 58
Earl of Dartmouth, Fifth 85
Earl of Dartmouth, Sixth 85
Earl of Derby 8, 64, 76
Ebsworth, J.W. 142
eclipse of the moon 63, 64
education 150
eeny meeny miny mo 24
eggs 85, 158
Eiffel, Gustave 161
Eiffel tower 161
8, 8 169
8, 08 169
elderly sow 152
Elephant in the room 50
Elisha 86
Eltham 195
English, Uilliam 48, 49
Epitaph on a Fowler 18
Epstein, Jacob 19
Espy, Willard 13
Exodus 105
exploding ladies 75, **76**
explosive machines 129
eye 117, 141

fagot 104
Fall's Road 71
fancy dress ball 164–166
farina 121
Farsi 17
feared 152
feats 85
fellow of Trinity 121, 129
Felo-de-se 154
female interest in limericks *see* ladies who limerick
fermented 14
Ferry 35
fiddle-de-dee 153
fidgets 121
Fife 95
fifty-three 134
Fili na Máighe 41; *see also* Maigue poets
Filidhe na Máighe 45; *see also* Maigue poets
Fir-tree of Bosnia 125
Fisher, Sydney George 119
Fla *see* Florida
flagitious 97
fleas 66, 129
Flirter 131
Florida 157
flurry 168, 177
Fonn Fáil 49
Fontaine, Dr. Carol R. 13

fools 139
forehead 149–150
foreskin 149
fork 109
foul 198
fowls 70
France, suggested birthplace of limericks 25; comment by Robert Herbert 45
Frederick II of Prussia 49
Free Mason's Hall 116
French, limericks in 26, 137, 140–141, 165
fright 136
frighten 158
The Frogs (play) 18
Frome 83
fuck 126, 195
fucked her 126
fucks 'em 126
fun 94, 164, 165
Fun Magazine 90, 96–97, 105, 167
Funnyman, A. *see* Bede, Cuthbert
fury 160

Gaelic Society of Inverness 47
Galt, John 63
gambling 186; *see also* National Anti-Gambling League
Gammer Gurton 59, 60
Gamow, George 122
gaol 93
Garfield, President James A. 113
garter 79
Genesis 105
Geneva 92, 93
German television program 42–43
ghost 173
giants 13
Gilbert, W.S. 18, 96, 148
GINGER 106
Giolla Na Sgríob 46
Gladstone, Sir William Ewart 82, 89, 97, 99
globular Person of Hurst 69
Gloomy Dean *see* Inge, William Ralph
Glo'ster 120
Gloucester 126, 142
glue 138
glutton 70
Glynne, Sir Stephen Richard 92, 93
glyster 102
Gogarty, Oliver St. John 139
goggle-eyed 70
good curate at Eltham 195
gourmand 129
grandmother's wedding 132, 133
grapple 130
grass 120, 139, 140

Index

Graves, Charles Larcom 130; articles by 192, 199; biography by 132
Graziosi, Marco 36
great congregational preacher 134
great country of old 191
Great Pale Ale Controversy 74
great person called G. 89
Greece *see* Ancient Greece
Greek, limericks in 17–19
Greeks 120
green apples 14
Grimsby 181
grist 142
Groninger Swaffel Choir 25
Grove, Sir George 132
Grove's Dictionary of Music and Musicians 132
growl 198
guile 178

The Haileybury Observer 73; reference to limericks in this magazine 69
hair-dresser 75, 86
hall 116, 133, 134, 164, 165, 166
Halliwell, James Orchard 65–66, 72
Harris, Frank 68
Harrow 147, 167
Harrowven, Jean 6, 21, 41, 44, 45, 48, 205
Harte, Bret 105
Hass, Henry Bohn 14, 15
Hatham 158
heart of this cow 112, 113
hearty 135
hen 134, 152
hen reward BEECHER 135
Henry, O. *see* Porter, William Sydney
Herbert, Robert 38, 39, 45
heresies 104
Herrick, Robert 30, 215, 216, 230, 233
Hickory Dickory Dock 25, 26, 27, 28, 37, 233; *see also* Dickory Dickory Dock
hieroglyphics, limericks in 13–14
Higginson, Thomas Wentworth 97
high station 150
Hilton, Arthur Clement 127–130
hind legs 158
The History of Sixteen Wonderful Old Women 55, 56, 57, 58, 59, 61, 65, 70, 71, 72, 85
The History of the Limerick 36, 47
Hockcliffe collection 58
Holland, suggested birthplace of limericks 24–25
Homer 90
The Horn Book 4, 36
hornet 148

horrible cow 113
Hottentot gal 195
Houses of Parliament 62
How, Bishop William Walsham 69–70
Hull 92
Hummel's grand trio 120
Hunt, Leigh 62–63, 230
Hurst 68, 69
Huxham 126
Hyde Park 19

Ichthyosaurus 158, *159*, 167
Ifield 131
immersion 66
indicted 135
infinity 121
Inge, William Ralph 77–78
Inner Temple 136
inside 14
inspector of schools 139
invited 135
The Isis 162, 167

Jack 142
Jackson, Dr. Wyse 48
jam 157
Jamaica 154
Janseniste 26
Japan 147
Jew 136
jewel 66
John's 129
Johnson, Dr. Samuel 26, 34, 35, 217
jokes 79
Jonson, Ben 31, 212, 213
Journal of Education 160
Journal of the Irish Folk Song Society 46
Judy Magazine 119, 167, 168
juggler 85
Juice 198
Jury 160

K 150
Kaiser Will 197
Kenney, Charles Lamb 110, 123
Kent 198
Kew 177
Kildare 83, 84
Kilkee 144
Kilty M'G 71
King Edward VII 68, 175
King George II 49
King of Siam 195
King of the Greeks 120
King William IV 63, 64
King's College 130

Index

Kinsale 15
kitten 84, 136
Knox, Ronald Arbuthnott 22, 224
Kynaston, Dr. Herbert 163

Labouchere, Henry 151, 153; see also *Truth* magazine
ladies of Huxham 126
ladies who limerick 80–81, 82–83, 97–98, 119, 169–171, 189
lady reporter in Kent 198
lamb 157
lame 116
lamented 14
Langham Sketching Club 95–96
lap 101
last line competitions 175–190
last line too long 147, 157–158
last lines which don't rhyme 157–158
Latin limericks 20, 24, 74, 110, 121
Laxo-Tonic Company 187–188
The Lays of Modern Oxford 133–134
Lear, Edward 4, 8, 19, 57, 58, 62, 64, 65, 68, 69, 70, 72, 73, 76, 84, 85, 86–94, 99, 104, 109, 112–113, 117, 122, 126, 127, 137, 151, 152, 196, **197**
Leary, Dr. Patrick 96, 101, 120
Leary, Edward 129; see also Hilton, Arthur Clement
legions of hell 191
Legman, Gershon 4, 5, 26, 29, 36, 56, 100, 111, 114, 156, 162, 203, 204, 205, 206, 207, 208, 209, 210, 211, 213, 214, 215, 217, 218, 220, 222, 223, 224, 228, 233
Leicester 126
Leland, Charles Godfrey 111, 114, **115**
Leviora: being the rhymes of a successful competitor 160
Levitical 103, 104
lexicons 110
life 199–200
lifeboat 156
The Light Green 128, 130
Light Greens 130
Limerick (city) 38, 40, 42, 43, 44, 48
Limerick (county) 38, 40, 41, 42, 43
limerick competitions 146, 151–153, 172–173, 175; see also dishonesty in limerick competitions
limerick last-lining 175–190
The Limerick Leader 39, 43, 44
The Limerick Makers 6, 41
limericks, use in advertising see advertisements in limerick form
Lincoln, President Abraham 107, 112, 114, 118

liquor 39
Liszt 143
The Little Book of Limericks 30
Little Rhymes for Little Folks: or, a Present for Fanny's Library 55
London 105
London Opinion 176, 178, 179, 180, 181, 182, 183
Loomis, Dr. C. Grant 154–155
Lord Palmerston 77
Lord Thomasine 30
lotions 83
loud cheers 195
luncheon 171
The Lure of the Limerick 5
lustre 34, 35
Lyon, Ralph A. 30, 216, 226, 233
Lyttelton, Lucy Caroline see Cavendish, Lucy

Macassar of Rowland 131
machine 3, 129
Magdalen Hall 133, 134
Maigue poets 38–42, 43, 44, 45; see also Fili na Máighe and Filidhe na Máighe
Maine 189
man named McCall 165
Man of Tobago (sick/old) see Tobago
Mangan, James Clarence 39, 40, 41, 47, 48, 49
marred 25
marrow 139, 147
masquerade ball 165
Mayfair 86
McCall 165
McGrath, Andrew 39, 40
McLean, Thomas 68, 76, 87
Me see Maine
merry 34, 35, 39
mettle 47
Mexicans 110
military limericks see soldierly interest in limericks
miller's son 142
Milnes, Richard Monckton 110
Milton, John 94, 183
Ming limerick, priceless 24
Minkowski, Professor Christopher 15
Mr. Punch see Punch, Mr.
Mnasalcas 18
Moliniste 26
The Monthly Packet of Evening Readings for Members of the English Church 119
Moore, Thomas 30, 48, 216, 226, 227, 228, 229, 230, 233
Morgan, Godfrey 101–102, 149

mortar 69
Moses 102, 103, 105
Mother Goose 27–28
Mull 92
munchin' 171
Munitions 199
Murray, Gilbert 18
The Musical World 104, 110
myth 143

N.B. 100
Nagtegeijl, Drs. 25
Nanteuil **140**, 141
Nantucket 157
Napier 110
Napoleon, Louis 110
narrow 139, 147
Natal 102, 104, 105, 106, 195
National Anti-Gambling League 182, 183, 190
needle 99
Neigh 119
Nepal 165
Nepaul 126, 164
Neumann, John von 3
A New Book of Nonsense 4
new bread 126, 127
New Year resolves 179
The New York Times 28, 30, 39, 42, 58, 216, 228, 233
The New York Times Book Review 40
The New York Times Magazine 40
The New York World 107
niches stir 139
Nigger 181
Nile 14
ninety-ninth stroke 3
Noakes, Vivien 41
Nolly 91
non-existent book 27–28
non-rhyming limericks 148
Nonsense for Girls 137
Nonsense Scribbles at Cambridge 148–149
Norway 90
Notes & Queries 21, 30, 57, 104
A Nursery Companion 53
Nursery Rhymes for the Army 111
The Nursery Rhymes of England 65
Nuttall, Dr. Jenni 36–37

oak 27, 57
Ó Baoill, Dr. Colm 47
Occam's razor 53
odd o' me 37, 195
O'Finner, Lucy 69
Ó Floinn, Críostóir 48, 49, 50

old Bishop of London 105
old bore of Torbay 198
Old Chap 101
Old Doctor of Churchill 83
old Doctor of Trinity 121
old Duchess of Como 75
old fellow called Spedding 133
old fellow named Teedie 132
old fellow of Cadiz 93
old Fellow of Peterhouse 129
old Fellow of Trinity 121, 129
old king of Siam 195
old lady at Staines 90
old lady of Kew 177
old lady of Putney 81, 120
old lady of Rookwood 144
old lady of Thurston 163
old Louis Napoleon 110
old man at Belgrade 160
old man named Skinner 195
old man of Barbadoes 74
old man of Bombay 72
old man of Cadiz 199
Old Man of Calcutta 84
old man of Dumbarton 198
Old Man of Kildare 84
old man of Kilkee 144
old man of New York 85
old man of Peru 136
old man of St. Bees 148
old man of Tabreez 66
Old Man of Tobago 58, 60, 65, 72, 73
old man of Tralee 148
Old Man on a hill **197**
old man who said "Cor 117
old man who said "Do 116
old man who said "Gee! 117
old man who said "how 113
old man who said "Oh! 116
old man who said "What 116
old man who said "Why 117
old man with a beard 152
old party at Waterloo 90
Old Person of Cheadle 84, 99
old person of Cromer 90
old Person of Hurst 68
old person of Ware 137
Old Persons 83, 84
old priest of Peru 136
old soldier of Bicester 57, 82, 101, 149
old soldier of Bister 27, 28, 79
old waiter at Wapping 136
The Old Woman and Her Three Sons 60
old woman in Cyprus 145
Old Woman of Broom 83
old woman of Broughton 97

268 Index

old woman of Churston 163
Old Woman of Ealing 58
Old Woman of Frome 83
old woman of Sutton 70
old woman who lived in Fla. 157
omnibus 126
ooftish 142, 143
Opie, Iona and Peter 28, 53, 56, 225, 232
oration 147
Orbilius Flagellator 131
organs 142
orifice 77, 78
ostrich plume 83
O'Sullivan, D.J. see Bunting collection
O'Tuama, Séan 40, 41, 42, 46, 48
O'Tuomy, John 39, 40
Ourse 137
Out on a Limerick 135
ovation 147
ovina 121
owls 70
The Oxford Dictionary of Nursery Rhymes 232

pail 16
The Pall Mall Magazine 192
pantacow 128
Pantasote 189–190
panties 120
The Papers of the Bibliographical Society of America 47
Paradise Lost 183
Parke, Walter 135–136
Parma 83, 84
Parry, John Orlando 75, **76**
party 135
Pastoral Music magazine 23
patent digester 92
Patmore, Coventry 93
pay-per-view 138
The Pearl 102, 145, 147, 149–150, 195
pedant 37
pee 68
A Peep at the Geography of Europe 55, 56
peer 110
peer-amid 14
Penmaenmawrs 97
Pentateuch 102, 103, 104, 105, 106, 132
Persia, suggested birthplace of limericks 15–17
Persian 16, 66
personal limericks 8, 9, 66, 67, 79, 91, 106–107, 119, 122, 125, 131, 132, 133, 138–140
Peru 136
perversions 16
Peterhouse 129

phallus 125
philosophical limericks 18, 75, 116, 198
physician 57
picturesque coon 181
Pigott, Mr. Mostyn 185
pill 92, 126, 154, 187
Pimander 18
Pink 'Un 157; *see also Sporting Times*
Piozzi, Signora / Mrs. see Thrale, Mrs.
pissed with 142
plesiosaurus 159
plume 83
pockets **76**
Poema Militare 106–107
poke 27, 57, 79
Poland 131
policeman of Adelaide 93
Polyphemus's song 34, 35
poor devil named Dallas 125
poor lady grown sadder 96
popping 136
porous 159
porter 168, 177
Porter, William Sydney 156–157
Portslade 179
potions 83
Potter, Dr. Matthew 43–44, 204, 206, 207
powder 154
pox 195
Pozz up 34
Prague 89
prayer 99; *see also* Aquinas, St. Thomas
pre-limericks 31, 37
Prince Makaroo 181
print of her ass 120
Procrustean method 75, 81, 86
profane limerick 173
professor 75
Professor Dingo see Dingo, Professor
proto-limerick 4, 6, 11, 29, 30, 31, 36, 203
proud Chieftain of Fife 95
Pryce, Mostyn 136–137
Punch magazine 19, 67, 72, 82, 89, 96, 98, 99, 100, **101**, 107, 110, 126, 131, 140, 141, 149, 156, 167, 182
Punch, Mr. 67, 89, 98, 99–100, **101**, 131, 156
Punch's Almanac 99, 131, 167
Putney 81, 120
pyramid 14

quaint party in Brighton 139
Queen Elizabeth I 206
Queen Victoria 67, 68, 82, 106, 175
Queen Victoria's children 67–68
Queens 129

Index

questions 139
quim 166

rabbits 117
Racine 3
raccoon 162
rail 126
raven 67
recruit 98
Reed, Langford 3, 20, 22, 25, 26, 28, 29, 44, 45, 60, 61, 66, 67, 77, 85, 92, 100, 136, 153, 156, 157, 170, 171, 175, 181, 223, 228, 233
Remarks on the Proper Treatment of Polygamy 102
revel 25
Rhyll 126
Rhymes of Nonsense Truth & Fiction 134–135
Rice, Wallace and Frances 30–31, 212, 213
rice-gruel 57
Ridiculous Things, Scraps and Oddities 75, **76**
Rio 119–120
riotous glutton 70
roast leg of mutton 57
rockets **76**
Ronan's Lament 45
Rontgen, Herr 171
Rookwood 144
Roosevelt, President Theodore 131–132
rooster 155
rope 104, 192
ros'nier 125
Ross, Charles Henry 108
Rossetti, Dante Gabriel 91, 92, 103, 124–125
Routledge & Warne 87, 88, 89
Rubáiyát of Omar Khayyam 15
rude H. of C. 89
Rule of Three sums 106
Rummical Rhymes 107, 108, 109

sago 57, 67
St. Bees 148
St. John's College, Cambridge 102, 127, 128
St. Just 126
St. Kitts 63–64
St. Neots 85, 86
St. Nicholas Magazine 158–159
St. Paul 164
St. Stephen's chapel 67
saints 139
Salamanca 195
Sam of the Soap 104
Samuda, Mr. 183–186

Sanitary Commission 118
Sanskrit, suggested limericks in 14–15
Satan 179
scan 147
scanty 120
schoolboy interest in limericks 63–64, 73–74, 77–78, 121, 155
schools 139
Scribner's magazine 155
sculptor of mark 19
sea 68, 103, 190
sea level 25
seas 161
seedy 132
Selver, Paul 15, 16, 18
sermons and teas 80
seven by three 117
severe 77, 78
Shakespeare, William 43, 207, 208, 209
Shakspeare [sic] 61
SHAM 37
Shanghai rooster 155
shape 166
Sharpe, Richard Scrafton 56, **59**
shawl 164
sherry 39
Shihuri 160
shill'ns 110
shorter 69
short-kilted North Briton 84, 85
Siam 195
sick man of Tobago 57, **59**, 67, 121
Sid. Sussex 129
siesta 111
silent orgasm 143
Silver diary 96, 101, 120, 144
Simons, Miss 77
Simpson, Reverend Abraham Calovius 70–71
Singer of Avon 67
Singing of limericks 25, 136–137, 144, 194
Sioux 155
Sir Cresswell 92
sister 27, 102, 138
Sivret, Mrs. 97–98
Skinner 195
slighted 135
sluggard 195
Small Latin and Less Greek 112, 113, 167, 178
smile 112, 113, 167, 178
smisle 154
smoke 93
Soapy Sam 104
sodomy 195
soft chancre 195

Index

Soho 185
soldierly interest in limericks 26, 106, 111, 113, 195
Song to Ceres 63, 230, 231
Songs of Singularity 135–136
soot 98
Southall 166
spade 111
Sparta 79
The Spectator 21, 89, 133, 199
Spedding, James 66, 67, 132, 133
spellings, non-traditional 154–157, 162–163
Sphinx 14
spider 116
spinster of Swansea **76**
The Sporting Times 142, 146, 157, 161, 164, 166, 167
Springfield, Lincoln 181
Staines 90
Stelts, Sandra 85
Stevenson, Robert Louis 166
stiff 90
stifled 131
stile 112, 113
stink finger 195
Stobæus 19
Stockholm 160
Stokes 79
store of vice 78
store office 77
street plaques, limericks adorning 43
strychnine 74, 83
student interest in limericks 45, 69, 80, 127–130, 133–134, 148–149, 156, 162, 167
stunt 166
Stygian Ferry 35
sucks 'em 126
Sue 138, 169, 170, 171
suicidal 92
The Sunday Times 106
Sutton 70
swans 129
Swansea 75, **76**
Sweetie called Will 149
Swinburne, Algernon 91, 103, 104, 143
swoon 63, 64
Sydney Once A Week Magazine, The 144
Synge, William Webb Follett 77, 95

The Table 23
Tabreez 66
Tait 169, 171, 173
tall soph. from Toledo 147
tap 101
Tate 169, 171

tear 166
teas 80
Teedie 132
telephone 198
temperance light 192
temple, outside of 173
Tenby 100, 152
tête-à-tête 169
Thackeray, William Makepeace 66–67, 77, 86, 95, 96, 104, 132, 133
thinking 129
thinner 69
third husband 163
Thomond 38
Thrale, Mrs. Hester Lynch 34, 35
thumb up her ass 120
thumbs 91
Thurston 163
The Time I've Lost in Wooing 30, 216, 232, 233
Times Literary Supplement 21, 39
tipple and swill 47
Tobaginâ 121
Tobago 57, 58, **59**, 60, 65, 67, 72, 73, 121
toe 116
Toledo 147
Tomkins, W.M. 77
tongue-twisters 167–171
Torbay 198
tornadoes 74
torpedo 147
Torquay 114, 115, 116, 156
toss up 34
Traill, William Frederick 134
train 90, 153
Tralee 148
Traylee cigarettes 183, 184, 185
Treadle 145
tree 165
Treglown, Jeremy 5
trichinosis 152
trifled 131
Trinity 121, 129
Trossley 163
Trottersclifffe 162
Truefitt & Hill, barbers 86
Truth magazine 151–153, 168, 169, 172–173, 176
Tuer, Andrew White 30, 57–58, 59
Turvey, Bob, limericks written by 25, 37, 117, 138, 141, 143, 146, 158
twenty 117
twenty-three 190
twenty-two cats 136
two and two 116
two two 153

Index

2, 2 (two-two) 168
twopenny Pieman's 77

un-arithmetical 104
uncommonly beautiful spot 116
uncritical 103
University of Cambridge 45, 80, 82, 102, 103, 121, 127, 128, 130, 132, 148, 167
University of Durham 70, 163
University of Florida 109, 117, 138
University of Limerick 43
unorthodox orthography *see* spelling, non-traditional
Untermeyer, Louis 28
Uxbridge 127–128
uxurious [*sic*] 111

Vallandigham, Clement 113, **115**
vice 77–78
vicinity 129
Victoria & Albert Museum 66, 96
Victoria Cross, self-awarded 181
vip'rous 145
VIRESCO 173

w + x 129
wanking machine 3
Wapping 136
War Office 77, 78
wasp 148
The Wasps (play) 17, 18
Waterloo 90
wealthy old man of Tabreez 66
wedding 66, 132, 133
well hung 125
Wells, Carolyn 63, 64, 153, 169–171, 190
Werner, Jack 21
whim 166
white satins 139
Who's Who 181
whore 195
wife 95
Wilberforce, Bishop Samuel 104
Wilton 94
Winchester 111
women writing or illustrating limericks *see* ladies who limerick
Wood, Clement 27
Worcester 98, 142, 155
Worthies of Thomond 38, 39
wren 152
writ properly 37

xyz 121

young critic of King's 130
young curate of Worcester 98
young fellow at Bicester 101, 149
young fellow called Tait 169
young fellow of Crewe 153
young Fir-tree of Bosnia 125
young genius of Queens' 129
young girl from Aberystwyth 142
young girl of Aberystwyth 142
young girl of Nantucket 157
young gourmand of John's 129
young lady from Clyde 14
young lady in Shihuri 160
young lady named Sue 138, 169, 170
young lady of Bray 119
young lady of Brighton 158
Young Lady of Bute 83, 84
young lady of Cheadle 99, 145
young lady of Chester 92
young lady of Chichester 139
young lady of Cork 109
young lady of Crewe 168
Young Lady of Denbigh 100
young lady of Glo'ster 120
young lady of Harrow 147, 167
young lady of Hull 92
young lady of Ifield 131
young lady of Norway 90
Young Lady of Parma 84
young lady of Prague 89, 93
young lady of Rhyll 126
young lady of Rio 120
young lady of Sparta 79
young lady of Stockholm 160
young lady of Uxbridge 128
young lady of Wilton 94
Young Lady of Wilts 173
young maid in Jamaica 154
young maid of Aberystwith 142
young maiden of Gloucester 142
young man at St. Kitts 63, 64
young man at the War Office 77, 78
young man from near Aberdeen 3
young man named Colquhoun 162
young man of Aberystwith 143
young man of Antietam 111
young man of Bengal 164, 165, 166
young man of Bombay 149
young man of Carlisle 154
young man of Geneva 92–93
young man of Japan 147
young man of Kinsale 16
young man of Natal 195
young man of Nepal 165
young man of Nepaul 126, 164
young man of Oporta 69
young man of Portslade 179

Young Man of Racine 3
young man of St. Just 126
young man of St. Kitts 64
young man of St. Paul 164
young man of Salamanca 195
young man of Sid. Sussex 129
young man of Soho 185
young man of Southall 166
young man of the Cape 166
young man of Winchester 111
young man so benighted 135
young man they call GINGER 106
young man who was bitten 136
young man who would Growl 198
young Neddy from Dover 139

young party named Spedding 132
young person in Poland 131
young person named Tate 169
young poet of Chelsea 103
young princess called Dagmar 120, 126
young rascal called Nolly 91
young student of Caius 129
young violinist in Rio 120
young woman [...] at Chester 126
young woman named Sue 170
young woman of Durston 163
young woman of Worcester 155

Zamiel's Owl 110
Zulu 104

www.ingramcontent.com/pod-product-compliance
Lightning Source LLC
Chambersburg PA
CBHW032034300426
44117CB00009B/1049